T0215851

Implementing Always On VPN

Modern Mobility with Microsoft Windows 10 and Windows Server 2022

Richard M. Hicks

Apress®

Implementing Always On VPN: Modern Mobility with Microsoft Windows 10 and Windows Server 2022

Richard M. Hicks
Mission Viejo, CA, USA

ISBN-13 (pbk): 978-1-4842-7740-9   ISBN-13 (electronic): 978-1-4842-7741-6
https://doi.org/10.1007/978-1-4842-7741-6

Managing Director, Apress Media LLC: Welmoed Spahr
Acquisitions Editor: Smriti Srivastava
Development Editor: Laura Berendson
Coordinating Editor: Shrikant Vishwakarma

Cover designed by eStudioCalamar

Cover image designed by Pexels

Distributed to the book trade worldwide by Springer Science+Business Media LLC, 1 New York Plaza, Suite 4600, New York, NY 10004. Phone 1-800-SPRINGER, fax (201) 348-4505, e-mail orders-ny@springer-sbm. com, or visit www.springeronline.com. Apress Media, LLC is a California LLC and the sole member (owner) is Springer Science + Business Media Finance Inc (SSBM Finance Inc). SSBM Finance Inc is a **Delaware** corporation.

For information on translations, please e-mail booktranslations@springernature.com; for reprint, paperback, or audio rights, please e-mail bookpermissions@springernature.com, or visit http://www.apress.com/ rights-permissions.

Apress titles may be purchased in bulk for academic, corporate, or promotional use. eBook versions and licenses are also available for most titles. For more information, reference our Print and eBook Bulk Sales web page at http://www.apress.com/bulk-sales.

Any source code or other supplementary material referenced by the author in this book is available to readers on GitHub via the book's product page, located at www.apress.com/978-1-4842-7740-9. For more detailed information, please visit http://www.apress.com/source-code.

Printed on acid-free paper

To my loving wife, Anne. I am nothing without you.

Table of Contents

TABLE OF CONTENTS

About the Author

Richard M. Hicks is the founder and principal consultant at Richard M. Hicks Consulting, Inc. He is a widely recognized enterprise mobility and security infrastructure expert with more than 25 years of experience implementing secure remote access and public key infrastructure (PKI) solutions for organizations around the world. Richard is a former Microsoft Most Valuable Professional (MVP 2009–2019) and is active in the online community, sharing his knowledge and experience with IT professionals on his blog and through various social media channels. Visit his website www.richardhicks.com/ or connect with him on Twitter at @richardhicks.

About the Technical Reviewer

Natalie Jackson is a specialist security principal consultant at risual Limited. Using her 20-year Microsoft experience, she designs and manages the implementation of large and complex security solutions for a range of clients. Her passion is ensuring clients understand the entire security capability of Azure and Microsoft 365 to improve their security posture and protection.

Acknowledgments

Countless people deserve credit for this book – too numerous to count for sure. However, there are a few essential individuals I would like to mention.

To begin, I would like to thank my good friends Philipp Kuhn and Jason Jones at Microsoft. Both have been tremendously helpful and supportive over the years, answering countless questions about Always On VPN configuration and operation, in addition to implementation and security best practices. Thank you so much for always being there for me. I owe you both a tremendous debt of gratitude.

Thank you also to Natalie Jackson, who serves as the technical reviewer for this title, for stepping up and volunteering to take on the monumental task of reading every word of this book and ensuring its clarity and accuracy. Your feedback and suggestions have been instrumental, and your contributions have undoubtedly made this a better book for everyone.

There is a lot of PowerShell in this book, and although I am no expert in this field, my good friend Jeff Hicks is. I have read many of his books and watched most of his video training courses on Pluralsight, so if any of the PowerShell commands or scripts in this book are helpful, I have Jeff to thank for that. The more complicated tools I developed over the years for Always On VPN were primarily written by him. And though we are not related, we do share an affinity for single-malt Scotch whisky.

Finally, this book would not be possible without my wonderful wife's unconditional love and unwavering support. Anne, you're the best, and I love you the most.

Introduction

The book you are about to read results from many years of experience implementing secure remote access using Windows 10 Always On VPN. I have deployed this technology for organizations large and small and have learned many lessons over time. I have included as much practical, real-world experience as possible in this text to save administrators many hours of frustration in the future.

This book is not a technical reference. In these pages, you will not find detailed information about underlying technologies such as cryptography, IPsec, TLS, etc. Those are well documented in countless other publications. I encourage the reader to have a strong understanding of these foundational components, but I chose not to rehash those subjects here.

Instead, this book intends to be a practical implementation guide for planning, designing, and deploying Windows 10 Always On VPN using current implementation and security best practices. It will help administrators get up to speed quickly on this technology and allow them to implement Always On VPN to best meet their specific needs and requirements.

It is essential to note this book does not cover every possible deployment scenario available for Always On VPN. It focuses on the most common configuration options used by organizations worldwide. Administrators will find advanced configuration options and deployment guidance on my blog at https://directaccess.richardhicks.com/.

The book begins with a detailed discussion about the planning and design of an Always On VPN infrastructure. This is the most crucial part of an Always On VPN project, without a doubt. All aspects of the supporting infrastructure are covered in detail, including Windows Server infrastructure components, certificate requirements, networking models, VPN protocol options and selection, VPN client IP address assignment methods, and much more.

Deploying Routing and Remote Access Service (RRAS) and Network Policy Server (NPS) on Windows Server 2022 is included, and Always On VPN clients provisioning using Intune and PowerShell is outlined. Advanced Always On VPN client configuration options are discussed, and guidance for implementing Always On VPN in Azure is provided.

Always On VPN relies heavily on certificates, so certificate provisioning on-premises and using Intune is documented thoroughly. Azure MFA integration options are covered, and details about high availability and redundancy configuration are provided as well.

Finally, administrators will learn how to troubleshoot common Always On VPN configuration and connectivity issues, and guidance for ongoing system maintenance, operational support, and monitoring and reporting is provided.

Best of luck with your Always On VPN implementation!

CHAPTER 1

Always On VPN Overview

The concept of Enterprise Mobility has been around for many years and has taken on various forms during that time. In the beginning, virtual private networking (VPN) was used to establish remote network connectivity. Typically employed by IT administrators to provide remote support, the technology eventually made its way to privileged users; then when mobile computers became more ubiquitous, VPN adoption for the general user population became more prevalent.

In the past, remote access was considered a luxury. It was a "nice to have" or a perk for a select few. Currently, however, having secure remote access to on-premises data and applications is vital. With today's highly mobile workforce, Enterprise Mobility is no longer an option, it is a requirement.

Not only does an Enterprise Mobility solution allow field-based workers to be productive, but numerous studies also show that remote workers are more productive[1] and have a better work–life balance.[2] Of course, there are tangible benefits for organizations supporting remote work too. Companies supporting remote work have access to a global talent pool when employees aren't restricted to a single geography. There are also cost savings associated with having fewer workers in a physical building.

VPN

Virtual private networking (VPN) is not a new technology. Most IT administrators today will be familiar with enterprise VPNs in one form or another. Conceptually, VPN is used to establish a secure, encrypted communication channel over an untrusted network such as the public Internet.

---

[1] https://www.greatplacetowork.com/resources/blog/remote-work-productivity-study-finds-surprising-reality-2-year-study

[2] https://medium.com/react-rangers/remote-workers-benefit-by-maintaining-a-work-life-balance-289ab94d9bec

© Richard M. Hicks 2022
R. M. Hicks, *Implementing Always On VPN*, https://doi.org/10.1007/978-1-4842-7741-6_1

Historically though, VPNs have been cumbersome to use. Users had to manually initiate the VPN connection when they needed access to the remote network. Sometimes this involved entering a username and password along with multifactor authentication one-time password (OTP) or PIN. Before the proliferation of smartphones, this often meant a physical hardware token was required to access on-premises resources.

DirectAccess

To address the limitations of traditional VPN, Microsoft introduced DirectAccess in 2009 with the release of Windows Server 2008 R2 and Windows 7. DirectAccess was a tremendous success because it greatly simplified connecting to the corporate network remotely. DirectAccess connections happened automatically and transparently. No user interaction was required at all in the default configuration.

DirectAccess was revamped with the release of Windows Server 2012, making it a native feature of the operating system and integrating new capabilities such as high availability and geographic redundancy. The adoption of DirectAccess in the enterprise has grown exponentially since this release.

Demise of DirectAccess

Since Windows Server 2012 was introduced, there have been no new features or functionality added to DirectAccess. Although Microsoft has not formally deprecated DirectAccess (it is still supported in Windows Server 2022 and Windows 11), it is *effectively* end of life. Clearly, Microsoft is no longer investing in DirectAccess.

Why did Microsoft apparently give up on DirectAccess when it was such a success? Simply put, because of the cloud. DirectAccess relies on classic technologies such as Active Directory and group policy. DirectAccess servers and clients must be joined to a traditional Active Directory domain. Today, Microsoft is focused predominantly on cloud technologies in Azure. DirectAccess just does not align with their goals of driving cloud adoption.

DirectAccess Replacement

With DirectAccess widely deployed, Microsoft needed a replacement solution that provided feature parity with DirectAccess but also better integrated with Azure cloud services. To that end, Microsoft introduced Always On VPN with Windows 10.

Always On VPN

Always On VPN provides the same seamless, transparent, and always on experience as DirectAccess but does so in a fundamentally different way. Specifically, Always On VPN leverages the integrated VPN client in the Windows 10 operating system and uses traditional VPN protocols such as Internet Key Exchange version 2 (IKEv2) and Secure Socket Tunneling Protocol (SSTP) to establish a secure remote network connection.

Where DirectAccess leveraged many platform technologies such as the Connection Security rules in the Windows Firewall with Advanced Security, along with various IPv6 transition and translation technologies to establish a secure communication channel with the remote network, Always On VPN is much simpler and less complex. Always On VPN does not require IPv6 as DirectAccess did; IPv6 is optional. Always On VPN performs trusted network detection differently and does not require the DirectAccess Network Location Server (NLS).

Additionally, Always On VPN can be deployed to Windows 10 Professional. Also, Always On VPN supports non-domain joined clients. Non-Microsoft clients can also connect to the Always On VPN infrastructure as long as the client supports the VPN protocol and authentication scheme configured on the VPN server. However, the user will have to manually establish the VPN connection.

Always On VPN Infrastructure

Always On VPN supporting infrastructure can be implemented using existing, native Windows Server operating system features such as the Routing and Remote Access Service (RRAS) for VPN and the Network Policy Server (NPS) for VPN user authentication.

The advantage to using native Microsoft technologies for Always On VPN infrastructure is that they are mature, stable, and reliable solutions. They are also cost-effective and require no additional per-user or per-device licensing.

3

Routing and Remote Access Service

Routing and Remote Access Service (RRAS) has been around for quite some time. Originally introduced as an optional download for Windows NT4, it was first integrated with the operating system with the release of Windows 2000 Server.

Today, RRAS supports numerous VPN protocols. The two predominant protocols used with Always On VPN are the industry standard IKEv2[3] and the Microsoft proprietary SSTP.[4]

Network Policy Server

Network Policy Server (NPS) is Microsoft's implementation of the Remote Access Dial-In User Service (RADIUS) protocol. It is used for authentication and authorization of Always On VPN user-based VPN connections. NPS supports authentication with many different protocols. Always On VPN is typically configured to use Protected Extensible Authentication Protocol (PEAP) with Client Authentication certificates. However, other protocols such as MSCHAPv2 can be used if required.

Infrastructure Independent

Because Always On VPN is implemented entirely on the client, administrators are by no means strictly limited to using Windows services for VPN and authentication. For example, administrators can deploy a network security device that supports client-based VPN from their preferred vendor. Examples include Cisco, Palo Alto Networks, Fortinet, and many more.

In addition, authentication and authorization can be provided by non-Microsoft platforms as well. Many proprietary RADIUS implementations such as Cisco ISE and PulseSecure Steel-Belted RADIUS (SBR) can be used. Open-source RADIUS implementations such as FreeRADIUS can also be leveraged.

---

[3] https://tools.ietf.org/html/rfc7296

[4] https://docs.microsoft.com/en-us/openspecs/windows_protocols/ms-sstp/
c50ed240-56f3-4309-8e0c-1644898f0ea8

Modern Management

The most significant change with Always On VPN is configuration deployment and management. Unlike its predecessor, DirectAccess, it does not use Active Directory and group policy. Instead, Always On VPN uses modern management platforms like Microsoft Endpoint Manager (Intune) to configure and manage Always On VPN on endpoints. Non-Microsoft mobile device management (MDM) platforms can also be used.

Endpoint Manager/Intune or MDM is not strictly required to support Always On VPN, however. Always On VPN profiles can be provisioned and managed using traditional systems management solutions like Microsoft Endpoint Configuration Manager (MECM, formerly SCCM) or a variety of non-Microsoft systems management solutions such as ManageEngine and PDQ.

Cloud Integration

The primary motivating factor for Microsoft to pivot from DirectAccess to Always On VPN is better cloud integration. Not only is Always On VPN designed to be managed using Microsoft Endpoint Manager, it also includes support for Azure Active Directory authentication using cloud-native identities or user accounts synchronized to Azure Active Directory from an on-premises Active Directory.

Importantly, Always On VPN also supports integration with Azure multifactor authentication (MFA), Conditional Access, Windows Information Protection, and Windows Hello for Business.

Summary

As organizations continue to adopt Microsoft cloud technologies like Microsoft Azure and Active Directory, along with complementary technologies like Azure MFA and Conditional Access, migrating from DirectAccess to Always On VPN will have to be considered.

DirectAccess was great while it lasted, but in the end, Always On VPN is well-positioned to continue the legacy of its predecessor by providing seamless, transparent, always on access to on-premises resources yet integrate with today's modern management paradigms and advanced cloud-based security capabilities as well.

CHAPTER 2

Plan for Always On VPN

As with most technology implementations, identifying prerequisites and making design decisions are often the most tedious and time-consuming aspects of the process. There are many ways to deploy Always On VPN and lots of consideration to be made regarding which features and capabilities are required and how the solution will integrate with existing infrastructure.

Administrators must decide where to place VPN and authentication servers, if they should be joined to the domain, and which networking models are required. VPN protocols must be chosen, and IP address assignment methods and address ranges must be decided upon.

In addition, there are firewall and routing decisions to be made and configuration deployment methods to be selected.

The planning phase is the most critical aspect of the project, though, and attention to detail here will ensure the solution is well designed, reliable, scalable, and secure.

VPN Server

Always On VPN is infrastructure independent and is designed to work with both Microsoft and non-Microsoft VPN servers. Both options have their own advantages and disadvantages. Although we'll discuss non-Microsoft VPN solutions here briefly, this book focuses exclusively on the implementation of Always On VPN using Microsoft technologies.

Windows Server

Any supported version of Windows Server can be used to support client-based VPN connections for Always On VPN. However, it is recommended that Windows Server 2019 or newer be used, as it includes some important new features that will be helpful in some deployment scenarios. VPN services are provided with the Routing and Remote Access Service (RRAS) which is part of the DirectAccess-VPN role.

© Richard M. Hicks 2022
R. M. Hicks, *Implementing Always On VPN*, https://doi.org/10.1007/978-1-4842-7741-6_2

RRAS provides some important advantages over non-Microsoft VPN servers. RRAS is easy to install and configure and does require a specialized or proprietary skill set to configure and maintain. Also, RRAS does not need dedicated hardware and has no additional costs associated with per-user or per-device licensing, as many non-Microsoft solutions do.

RRAS can also be scaled out quickly and easily. To add capacity or redundancy, all that is required is to deploy additional RRAS servers and place them behind a network load balancer.

The main disadvantage to using RRAS is that it lacks built-in security controls. RRAS is essentially a router, and once a client connection is authenticated, the client will have access to any resources reachable by the VPN server.

Domain Join

Joining the Windows VPN server to a domain is optional. In this scenario, the server must be managed using locally configured user accounts. It also means that certificates must be manually deployed and updated.

Server Core

The DirectAccess-VPN role is fully supported and recommended on Windows Server Core. Server Core is a GUI-less version of Windows Server that provides numerous benefits such as reduced resource requirements, faster startup times, less maintenance (patching) requirements, and reduced attack surface.

Note   Although fully supported, it is not recommended to deploy RRAS on Windows Server Semi-Annual Channel (SAC) releases. Choose Windows Server Core Long-Term Servicing Channel (LTSC) instead. Visit *https://docs.microsoft.com/en-us/windows-server/get-started-19/servicing-channels-19* for more information.

Network Interfaces

The Windows VPN server can be deployed with one or two NICs. Using a single network interface is easier to configure. However, having two NICs, one internal-facing NIC and another external-facing NIC, is recommended to segregate network traffic between internal and external connections. Having two NICs allows the administrator to configure a more restrictive Windows Firewall policy on the external interface, reducing the attack surface of the server in perimeter/DMZ network. It may also improve performance and reduce network interface utilization by spreading the network load across multiple network adapters.

Network Placement

The Windows VPN server can be configured on the local area network (LAN), in a perimeter/DMZ network, or in a hybrid model with two NICs, one in an external-facing DMZ and one in the LAN or internal-facing DMZ. Although LAN deployments with a single NIC are easy to configure and manage, they are inherently less secure. For best security, consider deploying the VPN server in a perimeter/DMZ network to reduce network exposure.

IPv6

Always On VPN supports both IPv4 and IPv6. If IPv6 is deployed on the internal network, IPv6 addresses can be assigned to Always On VPN clients to provide full end-to-end IPv6 connectivity.

It's worth noting, however, that using IPv6 with Always On VPN is much less problematic than it was with DirectAccess. With DirectAccess, most issues were caused by applications making calls directly via IPv4, which would fail. However, Always On VPN supports both IPv4 and IPv6, so those applications that insist on using IPv4 will continue to work.

Non-Microsoft VPN Devices

Always On VPN is implemented in the Windows 10 client and can establish a VPN connection to any server or device if the VPN protocol and authentication scheme match. Not all VPN devices will work with Always On VPN, however.

The advantage of using a non-Microsoft VPN device is security. Most firewalls also support VPN services. This allows administrators to strictly control network access in a central location and apply unique policies to VPN client traffic.

The following requirements must be met to support Always On VPN using non-Microsoft VPN devices.

IKEv2

Any non-Microsoft VPN device must support Internet Key Exchange version 2 (IKEv2) for client VPN connections to support Windows 10 Always On VPN.

Windows Store Client

Optionally, a non-Microsoft VPN device can be configured to support Always On VPN if the vendor provides a plug-in provider VPN client for Windows 10. These VPN clients are commonly found in the Windows Store. As of this writing, the following vendors offer plug-in providers for their VPNs:

- Checkpoint
- Cisco
- F5
- Fortinet
- Palo Alto
- PulseSecure
- SonicWall

Note   Configuration for non-Microsoft VPN devices is outside the scope of this book. Consult the vendor's documentation for configuration guidance.

Authentication Server

An authentication service is required to support client-based Always On VPN connections. The RADIUS[1] protocol is used by the VPN server to communicate with the authentication server. As stated previously, Always On VPN is infrastructure independent and does not explicitly require a Windows-based RADIUS server. Any server that supports the RADIUS protocol can be used. However, this book will focus on using the Microsoft RADIUS implementation.

Note   Device-based Always On VPN connections do not use RADIUS for authentication. Instead, the VPN server validates the certificate presented by the device to authorize the connection.

Windows Server

Network Policy Server (NPS) is Microsoft's implementation of RADIUS in Windows Server. The NPS server must be joined to a domain to perform authentication. NPS is not a supported role in Windows Server Core, however. It must be installed using Windows Server with the Desktop Experience (GUI).

PKI

Most Always On VPN deployments use digital certificates for authentication. The issuance and management of certificates are performed using public key infrastructure (PKI). The term "public" is a bit misleading here because certificates used for user and device authentication are commonly issued by an internal, private PKI. Again, Always On VPN supports any PKI, public or private, and does not have to be Microsoft-based. This book focuses on the use of Microsoft Active Directory Certificate Services (AD CS) for PKI functionality.

---

[1]https://tools.ietf.org/html/rfc3579

> **Note**   The setup of Microsoft Active Directory Certificate Services (AD CS) is outside the scope of this book. Refer to `https://docs.microsoft.com/en-us/previous-versions/windows/it-pro/windows-server-2012-R2-and-2012/hh831348(v=ws.11)` for guidance on configuring a two-tier PKI using Microsoft AD CS.

VPN Protocols

There are a few different VPN protocols to choose from when planning an Always On VPN deployment. Windows Server RRAS supports several open standard protocols and one Microsoft proprietary protocol.

IKEv2

Internet Key Exchange version 2 (IKEv2) is an open standard VPN protocol. Defined in RFC7926,[2] it uses IPsec and requires a certificate to be installed on the RRAS server. It uses UDP for transport, with the initial handshake taking place on UDP port 500. If a NAT device is detected during the initial handshake between the peers, it switches to UDP 4500. IKEv2 is the protocol of choice when the highest level of security is required.

IKEv2 has some operational limitations, however. It is common for firewalls to block outbound UDP 500 and 4500, preventing access to the VPN server using this protocol. IKEv2 message exchanges can sometimes be quite large, especially during the initial handshake, resulting in packet fragmentation at the IP layer. IP fragments are blocked by default on many firewalls, again resulting in failed connections.

In addition, consumer grade home networking equipment and some Internet service providers (ISPs) often interfere with IKEv2 operation, making IKEv2 VPN connections potentially unreliable.

---

[2] `https://tools.ietf.org/html/rfc7296`

SSTP

Secure Socket Tunneling Protocol (SSTP) is a Microsoft proprietary VPN protocol. Defined in the Microsoft Open Specifications,[3] SSTP uses HTTP over Transport Layer Security (TLS) and requires a TLS (SSL) certificate to be installed on the RRAS server. It uses TCP for transport over the standard HTTPS port 443.

SSTP is the protocol of choice for most deployments as it provides the most reliable access. It is a firewall-friendly protocol, ensuring ubiquitous access behind even the most restrictive firewalls. When configured correctly, SSTP can provide a high level of security.

L2TP

Layer Two Tunneling Protocol (L2TP) is an open standard VPN protocol. Defined in RFC2661,[4] it is an IPsec-based protocol that can be configured with a variety of authentication methods. L2TP is a legacy protocol and should not be used in most production deployments today. If IPsec is required, IKEv2 should be used instead.

PPTP

Point-to-Point Protocol (PPTP) is an open standard VPN protocol. Defined in RFC2637,[5] it was a popular VPN protocol in the late 1990s because of its simplicity and ease of configuration. However, PPTP suffers from serious security vulnerabilities[6] and should not be used under any circumstances.

Certificates

The use of digital certificates is required to support Always On VPN. At a minimum, a TLS (SSL) server certificate will be required. Depending on which VPN protocols are supported, additional certificates may be required. Also, it is recommended, though not strictly required, to use certificates for Client Authentication to provide the highest level of security and assurance for remote access users.

---

[3] https://rmhci.co/sstp
[4] https://tools.ietf.org/html/rfc2661
[5] https://tools.ietf.org/html/rfc2637
[6] https://www.schneier.com/academic/pptp/faq/

SSTP

The SSTP requires a TLS certificate to be installed on the Windows VPN server. The certificate must include the Server Authentication Enhanced Key Usage (EKU) Object Identifier (OID) 1.3.6.1.5.5.7.3.1. The VPN server's public fully qualified domain name (FQDN) must be in the Subject Name field or included as an entry in the Subject Alternative Name (SAN) field. A wildcard certificate is also supported for use with SSTP.

It is recommended the TLS certificate used for SSTP be issued by a public Certification Authority (CA). Public CAs have robust, high-performance, and highly available certificate revocation list (CRL) infrastructure, ensuring reliable operation for SSTP VPN connections.

However, a TLS certificate issued by the organization's private, internal CA can be used if the CRL is publicly accessible.

IKEv2

The IKEv2 protocol requires a certificate to be installed on the Windows VPN server. The certificate must include the Server Authentication EKU and the IP security IKE intermediate EKU (1.3.6.1.5.5.8.2.2). This certificate must be issued by the organization's internal CA. The VPN server's public FQDN (not the server's hostname or NetBIOS name) must be in the Subject Name field or included as an entry in the Subject Alternative Name (SAN) field.

NPS

The NPS server requires a certificate to perform user authentication for VPN client connections. The certificate must include the Server Authentication EKU. This certificate must be issued by the organization's internal CA. The NPS server's hostname must be in the Subject Name field.

Note   Subject Alternative Name (SAN) entries are NOT evaluated when performing authentication requests.

User Authentication

Using certificates for user authentication is recommended for Always On VPN. This provides the highest level of assurance for authenticating users remotely. The user authentication certificate should be issued by the organization's internal CA. At a minimum, the certificate must include the Client Authentication EKU (1.3.6.1.5.5.7.3.2). It is common to include additional EKUs to provide additional functionality, such as Encrypting File System (EFS) and secure email.

Device Authentication

For device-based authentication, a certificate is required on the endpoint. This certificate should be issued by the organization's internal CA. The certificate must include the Client Authentication EKU. The subject name must match the hostname of the device.

TPM

Certificates deployed to mobile devices (e.g., Windows 10 laptops and tablets) for device or user authentication should be configured to use a Trusted Platform Module (TPM). TPM is a hardware-based crypto-processor with advanced physical security mechanisms that greatly increase the security and protection of certificate private keys on the device.

VPN Client IP Addressing

An IP address is assigned to the Always On VPN client when it connects to the VPN server. This IP address is used when connecting to on-premises resources over the VPN tunnel. IPv4 addresses can be assigned using Dynamic Host Configuration Protocol (DHCP) or static address pool. IPv6 addresses can only be assigned using a static prefix.

DHCP

The VPN server can be configured to use a DHCP server to assign IPv4 addresses to VPN clients. VPN clients do not lease IPv4 addresses directly from the DHCP server, however. Instead, the VPN server leases a block of IPv4 addresses from the DHCP server when the

RemoteAccess service starts and manages those itself. When a VPN client connects to the VPN server, it will be given an IPv4 address from this block of leased addresses.

DHCP servers commonly provide additional configuration information to their clients, such as a default gateway, DNS suffixes, DNS servers, and more. By default, the VPN server discards this information and provides only the IPv4 address to the client.

Without this additional configuration information available to clients, the use of DHCP for VPN client IPv4 address assignment introduces an external dependency and provides no real value over static IPv4 address pool configuration. As such, static IPv4 address pool assignment is preferred over DHCP to reduce complexity and improve overall reliability.

Static Pool

Using a static address pool for VPN client IPv4 address assignment is the preferred method for address assignment on the Windows VPN server. Additional client configuration details (e.g., DNS servers and DNS suffix assignment) will be provided as part of the VPN client configuration and provisioning process.

Address Range

An IP address range must be defined for VPN clients. The address range must be large enough to accommodate the expected maximum number of concurrent VPN connections. It is recommended to be generous when defining the IP address range to allow room for future growth. Also, when deploying both device tunnel and user tunnels, each individual VPN connection will consume an IP address. This means enough IP address space must be provisioned to accommodate two IP addresses per endpoint.

IPv4 Subnet

When using DHCP, the IPv4 subnet will be assigned by a DHCP scope that corresponds to the interface which RRAS uses to send the DHCP requests. Ensure the configured DHCP scope includes enough available address space to support the maximum number of concurrent VPN connections expected.

When using static pool assignment, the IPv4 subnet can be configured using a range of IPv4 addresses from the same subnet as the VPN server's internal network interface. Optionally, it can be configured using a unique IPv4 address pool that is not in use on the internal network. Using a unique IPv4 subnet allows administrators to quickly identify VPN clients by their IPv4 subnet assignment and perhaps used to restrict network access via firewall access control list (ACL) configuration. However, it requires additional internal routing configuration to ensure VPN client traffic is routed back to the VPN server correctly.

IPv6 Prefix

Static address pool assignment is the only supported IPv6 address assignment method for VPN clients. Choose a unique /64 IPv6 prefix that is not in use on the organization's internal network. Configure routes internally to ensure this IPv6 prefix is routed back to the VPN server accordingly.

Split vs. Force Tunneling

Always On VPN clients can be configured in one of two tunneling modes: split tunnel or force tunnel.

Split Tunnel

In a split tunnel configuration, only network traffic destined for the on-premises network is routed over the VPN tunnel. All other communication goes directly to the Internet. For split tunnel configurations, the administrator must choose which IP networks are accessible over the VPN tunnel. These IP subnets are then added to the routing table configuration during the VPN client configuration and provisioning process.

As organizations move their applications and data to the cloud, using the split tunnel configuration is recommended to ensure optimal performance.

Force Tunnel

In a force tunnel configuration, all network traffic, including Internet communication, goes over the VPN tunnel. No special routing configuration is required on the client. Force tunnel is often configured to provide visibility and control of Internet communication using on-premises security gateways. However, this method has some serious drawbacks. The user experience is greatly diminished, and performance is generally quite poor. It also increases resource utilization on VPN servers and ISP links.

Note   For a detailed analysis of split and force tunneling considerations, visit
`https://directaccess.richardhicks.com/2020/04/14/always-on-vpn-split-vs-force-tunneling/`.

Firewall Configuration

It is recommended the Windows VPN server be deployed behind an edge firewall to provide additional protection for the server. Firewall requirements differ depending on the VPN protocol used.

IKEv2

IKEv2 requires UDP 500 and UDP 4500 be allowed inbound on the edge firewall. If the VPN server has a routable public IP address and is not behind a NAT device, IP protocol 50 can also be allowed inbound.

SSTP

SSTP requires TCP port 443 be allowed inbound on the edge firewall.

NAT Configuration

Network address translation (NAT) is required when the VPN server does not have a public IP address. It is important to configure NAT rules on the edge firewall to perform destination NAT (DNAT) only. Translating the client's original source IP address should be avoided as much as possible. Performing source NAT (or full NAT) results in meaningless log information on the VPN server (all client connections appear to come from the same source IP address). It can also lead to connectivity issues due to limitations in Windows on the number of client connections allowed from a single source address.

Client Provisioning

Always On VPN configuration can be deployed to Windows 10 clients using a variety of different methods.

Microsoft Endpoint Manager

The recommended method for deploying Always On VPN configuration to Windows 10 clients is using Microsoft Endpoint Manager (Intune). Using Microsoft Endpoint Manager, administrators can easily configure and deploy all of the necessary Always On VPN settings to their endpoints wherever they are. Deploying Always On VPN using Microsoft Endpoint Manager requires that Windows 10 devices be joined to Azure Active Directory and enrolled for Intune management. Azure AD Premium is recommended to ensure support for all Always On VPN features and capabilities.

Windows 10 devices can be joined to an on-premises domain but still require Azure AD join to support Intune management. This configuration is called hybrid Azure AD join. However, there is no explicit requirement for Always On VPN devices to be joined to a domain. Access to on-premises applications and data with full support for single sign-on is still available even without the device being joined to the on-premises domain.

PowerShell

A PowerShell script can be used to configure a Windows 10 client for Always On VPN. Obviously, this method does not scale well on its own, but it can be convenient for organizations with relatively few devices to configure. Another drawback is that running the script requires administrative access to the machine. PowerShell is helpful and often used for initial testing and evaluation of Always On VPN configuration prior to broad deployment.

MECM

Microsoft Endpoint Configuration Manager (MECM, formerly SCCM) is a popular solution for enterprise system management. Although VPN profiles for Windows 10 can be configured using MECM, it does not support configuring and provisioning for Always On VPN profiles. To deploy Always On VPN using MECM, a PowerShell script must be delivered and executed on Windows 10 devices.

Co-management

It is possible to manage endpoints using both Microsoft Endpoint Manager and SCCM. To provision Always On VPN using Microsoft Endpoint Manager, co-management must be enabled for the device configuration workload.

Note   Switching the device configuration workload to Microsoft Endpoint Manager also moves the Resource Access and Endpoint Protection workloads. More details can be found here: `https://docs.microsoft.com/en-us/mem/configmgr/comanage/workloads#device-configuration`.

Summary

Always On VPN has many supporting infrastructure requirements and touches upon numerous aspects of the enterprise, including servers, networking, certificates, authentication, security, and systems management. Once the planning phase is complete, the administrator can begin the task of configuring the individual components to support Windows 10 Always On VPN.

CHAPTER 3

Prepare the Infrastructure

There are many important prerequisites that must be addressed before deploying Windows 10 Always On VPN. Certificates will be required to support user and device authentication. This requires certificate templates to be configured and published for enrollment. Also, security groups are required to control access to certificates and to enable automatic certificate enrollment and renewal.

Security Groups

Security groups are required to be configured for Always On VPN. They will be used to restrict access to certificate templates and to control access to which users and devices can establish VPN connections. The following security groups should be configured in Active Directory, as shown in Table 3-1.

Table 3-1. *Active Directory Security Groups*

Group name	Group members
VPN users	AD user accounts that require an Always On VPN user tunnel
VPN devices	AD computer accounts that require an Always On VPN device tunnel
VPN servers (if domain-joined)	AD computer accounts of Windows VPN servers
NPS servers	AD computer accounts of Windows NPS servers

Certificates

Certificates will be deployed to Windows VPN servers to support IKEv2 VPN connections and to Windows NPS servers to support the authentication process. In addition, certificates will be issued to users to support Always On VPN user tunnel connections and to devices to support Always On VPN device tunnel connections. Finally, a

© Richard M. Hicks 2022
R. M. Hicks, *Implementing Always On VPN*, https://doi.org/10.1007/978-1-4842-7741-6_3

certificate is required on all domain controllers to support VPN user authentication with client certificates.

Certificate Templates

To access certificate templates in AD, open the Certificate Templates console (certtmpl. msc) on an issuing CA server or an administrative workstation with the Remote Server Administration Tools (RSAT) installed, and then follow the succeeding steps to create the required certificate templates for Always On VPN.

VPN Server

Perform the following steps to create the VPN server certificate template:

1. Right-click the **RAS and IAS Server** template, and choose **Duplicate Template**.

2. Click the **Compatibility** tab, and make the following changes as shown in Figure 3-1:

   a. Uncheck the box next to **Show resulting changes**.

   b. Select the latest version of Windows Server available from the **Certification Authority** drop-down list.

   c. Select the latest version of Windows client/Server available from the **Certificate recipient** drop-down list.

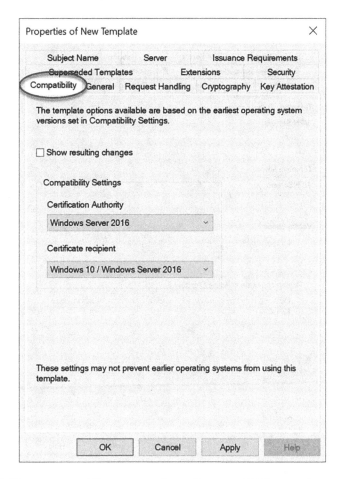

Figure 3-1. *VPN server certificate template Compatibility settings*

3. Click the **General** tab and make the following changes as shown in Figure 3-2:

    a. Enter **VPN Servers** in the **Template display name** field.

    b. Choose a suitable validity and renewal period.

    c. Do NOT check the box next to **Publish in Active Directory**.

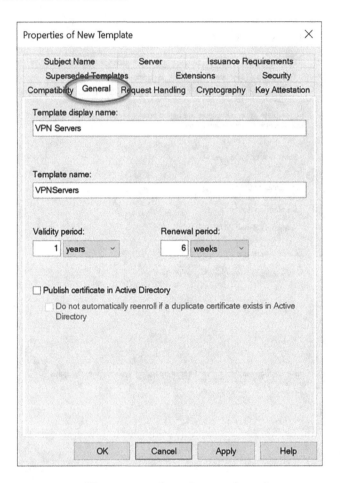

Figure 3-2. *VPN server certificate template General settings*

4. Click the **Cryptography** tab and make the following changes as shown in Figure 3-3:

    a. Select **Key Storage Provider** from the **Provider Category** drop-down list.

    b. Select **RSA** from the **Algorithm name** drop-down list.

    c. Enter **2048** in the **Minimum key size** field.

    d. Select **SHA256** from the **Request hash** drop-down list.

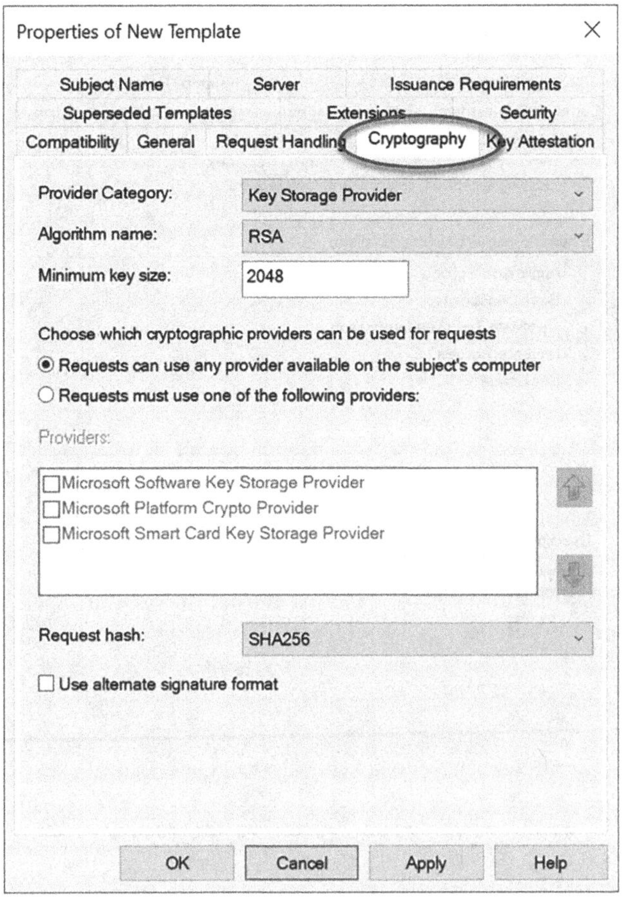

Figure 3-3. *VPN server certificate template Cryptography settings*

5. Click the **Extensions** tab and make the following changes as shown in Figure 3-4:

   a. Click **Application Policies** and click **Edit.**

   b. Click **Client Authentication** and click **Remove.**

   c. Click **Add.**

   d. Click **IP security IKE intermediate** and click **Ok.**

   e. Click **Ok.**

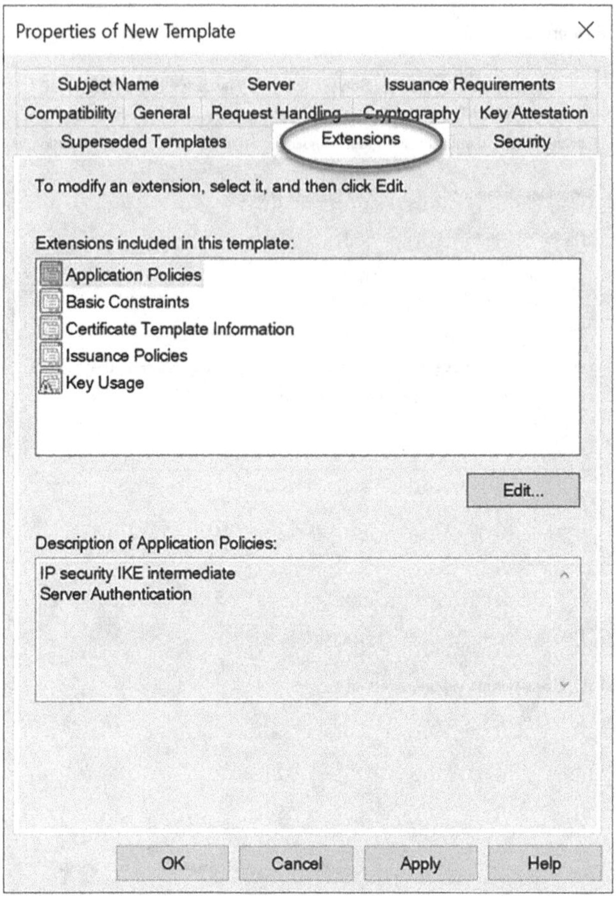

Figure 3-4. *VPN server certificate template Extensions settings*

6. Click the **Security** tab and make the following changes as shown in Figure 3-5:

    a. Click **RAS and IAS Servers** and click **Remove**.

    b. Click **Add**.

    c. Enter **VPN Servers** and click **Ok**.

    d. In the **Allow** column, check **Read**, **Enroll**, and **Autoenroll** boxes.

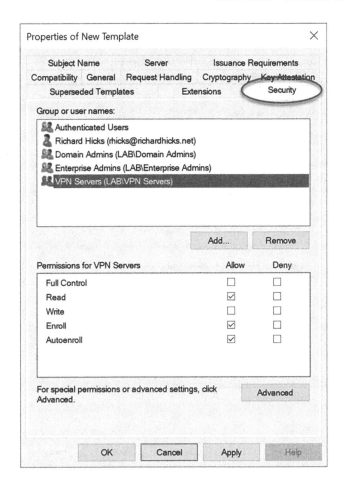

Figure 3-5. *VPN server certificate template Security settings*

7. Click the **Subject Name** tab and make the following changes as shown in Figure 3-6:

   a. Select **Supply in the request**.

   b. Click **Ok** on the certificate settings warning. Certificate approval, if required, will be configured later.

   c. Check the box next to **Use subject name information from existing certificates for autoenrollment renewal requests**.

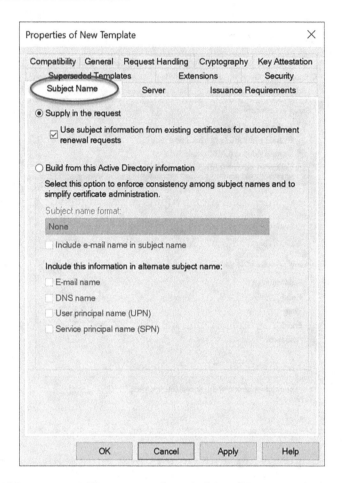

Figure 3-6. *VPN server certificate template Subject Name settings*

Note   The option to supply the subject name in the certificate request is required for the VPN server because the subject must be the public FQDN, not the server's hostname or NetBIOS name. Supplying the subject name in a certificate request presents a security risk, however. It is recommended, although not required, to complete the additional steps in the following to configure this certificate template to require approval before issuing.

---

8. Click the **Issuance Requirements** tab and make the following changes as shown in Figure 3-7.

   a. Check the box next to CA **certificate manager approval**.

   b. Click **Ok**.

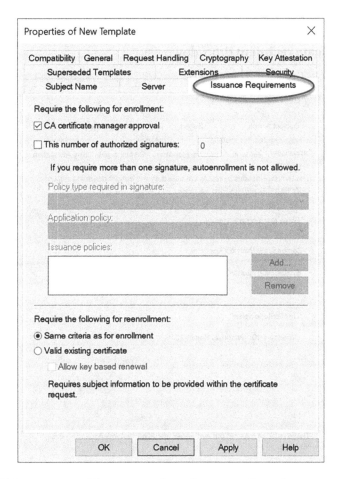

Figure 3-7. *VPN server certificate template Issuance Requirements settings*

NPS Server

Perform the following steps to create the NPS server certificate template:

1. Right-click the **RAS and IAS Server** template and choose **Duplicate Template**.

2. Click the **Compatibility** tab and make the following changes as shown in Figure 3-8:

    a. Uncheck the box next to **Show resulting changes**.

    b. Select the latest version of Windows Server available from the **Certification Authority** drop-down list.

    c. Select the latest version of Windows client/Server available from the **Certificate recipient** drop-down list.

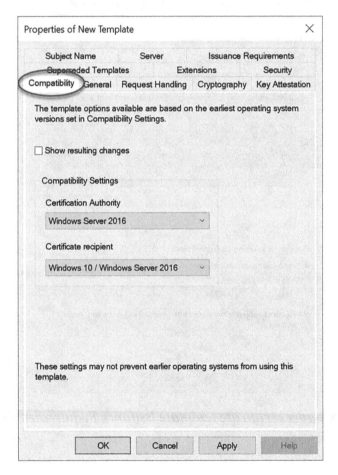

Figure 3-8. *NPS certificate template Compatibility settings*

3. Click the **General** tab and make the following changes as shown in Figure 3-9:

   a. Enter **NPS Servers** in the **Template display name** field.

   b. Choose a suitable validity and renewal period.

   c. Do NOT check the box next to **Publish in Active Directory**.

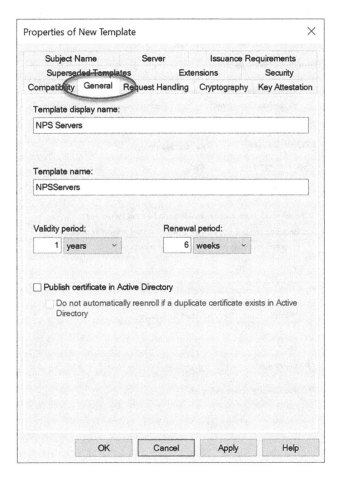

Figure 3-9. *NPS server certificate template General settings*

4. Click the **Cryptography** tab and make the following changes as shown in Figure 3-10:

    a. Select **Key Storage Provider** from the **Provider Category** drop-down list.

    b. Select **RSA** from the **Algorithm name** drop-down list.

    c. Enter **2048** in the **Minimum key size** field.

    d. Select **SHA256** from the **Request hash** drop-down list.

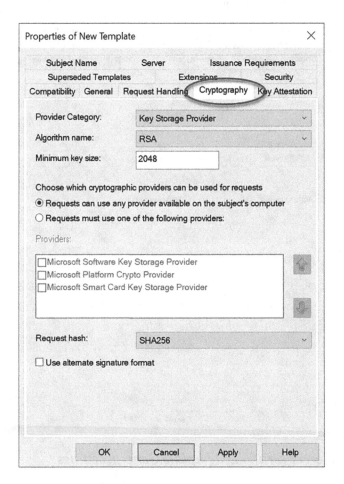

Figure 3-10. *NPS server certificate template Cryptography settings*

5. Click the **Extensions** tab and make the following changes as shown in Figure 3-11:

    a. Click **Application Policies** and click **Edit**.

    b. Click **Client Authentication** and click **Remove**.

    c. Click **Ok**.

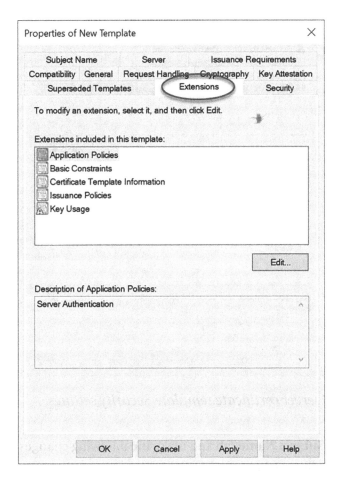

Figure 3-11. *NPS server certificate template Extensions settings*

6. Click the **Security** tab and make the following changes as shown in Figure 3-12:

    a. Click **RAS and IAS Servers** and click **Remove**.

    b. Click **Add**.

  c. Enter **NPS Servers** and click **Ok**.

  d. In the **Allow** column, check **Read**, **Enroll**, and **Autoenroll** boxes.

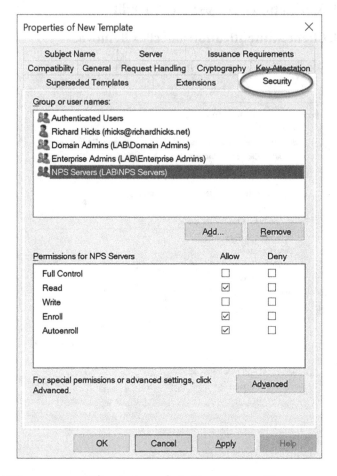

Figure 3-12. *NPS server certificate template Security settings*

7. Click the **Subject Name** tab and make the following changes as shown in Figure 3-13:

  a. From the **Subject name format** drop-down list, select **DNS name**.

  b. In the **Include this information in alternate subject name** section, check the box next to **DNS name** only.

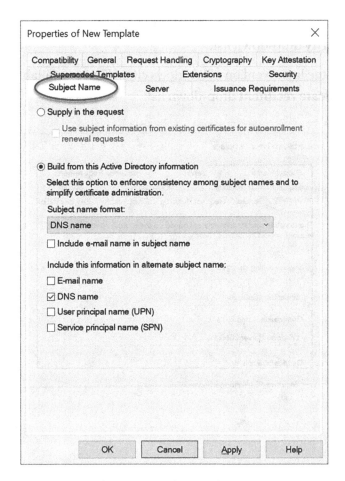

Figure 3-13. *NPS server certificate template Subject Name settings*

8.   Click **Ok**.

User Authentication

Perform the following steps to create the user authentication certificate template:

1.   Right-click the **User** certificate template and choose **Duplicate Template**.

2.   Click the **Compatibility** tab and make the following changes as shown in Figure 3-14:

a.   Uncheck the box next to **Show resulting changes**.

b. Select the latest version of Windows Server available from the **Certification Authority** drop-down list.

c. Select the latest version of Windows client/Server available from the **Certificate recipient** drop-down list.

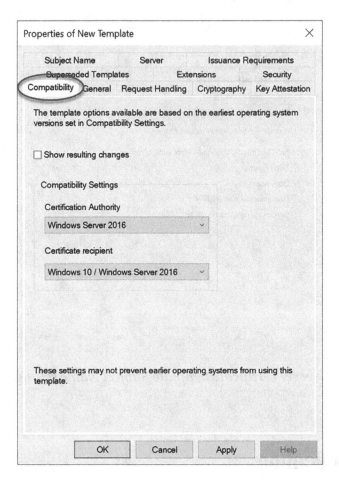

Figure 3-14. *User certificate template Compatibility settings*

3. Click the **General** tab and make the following changes as shown in Figure 3-15.

a. Enter **VPN Users** in the **Template display name** field.

b. Choose a suitable validity and renewal period.

c. Uncheck the box next to **Publish in Active Directory**.

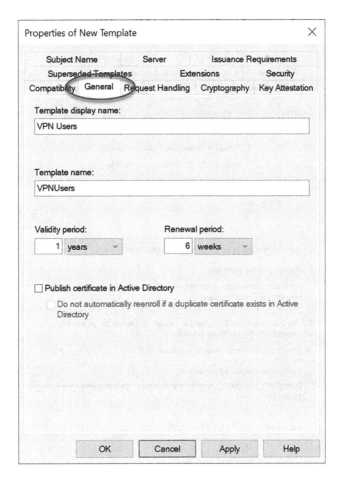

Figure 3-15. *User certificate template General settings*

4. Click the **Request Handling** tab and make the following changes as shown in Figure 3-16:

   a. Uncheck the box next to **Allow private key to be exported**.

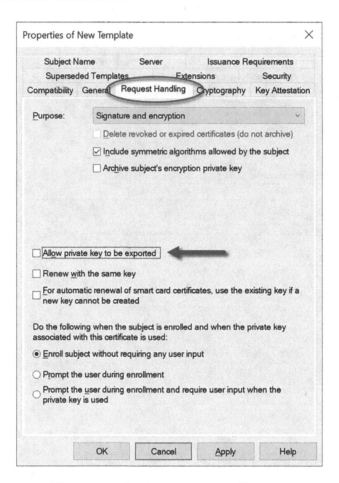

Figure 3-16. *User certificate template Request Handling settings*

5. Click the **Cryptography** tab and make the following changes as shown in Figure 3-17.

   a. Select **Key Storage Provider** from the **Provider Category** drop-down list.

   b. Select **RSA** from the **Algorithm name** drop-down list.

   c. Enter **2048** in the **Minimum key size** field.

   d. Select **Requests must use one of the following providers**.

   e. Check the box next to **Microsoft Platform Crypto Provider**.

   f. Select **SHA256** from the **Request hash** drop-down list.

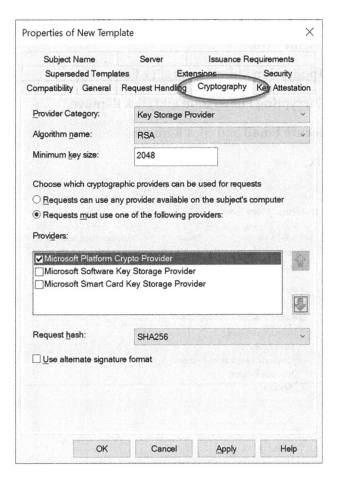

Figure 3-17. *User certificate template Cryptography settings*

Note   Selecting the Microsoft Platform Crypto Provider ensures that private key operations are protected by the Trusted Platform Module (TPM) on the client device. This is the recommended option for most deployments. If a user authentication certificate must be deployed to a device without a TPM, administrators can also select Microsoft Software Key Storage Provider. Ensure the Platform Crypto Provider is listed first so that it is preferred and used whenever a TPM is present. Also, consider using TPM Key Attestation for additional security and assurance. More details here: `https://docs.microsoft.com/en-us/windows-server/identity/ad-ds/manage/component-updates/tpm-key-attestation`.

---

6. Click the **Extensions** tab and make the following changes as shown in Figure 3-18:

   a. Click **Application Policies** and click **Edit**.

   b. Click **Encrypting File System** and click **Remove**.

   c. Click **Secure Email** and click **Remove**.

   d. Click **Ok**.

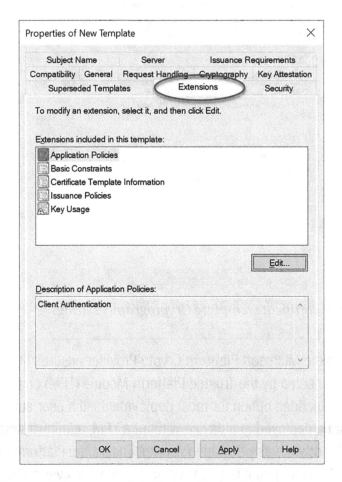

Figure 3-18. *User certificate template Extensions settings*

Note   Administrators can choose to leave the Encrypting File System and/or Secure Email application policies if those capabilities are needed. However, the Client Authentication application policy is the only policy required to support VPN user authentication.

7. Click the **Security** tab and make the following changes as shown in Figure 3-19.

    a. Click **Domain Users** and click **Remove**.

    b. Click **Add**.

    c. Enter **VPN Users** and click **Ok**.

    d. In the **Allow** column, check **Read**, **Enroll**, and **Autoenroll** boxes.

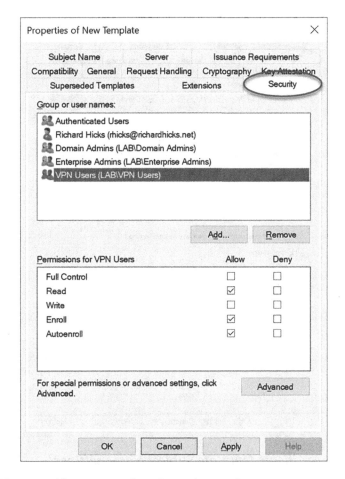

Figure 3-19. *User certificate template Security settings*

8. Click the **Subject Name** tab and make the following changes as shown in Figure 3-20:

    a. Select **Build from this Active Directory information**.

    b. Select **Common name** from the **Subject name format** drop-down list.

    c. Uncheck **Include e-mail name in subject name**.

    d. Uncheck **E-Mail name** in the **Include this information in the alternate subject name section**.

    e. Check the box next to **User principal name (UPN)**.

    f. Click **Ok**.

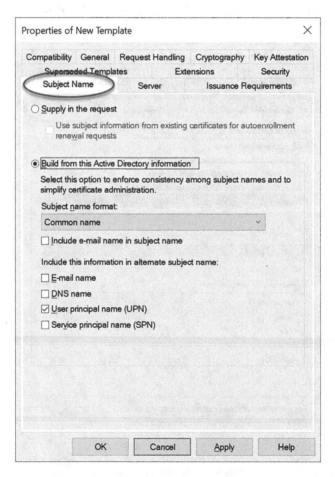

Figure 3-20. *User certificate template Subject Name settings*

Device Authentication

Perform the following steps to create the VPN device certificate template:

1. Right-click the **Workstation Authentication** template and choose **Duplicate Template**.

2. Click the **Compatibility** tab and make the following changes as shown in Figure 3-21:

   a. Uncheck the box next to **Show resulting changes**.

   b. Select the latest version of Windows Server available from the **Certification Authority** drop-down list.

   c. Select the latest version of Windows client/Server available from the **Certificate recipient** drop-down list.

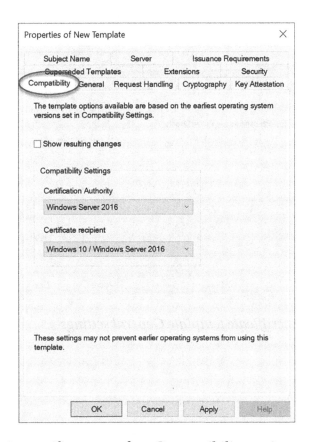

Figure 3-21. *Device certificate template Compatibility settings*

3. Click the **General** tab and make the following changes as shown in Figure 3-22:

   a. Enter **VPN Devices** in the **Template display name** field.

   b. Choose a suitable validity and renewal period.

   c. Do NOT check the box next to **Publish in Active Directory**.

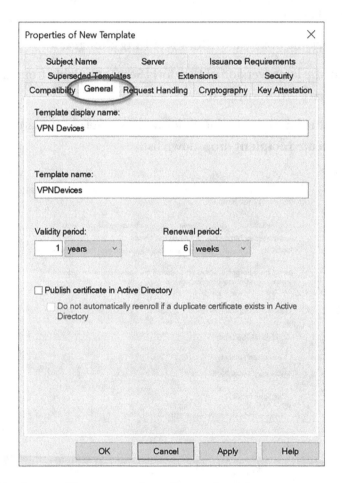

Figure 3-22. *Device certificate template General settings*

4. Click the **Cryptography** tab and make the following changes as shown in Figure 3-23.

   a. Select **Key Storage Provider** from the **Provider Category** drop-down list.

   b. Select **RSA** from the **Algorithm name** drop-down list.

   c. Enter **2048** in the **Minimum key size** field.

   d. Select **Requests must use one of the following providers**.

   e. Check the box next to **Microsoft Platform Crypto Provider**.

   f. Select **SHA256** from the **Request hash** drop-down list.

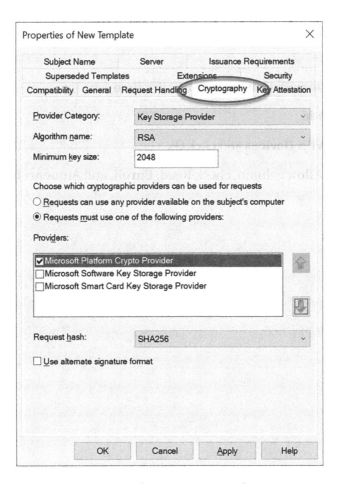

Figure 3-23. *Device certificate template Cryptography settings*

Note   Selecting the Microsoft Platform Crypto Provider ensures that private key operations are protected by the Trusted Platform Module (TPM) on the client device. This is the recommended option for most deployments. If a user authentication certificate must be deployed to a device without a TPM, administrators can also select Microsoft Software Key Storage Provider. Ensure the Platform Crypto Provider is listed first so that it is preferred and used whenever a TPM is present. Also, consider using TPM Key Attestation for additional security and assurance. More details here: `https://docs.microsoft.com/en-us/windows-server/ identity/ad-ds/manage/component-updates/tpm-key-attestation`.

5. Click the **Security** tab and make the following changes as shown in Figure 3-24:

    a. Click **Domain Computers** and click **Remove**.

    b. Click **Add**.

    c. Enter **VPN Devices** and click **Ok**.

    d. In the **Allow** column, check **Read**, **Enroll**, and **Autoenroll** boxes.

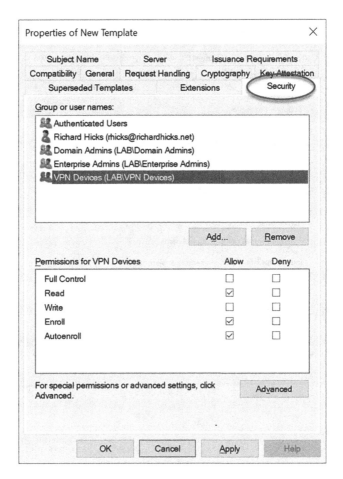

Figure 3-24. *Device certificate template Security settings*

6. Click the **Subject Name** tab and make the following changes as shown in Figure 3-25:

    a. Select **Build from this Active Directory information**.

    b. Select **DNS name** from the **Subject name format** drop-down list.

    c. Check the box next to **DNS name**.

    d. Click **Ok**.

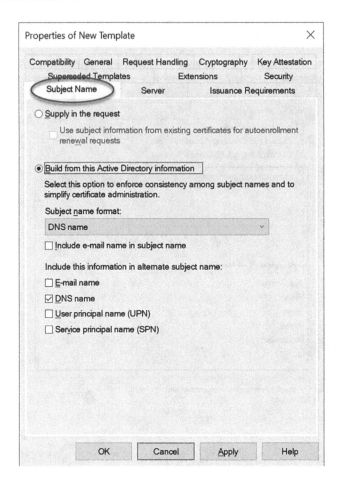

Figure 3-25. *Device certificate template Subject Name settings*

Kerberos Authentication

All domain controllers in the organization must have a Kerberos Authentication certificate to support client certificate authentication for Always On VPN. A Domain Controller Authentication will also suffice, but it is recommended to use the new Kerberos Authentication certificate template whenever possible.

Perform the following steps to create the Kerberos Authentication certificate template for enterprise domain controllers:

1. Right-click the **Kerberos Authentication** template and choose **Duplicate Template**.

2. Click the **Compatibility** tab and make the following changes as shown in Figure 3-26:

    a. Uncheck the box next to **Show resulting changes**.

    b. Select the latest version of Windows Server available from the **Certification Authority** drop-down list.

    c. Select the latest version of Windows client/Server that matches the oldest domain controller in the organization available from the **Certificate recipient** drop-down list.

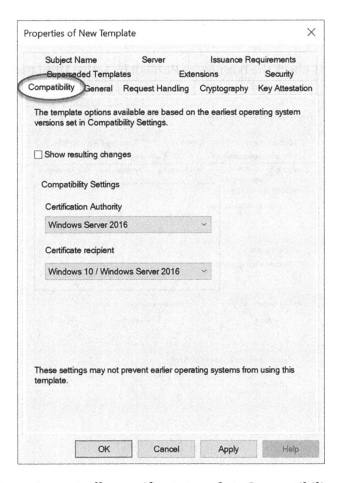

Figure 3-26. *Domain controller certificate template Compatibility settings*

Note   If all domain controllers in the organization are running Windows Server 2016, select Windows 10/Windows Server 2016 from the Certificate recipient drop-down list. If any domain controllers are running older versions of Windows, select a Certificate recipient value that matches the oldest version of Windows running on a domain controller in the environment.

3. Click the **General** tab and make the following changes as shown in Figure 3-27:

    a. Enter **DC Kerberos Authentication** in the **Template display name** field.

    b. Choose a suitable validity and renewal period.

    c. Do NOT check the box next to **Publish in Active Directory**.

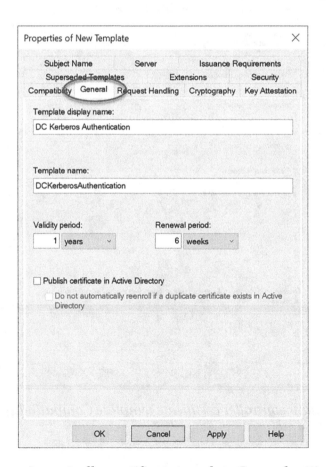

Figure 3-27. *Domain controller certificate template General settings*

4. Click the **Cryptography** tab and make the following changes as shown in Figure 3-28.

    a. Select **Key Storage Provider** from the **Provider Category** drop-down list.

    b. Select **RSA** from the **Algorithm name** drop-down list.

    c. Enter **2048** in the **Minimum key size** field.

    d. Select **SHA256** from the **Request hash** drop-down list.

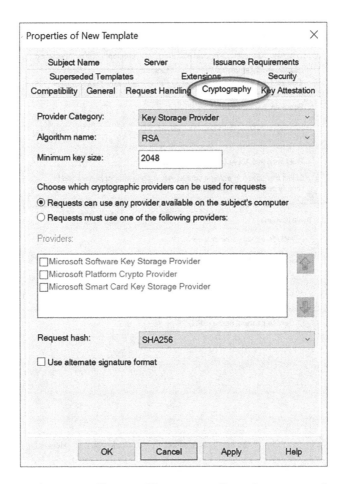

Figure 3-28. *Domain controller certificate template Cryptography settings*

5. Click the **Subject Name** tab and make the following changes as
    shown in Figure 3-29:

    a. Select **Build from this Active Directory information**.

    b. Select **DNS name** from the **Subject name format** drop-down list.

    c. Check the box next to **DNS name**.

    d. Click **Ok**.

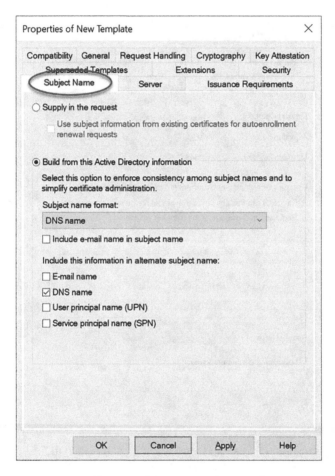

Figure 3-29. *Domain controller certificate template Subject Name settings*

Issue Certificate Templates

Once all the necessary certificate templates have been created, they must be made available for enrollment on all issuing CA servers in the organization.

Open the Certificate Authority console (certsrv.msc) on an issuing CA server or an administrative workstation with the Remote Server Administration Tools (RSAT) installed, and then follow the succeeding steps to publish the certificate templates.

Issuing CA Servers

Perform the following steps as shown in Figure 3-30 to publish certificate templates on all issuing CA servers in the organization:

1. Expand the Certification Authority.

2. Right-click **Certificate Templates** and choose **New ➤ Certificate Template to Issue**.

3. Select the **DC Kerberos Authentication**, **NPS Servers**, **VPN Devices**, **VPN Servers**, and **VPN Users** templates (use Ctrl-Click to select more than one).

4. Click **Ok**.

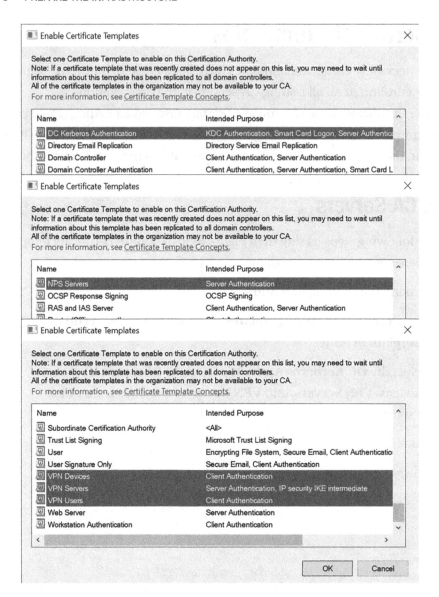

Figure 3-30. *Publish certificate templates*

Certificate Autoenrollment

It is recommended that certificate autoenrollment be enabled whenever possible. This will streamline certificate deployment for Always On VPN, ensuring that all servers, users, and devices receive the certificates necessary for Always On VPN. Crucially, it also ensures that certificates are renewed automatically before they expire.

Autoenrollment GPO

Open the Group Policy Management console (gpmc.msc) on a domain controller or an administrative workstation with the RSAT installed, and then perform the following steps to create the user and device certificate autoenrollment group policy object (GPO) and link it to the domain.

Note   Although it is recommended the certificate autoenrollment GPO be applied at the domain level, it is not strictly required. The certificate autoenrollment GPO can be applied to specific Organizational Units (OUs) if required. In this scenario, ensure the GPO applies to all VPN and NPS servers, as well as OUs containing VPN users and devices.

---

1. Right-click the target domain and choose **Create a GPO in this domain and link it here**.

2. Enter **Certificate Autoenrollment** in the **Name** field.

3. Click **Ok**.

4. Right-click the Certificate Autoenrollment GPO and choose **Edit**.

5. Expand **Computer Configuration ➤ Policies ➤ Windows Settings ➤ Security Settings** and highlight **Public Key Policies**.

6. Double-click **Certificate Services Client – Auto-Enrollment** and make the following changes as shown in Figure 3-31:

    a. Select **Enabled** from the **Configuration Model** drop-down list.

    b. Check the box next to **Renew expired certificates, update pending certificates, and remove revoked certificates**.

    c. Check the box next to **Update certificates that use certificate templates**.

    d. Click **Ok**.

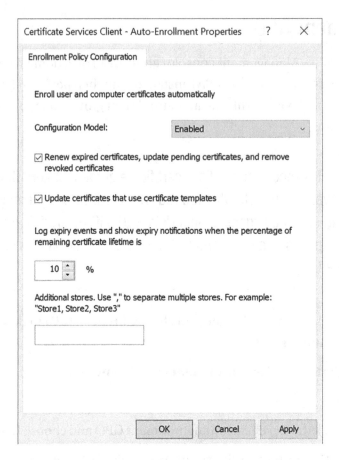

Figure 3-31. Computer certificate autoenrollment GPO settings

7. Expand **User Configuration ➤ Policies ➤ Windows Settings ➤ Security Settings** and highlight **Public Key Policies**.

8. Double-click **Certificate Services Client – Auto-Enrollment** and make the following changes as shown in Figure 3-32:

   a. Select **Enabled** from the **Configuration Model** drop-down list.

   b. Check the box next to **Renew expired certificates, update pending certificates, and remove revoked certificates**.

   c. Check the box next to **Update certificates that use certificate templates**.

   d. Click **Ok**.

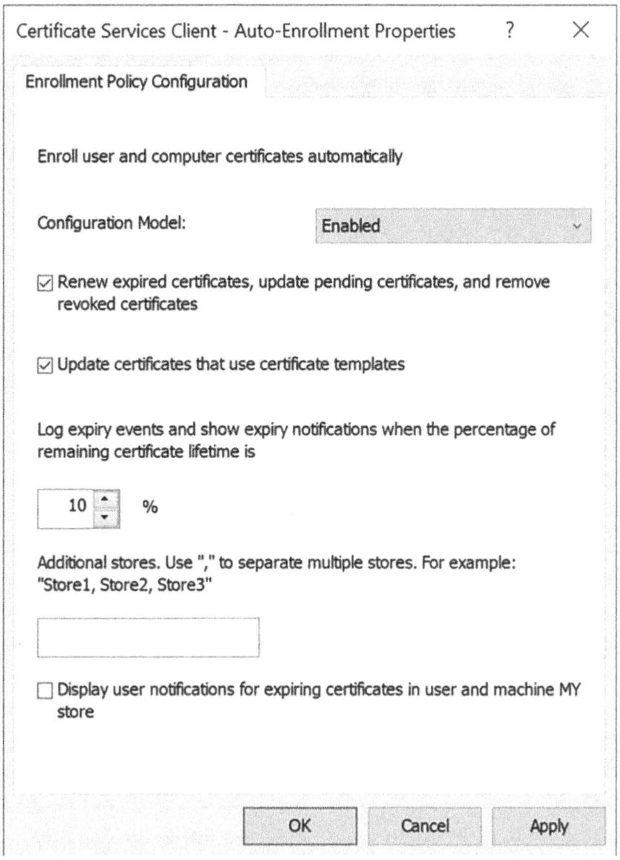

Figure 3-32. *User certificate autoenrollment GPO settings*

Summary

Proper certificate configuration is vital to ensuring the Always On VPN solution will be secure and resilient. Configuring certificate autoenrollment also ensures that certificates will be automatically provisioned, when required. Importantly, certificates will be renewed automatically before they expire, which improves the overall reliability of the solution.

Now that the supporting infrastructure is configured and prepared for Always On VPN, the process of building out the VPN and authentication infrastructure can begin.

## CHAPTER 4

Configure Windows Server for Always On VPN

A VPN server must be deployed to accept VPN connections from Always On VPN clients. In this book, Windows Server 2022 with Routing and Remote Access Service (RRAS) will be used. Of course, users must be authenticated when they connect to the VPN server. To support this, Windows Server 2022 Network Policy Server (NPS) will be configured. Certificates must be provisioned on both NPS and VPN servers. In addition, the DirectAccess-VPN and NPAS roles must be installed and configured on VPN servers and NPS servers, respectively. Finally, some of the default settings and parameters are suboptimal. Once the infrastructure is configured initially, some fine-tuning of the settings will be required prior to deployment.

Network Policy Server

The Network Policy Server (NPS) is Microsoft's implementation of the Remote Access Dial-In User Service (RADIUS) and is required to support user authentication for Always On VPN connections. The NPS server must be joined to the domain and be enrolled for the NPS server certificate created previously.

Note   The NPS role is not a supported role on Windows Server Core. The NPS role must be installed on Windows Server with Desktop Experience (GUI).

© Richard M. Hicks 2022
R. M. Hicks, *Implementing Always On VPN*, https://doi.org/10.1007/978-1-4842-7741-6_4

Preparation

To prepare the NPS server, provision a Windows Server 2022 server, assign an IP address, and join it to the domain. Next, add the NPS server to the NPS Servers security group in Active Directory. Reboot the NPS server, and then confirm the NPS server certificate was enrolled successfully.

1. In the **Search** window, enter **certlm.msc**.

2. Expand **Certificates – Local Computer ➤ Personal ➤ Certificates**.

3. Verify a certificate has been enrolled using the NPS Servers template as shown in Figure 4-1.

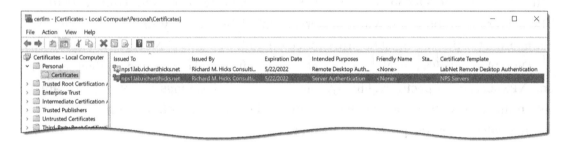

Figure 4-1. *NPS server certificate*

Install NPS

Once the NPS server is provisioned, joined to the domain, and has the NPS Server certificate installed, the NPAS role can be installed by opening an elevated PowerShell window and entering the following command.

```
Install-WindowsFeature NPAS -IncludeManagementTools
```

Next, to ensure that auditing is enabled for the NPS role, run the following command.

```
auditpol.exe /set /subcategory:"Network Policy Server" /success:enable /
failure:enable
```

Finally, to address a known issue in Windows Server 2019 where the Windows Firewall blocks incoming RADIUS authentication requests (even though there are firewall rules present and enabled by default to allow access), run the following command, and then restart the server.

```
sc.exe sidtype IAS unrestricted
```

Note   The Windows Firewall issue on NPS servers only affects Windows Server 2019. Earlier versions of Windows Server and Windows Server 2022 are not affected.

Configure NPS

To configure NPS, RADIUS clients must be configured, and a network policy must be defined to perform user-based authentication for Always On VPN connections.

RADIUS Client

The NPS server must be configured to accept incoming RADIUS requests from specific hosts, called RADIUS clients. Follow the succeeding steps to configure the VPN server as a RADIUS client on the NPS server as shown in Figure 4-2:

1. On the NPS server, open the Network Policy Server management console (nps.msc).

2. Expand **RADIUS Clients and Servers**.

3. Right-click **RADIUS Clients** and choose **New**.

4. In the **Name and Address** section, enter the fully qualified domain name (FQDN) or hostname of the VPN server in the **Friendly name** field.

5. Enter the FQDN, hostname, or IP address of the VPN server in the **Address (IP or DNS)** field.

6. If an FQDN or hostname was entered, click the **Verify** button, and
    then click the **Resolve** button and verify the FQDN or hostname
    resolves to the correct IP address.

7. In the **Shared Secret** section, enter a long, complex password in
    the **Shared secret** field. Alternatively, select the **Generate** option
    to automatically create the shared secret. Copy the shared secret,
    as it will be required later during VPN server configuration.

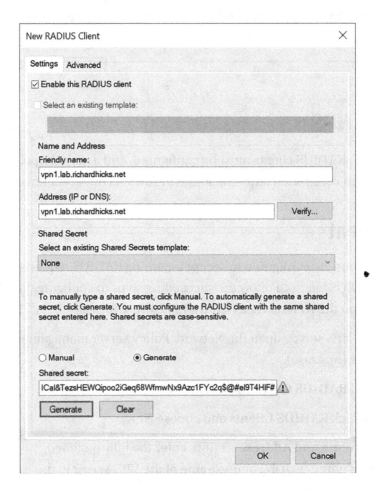

Figure 4-2. *New RADIUS client configuration*

Network Policy

The NPS server must be configured to perform user authentication for Always On VPN user tunnel connections. Follow the succeeding steps to configure a Network Policy using Protected Extensible Authentication Protocol (PEAP) with client certificates.

1. Expand **Policies** and select **Network Policies**.

   a. Right-click each default network policy and choose **Delete**.

2. Right-click **Network Policies** and choose **New**.

3. Enter **VPN Access** in the **Policy name** field.

4. Select **Remote Access Server (VPN-Dial up)** from the **Type of network access server** drop-down list (see Figure 4-3).

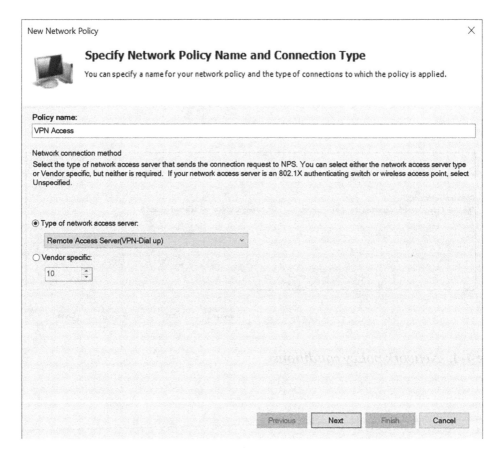

Figure 4-3. *Network policy name and connection type settings*

5. Click **Next**.

6. Click **Add**.

7. Select **User Groups** and click **Add**.

   a. Click **Add Groups**.

   b. Enter **VPN Users** and click **Ok**.

   c. Click **Ok** (see Figure 4-4).

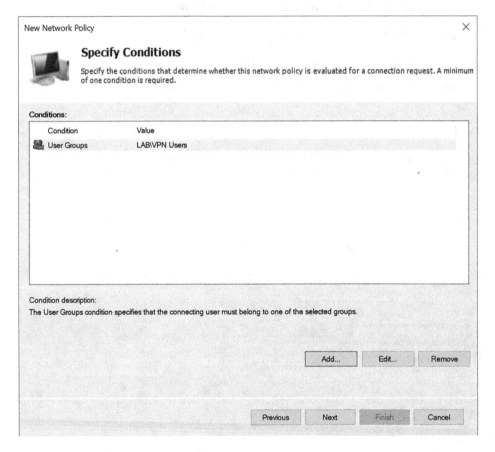

Figure 4-4. *Network policy conditions*

8. Select **Access granted** and click **Next** (see Figure 4-5).

Figure 4-5. *Network policy access permissions*

9. Below the **EAP Types** field click **Add**.

    a. Select **Microsoft: Protected EAP (PEAP)**.

    b. Click **Ok**.

10. Highlight **Microsoft: Protected EAP (PEAP)** in the **EAP Types** section and click **Edit**.

    a. Ensure the correct NPS server certificate is selected in the **Certificate issued to** drop-down list.

    b. Uncheck the box next to **Enable Fast Reconnect**.

    c. Check the box next to **Disconnect Clients without Cryptobinding**.

  d. In the **EAP Types** section, select **Secure password (EAP-MSCHAP v2)** and
     click **Remove**.

  e. Click **Add**.

  f. Select **Smart Card or other certificate**.

  g. Click **Ok**.

  h. Click **Edit**.

  i. Ensure the correct NPS server certificate is selected in the **Certificate
     issued to** drop-down list.

  j. Click **Ok**.

  k. Click **Ok** (see Figure 4-6).

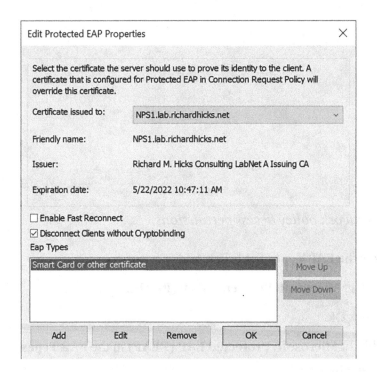

Figure 4-6. *Protected EAP configuration*

11. In the **Less secure authentication methods** section, uncheck all
protocols as shown in Figure 4-7 and click **Next**.

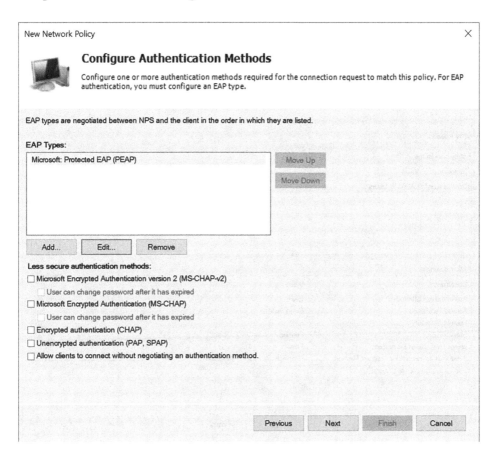

Figure 4-7. *Network policy authentication methods*

12. Click **Next** on the remaining menus, and then click **Finish** (see Figure 4-8).

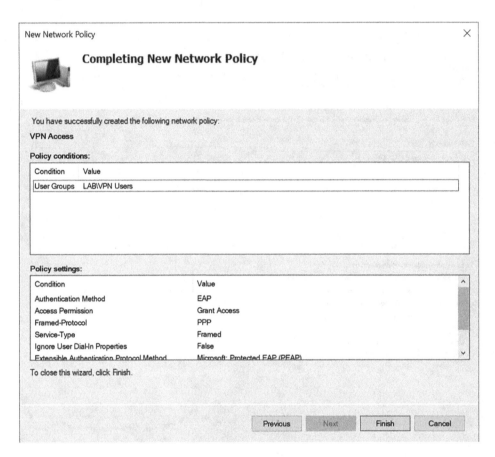

Figure 4-8. *Network policy configuration complete*

13. Right-click the VPN Access network policy and choose **Properties**.

14. Check the box next to **Ignore user account dial-in properties** and click Ok (see Figure 4-9).

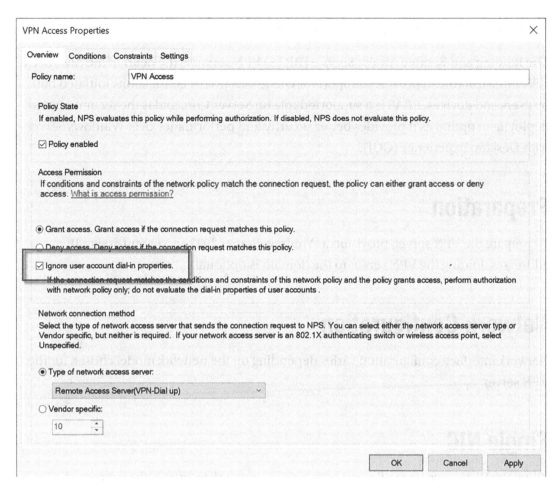

Figure 4-9. *Ignore user account dial-in properties*

Note   Administrators with NPS configuration experience may have noticed the option to register the server in Active Directory was not previously performed. This is optional and not required when using security group membership to control network access permissions. It is possible to allow or deny access to users by configuring their network access permission on the dial-in tab in the Active Directory Users and Computers management console. If this is required, then the NPS server must be registered in Active Directory to read the user account properties and allow or deny access accordingly. This configuration option is not generally recommended as it does not scale well in large environments.

Routing and Remote Access Service Server

The Routing and Remote Access Service (RRAS) VPN server is the heart of the Always On VPN infrastructure. It provides support for client-based VPN connections initiated both by users and devices. RRAS is a supported role on Server Core and is the recommended deployment option as it provides better security and performance over Windows Server with Desktop Experience (GUI).

Preparation

To prepare the VPN server, provision a Windows Server 2022 server and assign IP addresses. Joining the VPN server to the domain is optional.

Network Configuration

Network interface configuration varies depending on the network model chosen for the VPN server.

Single NIC

When the VPN server is configured with a single network interface, the process of assigning IP addresses is straightforward. In this scenario, assign an IP address, subnet mask, default gateway, and internal DNS servers to the network interface. No additional configuration is required.

Dual NIC

Network configuration is more complex when two network interfaces are used. Each network interface should be renamed to clearly indicate which network the interface belongs to. Each interface will require an IP address and subnet mask, but only the external interface should be configured with a default gateway. Static routes to remote internal networks must be configured on the internal interface. In addition, DNS servers capable of resolving internal hostnames must be configured.

Follow the succeeding steps to configure the internal and external network interfaces on the VPN server when using two network interfaces.

Note   IPv6 is not required to support Always On VPN. However, IPv6 will be configured in all examples for completeness. It is crucial that IPv6 not be disabled on the VPN server, however. This will result in the RemoteAccess service failing to start. See `https://directaccess.richardhicks.com/2021/01/11/ always-on-vpn-windows-server-rras-service-does-not-start/` for more details.

External Interface

The external network interface should be configured as follows:

- IP address.

- Subnet mask.

- Default gateway.

- Do NOT configure DNS servers on the external interface.

- Unbind all network protocols except for IPv4 and IPv6.

To configure the external network interface on Windows Server with Desktop Experience, open the Network Connections control panel applet (ncpa.cpl) and perform the following steps:

1. Right-click the external network interface and choose **Rename**.

2. Enter a descriptive name for the interface.

3. Right-click the external network interface and choose **Properties**.

4. In the **This connection uses the following items** section, uncheck the box next to all protocols and services other than **Internet Protocol Version 4 (TCP/IPv4)** and **Internet Protocol Version 6 (TCP/IPv6)** as shown in Figure 4-10.

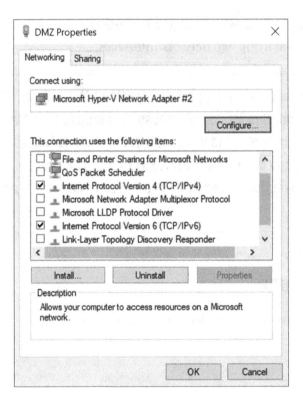

Figure 4-10. *External network interface configuration*

5. Select **Internet Protocol Version 4 (TCP/IPv4)** and click
    Properties.

    a. Select **Use the following IP address**.

    b. Enter the IPv4 address, subnet mask, and default gateway.

    c. Do NOT configure IPv4 DNS servers. Leave these fields blank
        (see Figure 4-11).

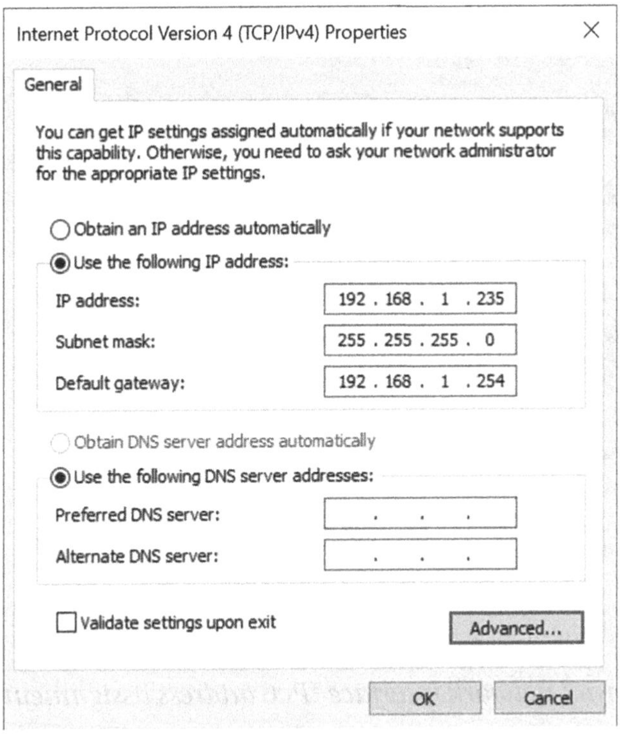

Figure 4-11. *External network interface IPv4 address assignment*

6. Select **Internet Protocol Version 6 (TCP/IPv6)** and click
    Properties (the following steps are optional and only required if
    IPv6 is deployed on the network):

    a. Select **Use the following IPv6 address**.

    b. Enter the IPv6 address, subnet mask, and default gateway.

    c. Do NOT configure IPv6 DNS servers. Leave these fields blank
        (see Figure 4-12).

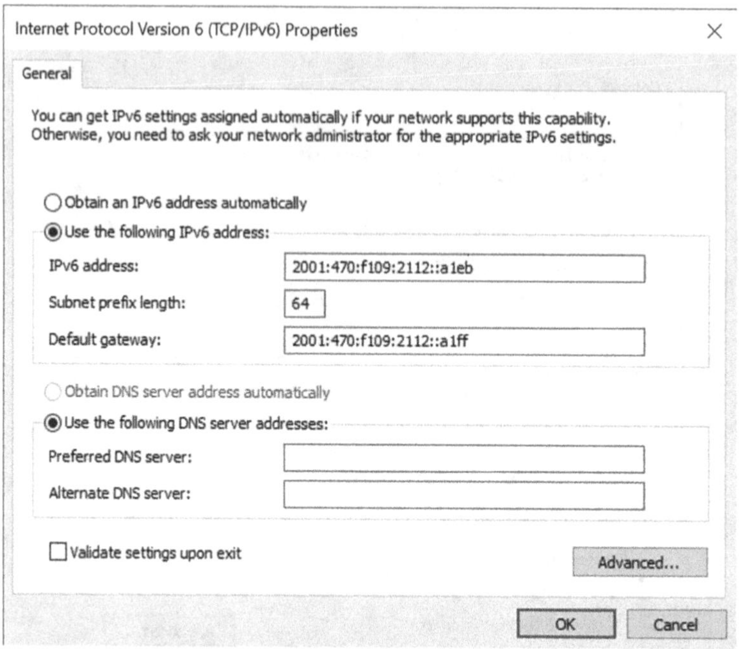

Figure 4-12. External network interface IPv6 address assignment

To configure the external network interface on Server Core, open an elevated PowerShell window and run the following commands to rename the network interface; assign an IP address, subnet mask, and default gateway; and unbind unused network protocols.

Note   Sconfig.cmd can also be used to configure network interfaces on Windows Server Core machines. In addition, sconfig.cmd can also be used to change the computer name, join the server to the domain, enable remote management, configure Windows Update settings, and more. However, IPv6 address assignment and network adapter bindings must be configured using PowerShell.

```
# // Rename Network Adapter

Get-NetAdapter Ethernet | Rename-NetAdapter -NewName DMZ

# // Configure IP Addresses

$Ipv4Address = '192.168.1.235'
```

```
$Ipv6Address = '2001:470:f109:2112::a1eb'
$Ipv4Gateway = '192.168.1.254'
$Ipv6Gateway = '2001:470:f109:2112::a1ff'
$Ipv4Prefix = '24'
$Ipv6Prefix = '64'

$NetAdapter = Get-NetAdapter -Name DMZ
$NetAdapter | Set-NetIPInterface -Dhcp Disabled
$NetAdapter | New-NetIPAddress -IPAddress $Ipv4Address -PrefixLength
$Ipv4Prefix -DefaultGateway $Ipv4Gateway
$NetAdapter | New-NetIPAddress -IPAddress $Ipv6Address -PrefixLength
$Ipv6Prefix -DefaultGateway $Ipv6Gateway
$NetAdapter | Set-DnsClient -RegisterThisConnectionsAddress $False

# // Disable Network Adapter Bindings

$NetAdapter | Set-NetAdapterBinding -DisplayName 'File and Printer Sharing
for Microsoft Networks' -Enabled $False
$NetAdapter | Set-NetAdapterBinding -DisplayName 'Client for Microsoft
Networks' -Enabled $False
$NetAdapter | Set-NetAdapterBinding -DisplayName 'Link-Layer Topology
Discovery Responder' -Enabled $False
$NetAdapter | Set-NetAdapterBinding -DisplayName 'Link-Layer Topology
Discovery Mapper I/O Driver' -Enabled $False
$NetAdapter | Set-NetAdapterBinding -DisplayName 'QoS Packet Scheduler'
-Enabled $False
$NetAdapter | Set-NetAdapterBinding -DisplayName 'Internet Protocol Version
6 (TCP/IPv6)' -Enabled $true
```

Once complete, run the following PowerShell command and confirm the external network interface appears as follows:

```
$NetAdapter | Get-NetAdapterBinding

Name DisplayName                                         ComponentID Enabled
---- -----------                                         ----------- -------
DMZ  Microsoft Network Adapter Multiplexor Protocol  ms_implat    False
DMZ  Link-Layer Topology Discovery Mapper I/O Driver ms_lltdio    False
```

```
DMZ  Internet Protocol Version 6 (TCP/IPv6)                ms_tcpip6   True
DMZ  Internet Protocol Version 4 (TCP/IPv4)                ms_tcpip    True
DMZ  Link-Layer Topology Discovery Responder               ms_rspndr   False
DMZ  File and Printer Sharing for Microsoft Networks ms_server   False
DMZ  Client for Microsoft Networks                         ms_msclient False
DMZ  QoS Packet Scheduler                                  ms_pacer    False
```

Internal Interface

The internal network interface should be configured as follows:

- IP address.

- Subnet mask.

- Do NOT configure a default gateway.

- Internal DNS servers.

To configure the network interface on Windows Server with Desktop Experience, open the Network Connections control panel applet (ncpa.cpl) and perform the following steps:

1. Right-click the internal network interface and choose **Rename**.

2. Enter a descriptive name for the interface. Do not use the name **Internal** as it is used in the RRAS configuration and can potentially cause a conflict.

3. Right-click the internal network interface and choose **Properties**.

4. Select **Internet Protocol Version 4 (TCP/IPv4)** and click **Properties**.

    a. Select **Use the following IP address**.

    b. Enter the IPv4 address and subnet mask. Do NOT configure a default gateway. Leave this field blank.

    c. Select **Use the following DNS server addresses**.

    d. Enter the IPv4 addresses of primary and secondary DNS severs capable of resolving hostnames on the internal network (see Figure 4-13).

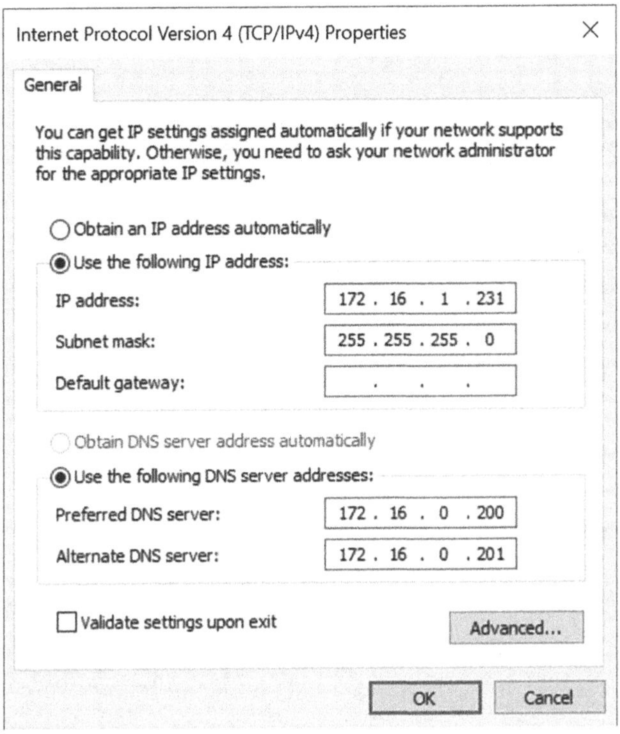

Figure 4-13. *Internal network interface IPv4 address assignment*

5. Select **Internet Protocol Version 6 (TCP/IPv6)**, and click
    Properties (the following steps are optional and only required if
    IPv6 is deployed on the network):

    a. Select **Use the following IP address**.

    b. Enter the IPv6 address and subnet prefix length. Do NOT configure a
        default gateway. Leave this field blank.

    c. Select **Use the following DNS server addresses**.

    d. Enter the IPv6 addresses of primary and secondary DNS severs capable of
        resolving hostnames on the internal network (see Figure 4-14).

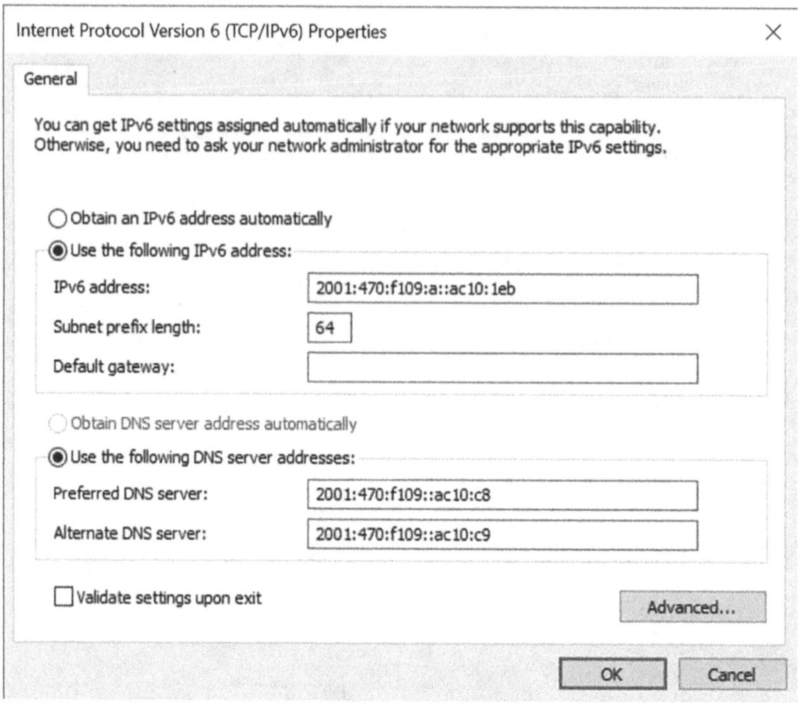

Figure 4-14. *Internal network interface IPv6 address assignment*

To configure the external network interface on Server Core, open an elevated PowerShell window and run the following commands to rename the network interface and assign an IP address, subnet mask, and internal DNS servers.

```
# // Rename Network Adapter

Get-NetAdapter 'Ethernet 2' | Rename-NetAdapter -NewName LAN

# // Configure IP Addresses

$Ipv4Address = '172.16.1.235'
$Ipv6Address = '2001:470:f109:a::ac10:1eb'
$Ipv4Gateway = '172.16.1.254'
$Ipv6Gateway = '2001:470:f109:a::fe'
$Ipv4Prefix = '24'
$Ipv6Prefix = '64'
$Dns = '172.16.0.200'
$Dnsv6 = '2001:470:f109::ac10:c8'
$DomainName = 'lab.richardhicks.net'
```

```
$NetAdapter | Set-NetIPInterface -Dhcp Disabled
$NetAdapter | New-NetIPAddress -IPAddress $Ipv4Address -PrefixLength
$Ipv4Prefix
$NetAdapter | New-NetIPAddress -IPAddress $Ipv6Address -PrefixLength
$Ipv6Prefix
$NetAdapter | Set-DnsClient -RegisterThisConnectionsAddress $true
Set-DnsClientServerAddress -InterfaceAlias LAN -ServerAddresses $Dns
Set-DnsClientServerAddress -InterfaceAlias LAN -ServerAddresses $Dnsv6
Set-DnsClientGlobalSetting -SuffixSearchList $DomainName
```

Static Routes

Since the internal network interface does not have a default gateway, it must be configured with static routes to any remote internal subnets. On Windows Server with Desktop Experience or Server Core, open an elevated PowerShell window and run the following commands to add static routes to the internal network interface. In the following example, the internal network is comprised of 172.16.0.0/16, 10.0.0.0/20, and 2001:470:f109::/48.

```
New-NetRoute -AddressFamily IPv4 -DestinationPrefix 172.16.0.0/16 -NextHop
172.16.1.254 -InterfaceAlias LAN
New-NetRoute -AddressFamily IPv4 -DestinationPrefix 10.0.0.0/20 -NextHop
172.16.1.254 -InterfaceAlias LAN
New-NetRoute -AddressFamily IPv6 -DestinationPrefix 2001:470:f109::/48 -NextHop
2001:470:f109:a::fe
```

Certificates

Two certificates must be installed on the VPN server to support client VPN connections. First, a certificate issued by the organization's internal Certification Authority (CA) must be installed to support IKEv2 VPN IPsec connections. In addition, a public Transport Layer Security (TLS) certificate must be installed to support SSTP VPN connections.

IKEv2 IPsec Certificate

A certificate to be used for IKEv2 VPN IPsec connections must be issued by the organization's internal CA. The procedure for requesting and installing the IPsec certificate varies depending on whether the server is joined to a domain, running Windows Server Core, or both.

Server GUI Domain-Joined

To install the IPsec certificate on domain-joined VPN servers configured with Windows Server with Desktop Experience, open the Local Computer Certificates management console on the VPN server (certlm.msc) and perform the following steps:

1. Expand **Certificates – Local Computer ➤ Personal**.

2. Right-click the **Personal** folder and choose **All Tasks ➤ Request New Certificate**.

3. Click **Next**.

4. Select **Active Directory Enrollment Policy** and click **Next**.

5. Check the box next to the **VPN Servers** template and click **More information is required to enroll for this certificate** (see Figure 4-15).

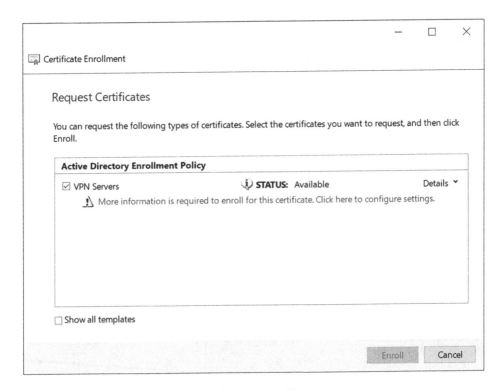

Figure 4-15. *VPN server IPsec certificate enrollment*

6. Select the **Subject** tab.

    a. In the **Subject Name** section, select **Common Name** from the **Type** drop-down list.

    b. Enter the public FQDN in the **Value** field.

    c. Click **Add**.

    d. In the **Alternative name** section, select **DNS** from the **Type** drop-down list.

    e. Enter the public FQDN in the **Value** field.

    f. Click **Add** (see Figure 4-16).

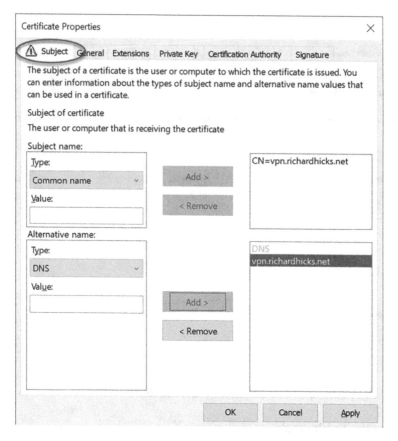

Figure 4-16. *VPN server IPsec certificate Subject Name settings*

If the certificate request requires approval, the submission will be pending. To approve the certificate request, open the Certification Authority management console on an issuing CA or a workstation with the remote administration tools installed and perform the following steps:

1. Expand the CA and select the **Pending Requests** folder.

2. Note the request ID. It will be required to retrieve the certificate later.

3. Right-click the certificate and choose **All Tasks ➤ Issue**.

To retrieve the certificate once it has been approved and issued, run the following command on the VPN server:

```
certreq.exe -retrieve [request ID] vpnipsec.cer
```

Next, run the following command to import the certificate:

```
certreq.exe -accept vpnipsec.cer
```

Once complete, refresh the certificates console, and then double-click the certificate to verify the private key is present and the subject name is correct (Figure 4-17).

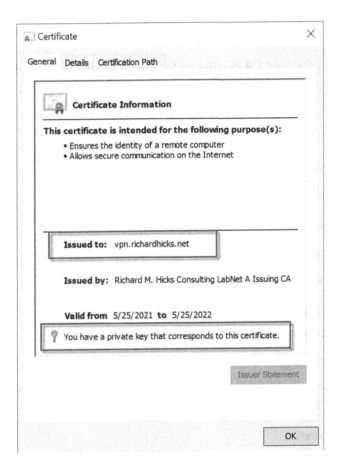

Figure 4-17. *VPN server IPsec certificate*

Server GUI Non-Domain Joined

Before installing the IPsec certificate on non-domain joined VPN servers, the root certificate and any intermediate certificates must first be imported on the VPN server.

Export CA Certificates

Perform the following steps on any domain-joined computer to export the root and intermediate CA certificates:

1. Click **Start** and enter **certlm.msc**.

2. Expand **Certificates – Local Computer ➤ Trusted Root Certification Authorities ➤ Certificates**.

3. Right-click the root CA certificate for the PKI that will be used to issue certificates to VPN servers and clients and choose **All Tasks ➤ Export**.

   a. Click **Next**.

   b. Click **Next**.

   c. Enter a name and path to save the file.

   d. Click **Next**.

   e. Click **Finish**.

   f. Click **Ok**.

4. Expand **Certificates – Local Computer ➤ Intermediate Certification Authorities ➤ Certificates**.

5. Right-click the intermediate CA certificate for the PKI that will be used to issue certificates to VPN servers and clients and choose **All Tasks ➤ Export**.

   a. Click **Next**.

   b. Click **Next**.

   c. Enter a name and path to save the file.

   d. Click **Next**.

   e. Click **Finish**.

Import CA Certificates

Copy the root and intermediate CA certificates to the VPN server. Open an elevated PowerShell window, navigate to the folder that contains the export root and intermediate CA certificates, and then run the following commands to import them:

```
Import-Certificate -FilePath C:\Config\RootCA.cer -CertStoreLocation
Cert:\LocalMachine\Root\
Import-Certificate -FilePath C:\Config\IssuingCA.cer -CertStoreLocation
Cert:\LocalMachine\CA\
```

Generate CSR

To install the IPsec certificate on non-domain joined VPN servers configured with Windows Server with Desktop Experience, a Certificate Signing Request (CSR) must be created. Open the Local Computer Certificates management console on the VPN server (certlm.msc) and perform the following steps:

1. Expand **Certificates – Local Computer ➤ Personal**.

2. Right-click the **Personal** folder and choose **All Tasks ➤ Advanced Operations ➤ Create Custom Request**.

3. Click **Next**.

4. Select **Proceed without enrollment policy**.

5. Click **Next**.

6. Select (**No template) CNG key** from the **Template** drop-down list.

7. For the Request Format, select PKCS #10.

8. Click **Next**.

9. Click the drop-down arrow next to **Details** and click **Properties** (see Figure 4-18).

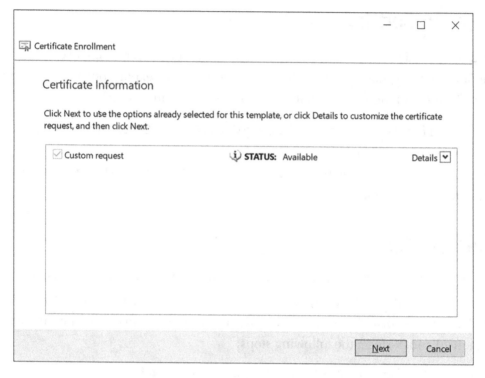

Figure 4-18. *VPN server IPsec certificate enrollment*

10. Select the **General** tab.

  a. Enter a descriptive name in the **Friendly name** field.

  b. Enter a description in the **Description** field (optional).

11. Select the **Subject** tab.

  a. In the **Subject Name** section, select **Common Name** from the
      Type drop-down list.

  b. Enter the public FQDN in the **Value** field.

  c. Click **Add**.

  d. In the **Alternative name** section, select **DNS** from the **Type**
      drop-down list.

  e. Enter the public FQDN in the **Value** field (see Figure 4-19).

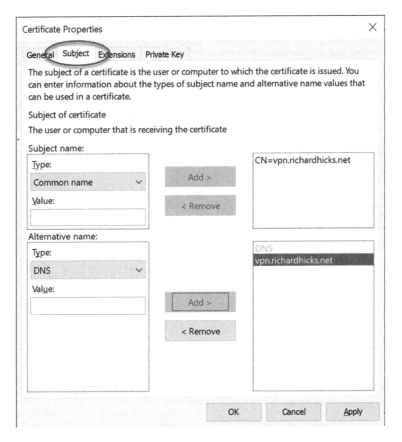

Figure 4-19. *VPN server IPsec certificate Subject Name settings*

12. Select the **Private Key** tab.

    a. Expand the Key options section.

    b. Select **2048** from the **Key size** drop-down list (see Figure 4-20).

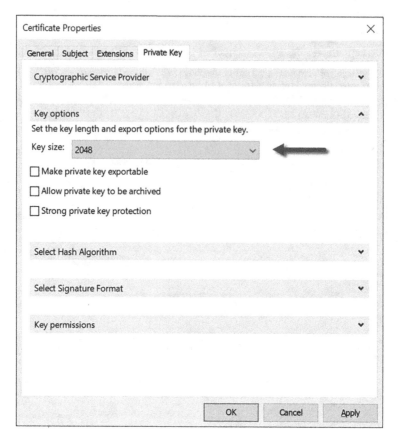

Figure 4-20. *VPN server IPsec certificate Private Key settings*

13. Click **Ok**.

14. Click **Next**.

15. Enter a name and path to save the file, and click **Finish**.

Request Certificate

Copy the CSR to a domain-joined system, open an elevated command window, and then run the following command to request the certificate:

```
certreq.exe -submit -attrib "CertificateTemplate:VpnServers" vpnipsec.csr
```

> **Note**   Be sure to run this command with a user account that has Read and Enroll permissions on the VPN servers certificate template.

If the certificate request requires approval, the submission will be pending. To approve the certificate request, open the Certification Authority management console on an issuing CA or a workstation with the remote administration tools installed and perform the following steps:

1. Expand the CA and select the **Pending Requests** folder.

2. Note the request ID. It will be required to retrieve the certificate later.

3. Right-click the certificate and choose **All Tasks ➤ Issue**.

To retrieve the certificate once it has been approved and issued, run the following command on the VPN server:

```
certreq.exe -retrieve [request ID] vpnipsec.cer
```

Next, copy the certificate file to the VPN server and run the following command to import the certificate:

```
certreq.exe -accept vpnipsec.cer
```

Once complete, refresh the certificates console, and then double-click the certificate to verify the private key is present and the subject name is correct (Figure 4-21).

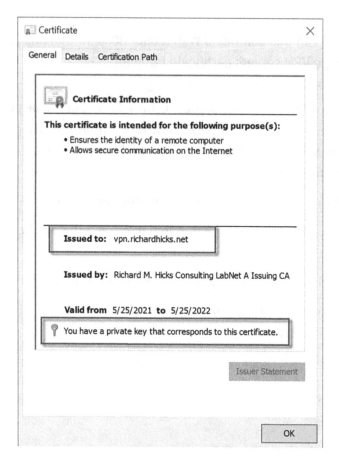

Figure 4-21. *VPN server IPsec certificate*

Server Core Domain-Joined

On Windows Server Core, there is no UI to create the CSR as there is with Windows Server with Desktop Experience. In this scenario, a configuration file must be created before creating the CSR.

Create INF File

On the VPN server, create a new text file that includes the following information. The subject name must be the public FQDN used to access the VPN server from the Internet. The CertificateTemplate name is the make of the certificate template (not the display name!) for the IKEv2 VPN certificate. Save the file with the .INF file extension.

```
[NewRequest]
Subject = "CN=vpn.richardhicks.net"
FriendlyName = vpn.richardhicks.net
KeyLength = 2048
MachineKeySet = true

[RequestAttributes]
CertificateTemplate = VPNServers

[Extensions]
2.5.29.17 = "{text}"
_continue_ = "dns=vpn.richardhicks.net&"
```

Create CSR

Run the following command to create the CSR using the information in the INF file:

```
certreq.exe -new csr.inf vpnipsec.csr
```

Next, submit the CSR to the issuing CA by running the following command:

```
certreq.exe -submit .\vpnipsec.csr -attrib "CertificateTemplate:VPNServers"
```

If the certificate request requires approval, the submission will be pending. To approve the certificate request, open the Certification Authority management console on an issuing CA or a workstation with the remote administration tools installed and perform the following steps:

1. Expand the CA and select the **Pending Requests** folder.

2. Note the request ID. It will be required to retrieve the certificate later.

3. Right-click the certificate and choose **All Tasks ➤ Issue**.

To retrieve the certificate once it has been approved and issued, run the following command:

```
certreq.exe -retrieve [request ID] vpnipsec.cer
```

To import the certificate, copy vpnipsec.cer to the VPN server and run the following command:

```
certreq.exe -accept vpnipsec.cer
```

Server Core Non-Domain Joined

The steps required to request an IPsec certificate for non-domain joined Windows Server Core servers is functionally similar to domain-joined Windows Server Core servers, with the exception that the CSR must be created from the command line, as demonstrated in the previous section. Also, the request must be submitted from a domain-joined system. See section "Server GUI Non-Domain Joined" for details.

SSTP Certificate

A certificate to be used for SSTP VPN connections should be issued by a public CA. A CSR must be generated on the VPN server and then submitted to a public CA for signing. Once the certificate has been issued, it can be installed on the VPN server.

It is recommended to use a TLS certificate with ECDSA keys for SSTP instead of RSA whenever possible. ECDSA provides better security and performance than RSA. However, some public CAs do not support issuing ECDSA certificates, so RSA is used in the configuration examples here. For detail information on configure an ECDSA certificate request for SSTP, visit https://directaccess.richardhicks. com/2018/08/20/always-on-vpn-ecdsa-ssl-certificate-request-for-sstp/.

The procedure for requesting and installing the SSTP TLS certificate is identical to IKEv2 IPsec, with the exception that the CSR is submitted to a public CA, not the organization's internal CA. Like the IPsec certificate, the Subject Name is the VPN server's public FQDN. The only exception is that when creating the INF file, omit the [RequestAttributes] section, as shown here. Optionally, the certificate can be marked exportable by adding Exportable = true to the [NewRequest] section.

```
[NewRequest]
Subject = "CN=vpn.richardhicks.net"
FriendlyName = vpn.richardhicks.net
KeyLength = 2048
```

```
MachineKeySet = true
Exportable = true

[Extensions]
2.5.29.17 = "{text}"
_continue_ = "dns=vpn.richardhicks.net&"
```

Once complete, submit the CSR to a public CA. When the certificate is issued, run the following commands on the VPN server to import the certificate, along with any root or intermediate certificates provided. In this example, a CSR was sent to DigiCert for signing. Once issued, three certificates were returned: the requested certificate, DigiCert's root certificate, and intermediate CA certificates.

```
Import-Certificate -FilePath C:\Configuration\vpn_richardhicks_
net_137714662TrustedRoot.crt -CertStoreLocation Cert:\LocalMachine\Root\
Import-Certificate -FilePath C:\Config\vpn_richardhicks_
net_137714662DigiCertCA.crt -CertStoreLocation Cert:\LocalMachine\CA\
certreq.exe -accept C:\Config\vpn_richardhicks_net_137714662vpn_
richardhicks_net.crt
```

Once complete, refresh the certificates console, and then double-click the certificate to verify the private key is present and the subject name is correct (Figure 4-22).

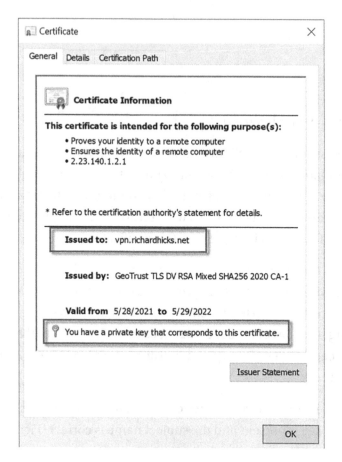

Figure 4-22. *VPN server SSTP TLS certificate*

In some cases, a certificate request may not be required. For example, an organization may already have a wildcard certificate, which is provided to the administrator in the form of a .PFX file. To import an existing PFX certificate on the VPN server, open an elevated PowerShell window and run the following commands:

```
$PwdTxt = 'SuPerS3crETpasSW@rd'
$Pwd = ConvertTo-SecureString -String $PwdTxt -Force -AsPlainText
Import-PfxCertificate -FilePath C:\Config\vpn_richardhicks_
net.pfx -CertStoreLocation Cert:\LocalMachine\My\ -Password $Pwd
```

> **Note**   It is common for PFX files to include all certificates in the chain. After importing a PFX file, only the end-entity certificate should be present in the Personal certificate store. If this store includes any other root and/or intermediate CA certificates, move them to their respective certificate stores before proceeding.

Install RRAS

Once all the necessary certificates are in place, the Routing and Remote Access Service (RRAS) role can be installed. On the VPN server, open an elevated PowerShell window and run the following command:

```
Install-WindowsFeature DirectAccess-VPN -IncludeManagementTools
```

When installing the role on Windows Server Core, the server must be restarted after the role is installed. Add the -Restart switch to restart the server automatically after the role is installed.

```
Install-WindowsFeature DirectAccess-VPN -IncludeManagementTools -Restart
```

Once complete, configure the RRAS role by running the following PowerShell command:

```
Install-RemoteAccess -VpnType Vpn -Legacy -PassThru
```

> **Note**   Administrators can install the DirectAccess-VPN role using Server Manager on Windows Server with Desktop Experience, if preferred. Select the DirectAccess and VPN (RAS) option below Remote Access in the UI. There is no need to enable the Routing role, however.

Install RSAT

The Routing and Remote Access Management console (rrasmgmt.msc) is installed automatically on Windows Server with Desktop Experience. To manage a Windows Server Core VPN server, the Remote Server Administration Tools (RSAT) must be installed on a Windows Server with Desktop Experience or a Windows 10 Workstation.

Windows Server

To install the Remote Access Management tools on Windows Server with Desktop Experience, open an elevated PowerShell window and run the following command:

```
Install-WindowsFeature RSAT-RemoteAccess
```

Windows 10

On Windows 10 1809 and later, open an elevated PowerShell window and run the following command:

```
dism.exe /online /add-capability /CapabilityName:Rsat.RemoteAccess.
Management.Tools~~~~0.0.1.0
```

Configure RSAT

To configure RRAS, open the Routing and Remote Access Management console (rrasmgmt.msc). If the management console is installed on a remote server or workstation, perform the following steps:

1. In the navigation tree, right-click the local server or client and choose **Delete**.

2. Right-click **Routing and Remote Access** and choose **Add Server**.

3. Select **The following computer**.

4. Enter the hostname or FQDN of the VPN server to be managed remotely.

5. Click **Ok**.

Configure RRAS

To configure RRAS, open the Routing and Remote Access Management console on the VPN server or a server or workstation with the RSAT tools installed and perform the following:

1. In the navigation tree, right-click the VPN server and choose **Properties**.

2. Select the **General** tab.

   a. If IPv6 is required, check the box next to **IPv6 Remote access server** (Figure 4-23).

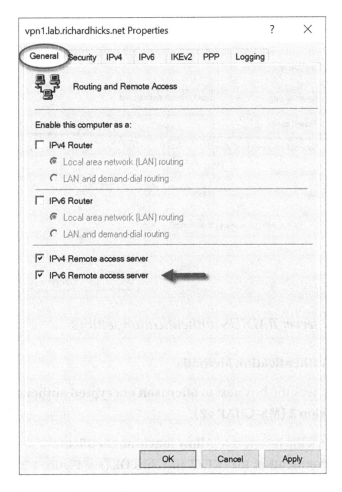

Figure 4-23. *VPN server General settings*

3. Select the **Security** tab.

   a. From the **Authentication provider** drop-down list, choose **RADIUS Authentication**.

   b. Click **Configure**.

      i. Click **Add**.

      ii. Enter the hostname or FQDN of the NPS server in the **Server name** field.

      iii. Click **Change**.

      iv. Enter the shared secret for the NPS server twice and click **Ok**.

      v. Click **Ok** (see Figure 4-24).

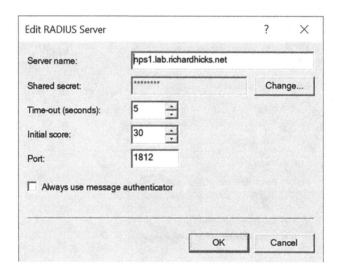

Figure 4-24. VPN server RADIUS authentication settings

   c. Click **Authentication Methods**.

      i. Uncheck the box next to **Microsoft encrypted authentication version 2 (MS-CHAP v2)**.

      ii. Check the box next to **Allow machine certificate authentication for IKEv2** and click **Ok** (see Figure 4-25).

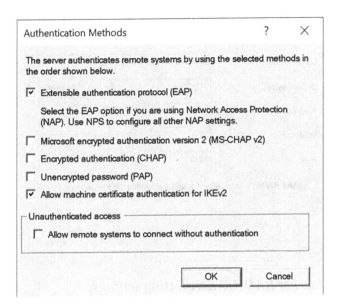

Figure 4-25. *VPN server authentication methods*

   d. From the **Accounting provider** drop-down list, choose **RADIUS Accounting**.

   e. Click **Configure**.

      i. Click **Add**.

     ii. Enter the hostname or FQDN of the NPS server in the **Server name** field.

    iii. Click **Change**.

    iv. Enter the shared secret for the NPS server twice and click **Ok**.

     v. Click **Ok** (see Figure 4-26).

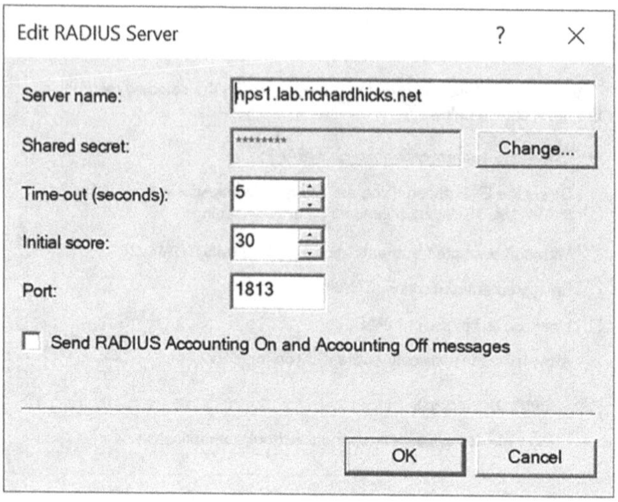

Figure 4-26. VPN server RADIUS accounting settings

    f. In the **SSL Certificate Binding** section, select the public TLS certificate from the **Certificate** drop-down list.

    g. Click **View** to confirm the correct TLS certificate has been selected.

Note   Clicking **View** when running the Routing and Remote Access Management console on a remote system will result in the following error:

The certificate used for Secure Socket Tunneling Protocol (SSTP) is missing. You must configure a new certificate for SSTP.

To select the correct certificate for SSTP, open the Local Computer Certificates management console (certlm.msc), and expand **Personal ➤ Certificates**. Double-click the public TLS certificate, click the **Details** tab, and then highlight **Thumbprint**. Copy the thumbprint to use in the following PowerShell commands.

To find the TLS certificate thumbprint on Windows Server Core servers, open an elevated PowerShell window on the VPN server, and run the following command:

```
Get-ChildItem -Path Cert:\LocalMachine\My\ | Select-Object
Thumbprint, Subject, Issuer | Format-List
```

Next, open an elevated PowerShell command on the VPN server and run the following commands:

```
$Thumbprint = 'SSL certificate thumbprint'

$Certificate = Get-ChildItem Cert:\LocalMachine\My\ | Where-
Object Thumbprint -eq $Thumbprint

Set-RemoteAccess -SslCertificate $Certificate –PassThru
Restart-Service RemoteAccess –PassThru
```

4. Select the **IPv4** tab.

   a. In the **IPv4 address assignment** section, choose **Static address pool**.

   b. Click **Add**.

      i. Enter the starting IP address in the **Start IP address** field.

      ii. Enter the ending IP address in the **End IP address** field (Figure 4-27).

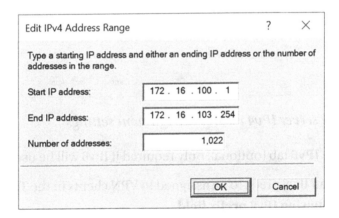

Figure 4-27. *VPN server IPv4 address range settings*

   c. On VPN servers configured with two network interfaces, select the internal network interface from the **Adapter** drop-down list (Figure 4-28).

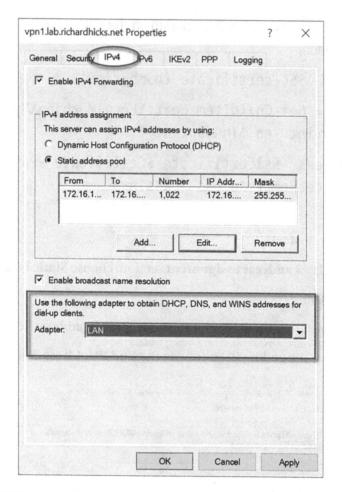

Figure 4-28. VPN server IPv4 address assignment settings

5. Select the **IPv6** tab (optional, only required if IPv6 will be used).

    a. Enter an IPv6 prefix to be assigned to VPN clients in the **This server assigns the following IPv6 prefix field**.

    b. On VPN servers configured with two network interfaces, select the internal network interface from the **Adapter** drop-down list (Figure 4-29).

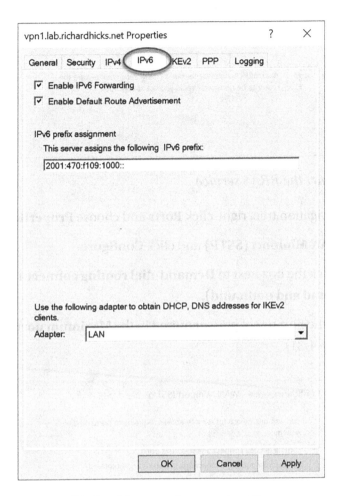

Figure 4-29. *VPN server IPv6 address assignment settings*

6. Click **Ok**.

7. Click *Yes* when prompted to restart the service (Figure 4-30).

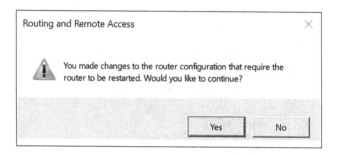

Figure 4-30. *Restart the RRAS service*

8. In the navigation tree, right-click **Ports** and choose **Properties**.

9. Select **WAN Miniport (SSTP)** and click **Configure**.

    a. Uncheck the box next to **Demand-dial routing connections (inbound and outbound)**.

    b. Enter the number of ports required in the **Maximum ports** field (Figure 4-31).

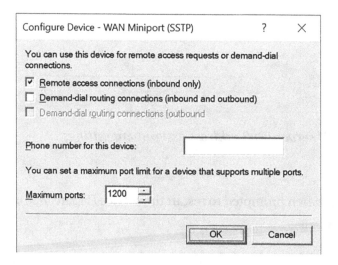

Figure 4-31. *VPN server SSTP port settings*

    c. Click **Ok**.

    d. Click **No** when prompted to restart the server (Figure 4-32).

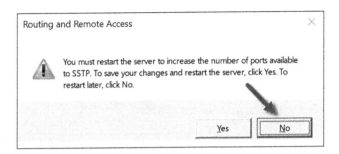

Figure 4-32. *Do not restart the server*

10. Select **WAN Miniport (IKEv2)** and click **Configure**.

   a. Enter the number of ports required in the **Maximum ports** field (Figure 4-33).

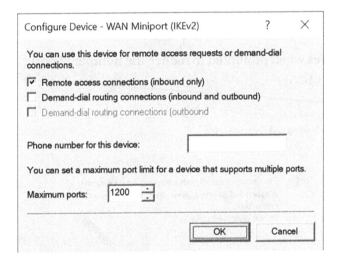

Figure 4-33. *VPN server IKEv2 port settings*

   b. Click **Ok**.

   c. Click **No** when prompted to restart the server.

11. Select **WAN Miniport (L2TP)** and click **Configure**.

   a. Uncheck the box next to **Remote access connections (inbound only)**.

   b. Enter **0** in the **Maximum ports** field (Figure 4-34).

105

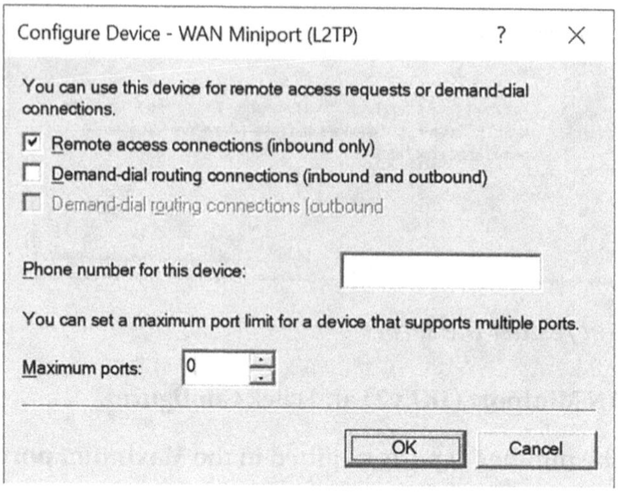

Configure Device - WAN Miniport (L2TP)   ?   ✕

You can use this device for remote access requests or demand-dial
connections.

☑ Remote access connections (inbound only)
☐ Demand-dial routing connections (inbound and outbound)
☐ Demand-dial routing connections (outbound

Phone number for this device:

You can set a maximum port limit for a device that supports multiple ports.

Maximum ports: 0

                                    OK   Cancel

Figure 4-34. *VPN server L2TP port settings*

c. Click **Ok**.

d. Click **Yes** when prompted to reduce the number of ports
(Figure 4-35).

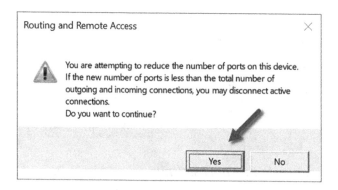

Routing and Remote Access   ✕

⚠ You are attempting to reduce the number of ports on this device.
If the new number of ports is less than the total number of
outgoing and incoming connections, you may disconnect active
connections.
Do you want to continue?

                                    Yes   No

Figure 4-35. *Confirm reducing the number of ports*

12. Select **WAN Miniport (PPTP)** and click **Configure**.

a. Uncheck the box next to **Remote access connections (inbound only)**.

b. Enter **1** in the **Maximum ports** field (Figure 4-36).

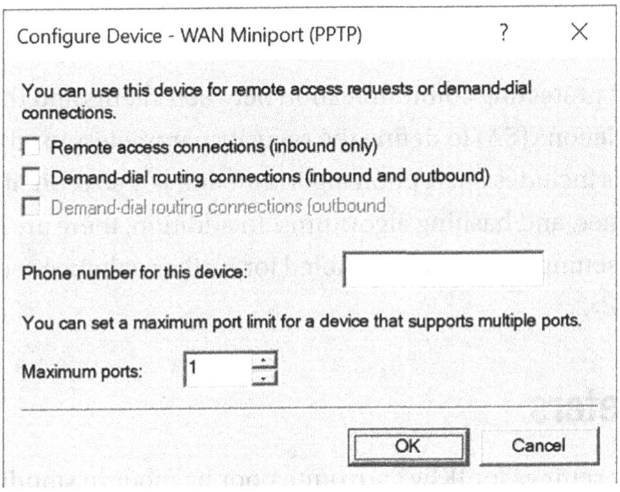

Figure 4-36. *VPN server PPTP port settings*

    c. Click **Yes** when prompted to reduce the number of ports.

Note   Intuitively, the administrator should be able to set the number of PPTP ports to "0", as you can with other ports on the RRAS server. However, "0" is not accepted for some reason, so in this case "1" will suffice. Technically speaking, it is not required to set the ports to 0 as they are disabled already. However, setting them to 0 makes it easier for administrators to visually identify which protocols are not in use.

Once complete, restart the VPN server to finalize the RRAS configuration.

Optimize RRAS

Many of the default settings configured with RRAS are less than optimal from both a security and performance standpoint. The following sections describe these limitations and how to improve them.

IKEv2 Settings

IKEv2 uses IPsec for protecting communication between clients and the server. IPsec uses Security Associations (SA) to define the security parameters used to establish the connection. This includes encryption algorithm and key size, SA lifetime and data renegotiation lifetimes, and hashing algorithms. In addition, there are some optional but recommended settings that can be enabled for further enhance security and performance for IKEv2.

IPsec Parameters

The default security settings for IKEv2 are quite poor by modern standards. For example, IPsec is configured to use 3DES for encryption, SHA-1 for the hash algorithm, and 1024-bit RSA keys. In addition, the default settings for Security Association (SA) lifetime and data size for renegotiation are less than optimal for client-based VPN.

Today, the minimum recommended security baselines for IPsec are AES-128, SHA-2, and 2048-bit RSA keys.

Note   AES-128 is recommended over AES-256 (in most cases) because the chances an attacker will brute-force (guess) the key is effectively zero. A brute force attack against AES-256 is obviously more difficult, but mitigating a risk that is already "effectively zero" provides no real value. Also, using AES-256 is slower and requires more CPU utilization on the client and the server. Use AES-256 only if data must be protected for extended periods of time (e.g., 50 years).

To update these settings on Windows Server 2019 and later VPN servers using minimum recommended security best practices (AES-128, SHA-2, and 2048-bit RSA keys), open an elevated PowerShell command and run the following command:

```
Set-VpnServerConfiguration -CustomPolicy -AuthenticationTransformConstants
GCMAES128 -CipherTransformConstants GCMAES128 -DHGroup Group14 -EncryptionMethod
GCMAES128 -IntegrityCheckMethod SHA256 -PFSgroup ECP256 -SALifetimeSeconds
28800 -SADataSizeForRenegotiationKilobytes 1024000 -PassThru
```

For Windows Server 2016 and earlier, run the following command:

```
Set-VpnServerConfiguration -CustomPolicy -AuthenticationTransform
Constants GCMAES128 -CipherTransformConstants GCMAES128 -DHGroup
Group14 -EncryptionMethod AES128 -IntegrityCheckMethod SHA256 -PFSgroup
PFS2048 -SALifetimeSeconds 28800 -SADataSizeForRenegotiationKilobytes
1024000 -PassThru
```

Once complete, restart the RemoteAccess service by running the following command:

```
Restart-Service RemoteAccess -PassThru
```

Note   The IPsec parameters previously defined must also be configured identically on the client. This will be covered in detail in the next chapter.

IKEv2 Fragmentation

It is common for IKEv2 messages to become quite large, especially during the initial handshake negotiation. Often these messages end up exceeding the Path Maximum Transmission Unit (PMTU) and must be fragmented at the IP layer. Many firewalls block IP fragments, which results in failed IKEv2 connection attempts.

IKEv2 fragmentation support was added to Windows 10 1803 and is enabled by default. IKEv2 fragmentation was added to Windows Server 1803 as well, but it is not enabled by default. To enable IKEv2 fragmentation support in Windows Server, open an elevated PowerShell window on the VPN server and run the following command:

```
New-ItemProperty -Path HKLM:\SYSTEM\CurrentControlSet\Services\RemoteAccess\
Parameters\Ikev2\ -Name EnableServerFragmentation -PropertyType DWORD -Value
1 -Force
```

Once complete, restart the RemoteAccess service for the change to take effect.

```
Restart-Service RemoteAccess -PassThru
```

IKEv2 Root Certificate

The Always On VPN device tunnel is authenticated by the VPN server using a device certificate installed on the Windows 10 endpoint. By default, Windows Server will accept a certificate issued by any of the CAs in its trust store. It is recommended that the VPN server be configured to accept device certificates issued only by the organization's internal, private CA. To do this, open the Local Computer Certificates management console (certlm.msc) on any domain-joined server or workstation and perform the following steps:

1. Expand **Certificates – Local Computer ➤ Personal ➤ Certificates**.

2. Double-click the **organization's root certificate**.

3. Select the **Details** tab.

4. Highlight **Thumbprint** and copy the thumbprint to be used later (Figure 4-37).

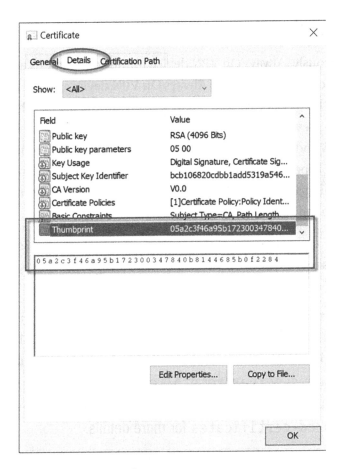

Figure 4-37. *Root certificate thumbprint*

Next, open an elevated PowerShell window and run the following commands:

```
$Certificate = Get-ChildItem -Path Cert:\LocalMachine\Root\ | Where-Object
Thumbprint -eq 05A2C3F46A95B172300347840B8144685B0F2284
Set-VpnAuthProtocol -RootCertificateNameToAccept $Certificate -PassThru
```

Once complete, restart the RemoteAccess service for the change to take effect.

```
Restart-Service RemoteAccess -PassThru
```

IKEv2 CRL Check

As mentioned previously, Always On VPN device tunnel connections are validated by the VPN server using a certificate issued to Always On VPN devices. If a device is lost, stolen, compromised, or is being deprovisioned and retired, administrators should revoke its device certificate to prevent access to the network via the device tunnel.

Unfortunately, Windows Server RRAS does not, by default, perform certificate revocation list (CRL) checking for device-based IKEv2 VPN connections. However, it can be enabled by opening an elevated PowerShell window on the VPN server and running the following command:

```
New-ItemProperty -Path HKLM:\SYSTEM\CurrentControlSet\Services\
RemoteAccess\Parameters\Ikev2\ -Name CertAuthFlags -PropertyType
DWORD -Value 4 -Force
```

> **Note**   Servers prior to Windows Server 2022 will require an update to support CRL checking for IKEv2 device connections. See https://docs.microsoft.com/en-us/windows-server/remote/remote-access/vpn/always-on-vpn/deploy/always-on-vpn-adv-options#blocking-vpn-clients-that-use-revoked-certificates for more details.

TLS Configuration

Secure Socket Tunneling Protocol (SSTP) VPN connections use TLS to secure communication between the client and VPN server. By default, both TLS 1.1 and TLS 1.0 are enabled on Windows Server 2022. Security best practices dictate these protocols should be disabled. To do this, open an elevated PowerShell window on the VPN server and run the following commands:

```
# // Disable TLS 1.1
New-Item -Path 'HKLM:\SYSTEM\CurrentControlSet\Control\SecurityProviders\
SCHANNEL\Protocols\TLS 1.1\Server' -Force
New-ItemProperty -Path 'HKLM:\SYSTEM\CurrentControlSet\Control\
SecurityProviders\SCHANNEL\Protocols\TLS 1.1\Server' -PropertyType
DWORD -Value 0 -Name Enabled
```

```
# // Disable TLS 1.0
New-Item -Path 'HKLM:\SYSTEM\CurrentControlSet\Control\SecurityProviders\
SCHANNEL\Protocols\TLS 1.0\Server' -Force
New-ItemProperty -Path 'HKLM:\SYSTEM\CurrentControlSet\Control\
SecurityProviders\SCHANNEL\Protocols\TLS 1.0\Server' -PropertyType
DWORD -Value 0 -Name Enabled
```

Once complete, reboot the server for the changes to take effect.

```
Restart-Computer -Force
```

Note   A PowerShell script to perform additional TLS hardening and optimization can be found here: `https://github.com/richardhicks/aovpn/blob/master/Optimize-VpnServerTlsConfiguration.ps1`.

Summary

With all the certificates in place, the VPN and NPS servers configured, and security and performance optimizations completed, the next step is to begin initial validation testing and then create and deploy Always On VPN user and device tunnels using Microsoft Endpoint Manager.

## CHAPTER 5

Provision Always On VPN Clients

With the infrastructure in place, the task of provisioning Always On VPN clients can begin. Before proceeding, though, it will be necessary to perform some initial testing to ensure the VPN infrastructure is configured correctly and that firewalls are passing traffic without issue and to ensure authentication is successful and that on-premises resources are accessible over the VPN tunnel as expected. Once the testing is complete, provisioning Always On VPN clients using Microsoft Endpoint Manager or PowerShell can move forward.

Validation Testing

Once the VPN/NPS infrastructure is in place, a test VPN profile must be created to validate the configuration. Connectivity, authentication, and access to resources over the VPN tunnel must be tested prior to production deployment. Before beginning, ensure the test user is in the VPN Users group, the Windows 10 device is in the VPN Devices group, and that the client authentication certificate and device certificates have been enrolled successfully.

Verify Certificates

Verify the user and device authentication certificates have been properly enrolled on the Windows 10 client. For the user authentication certificate, perform the following steps:

1. On the Windows desktop, click the **Start** button.

2. Click **Settings**.

115

© Richard M. Hicks 2022
R. M. Hicks, *Implementing Always On VPN*, https://doi.org/10.1007/978-1-4842-7741-6_5

3. In the search field, enter "certificate."

4. Click **Manage user certificates**.

5. Expand **Personal ➤ Certificates**.

If user certificate enrollment was successful, a user authentication certificate issued to the current user with the **VPN Users** template should appear in the certificate store, as shown in Figure 5-1.

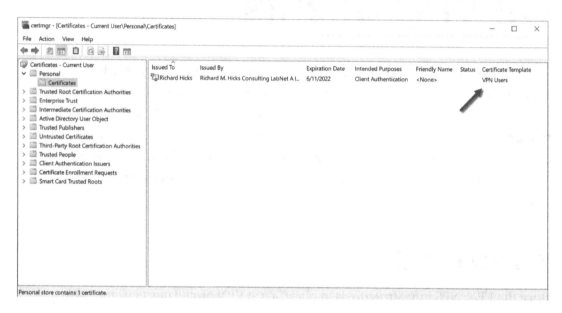

Figure 5-1. *Verify user certificate enrollment*

Perform the following steps to verify the device authentication certificate has been properly enrolled on the Windows 10 client:

1. On the Windows desktop, click the **Start** button.

2. Click **Settings**.

3. In the search field, enter "certificate."

4. Click **Manage computer certificates**.

5. Expand **Personal ➤ Certificates**.

If device certificate enrollment was successful, a device authentication certificate with the **VPN Devices** template should appear in the certificate store, as shown in Figure 5-2.

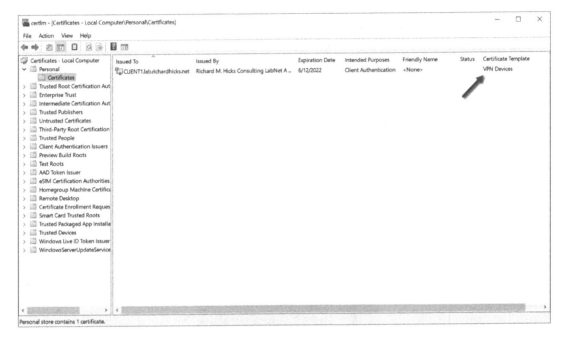

Figure 5-2.   *Verify device certificate enrollment*

Test Profile

A test VPN profile using the Secure Socket Tunneling Protocol (SSTP) VPN protocol and Protected Extensible Authentication Protocol (PEAP) using client certificates will be configured.

VPN Settings

Perform the following steps to create the test VPN profile:

1. Click the **Start** button on the Windows desktop.

2. Click **Settings**.

3. In the search field, enter "VPN."

4. Click **Add a VPN connection**.

117

5. Click the plus icon next to **Add a VPN connection**.

    a. Select **Windows (built-in)** from the **VPN provider** drop-down list.

    b. Enter "Test" in the **Connection name** field.

    c. Enter the VPN server's public fully qualified domain name (FQDN) in the **Server name or address field**.

    d. Select **Secure Socket Tunneling Protocol (SSTP)** from the **VPN type** drop-down list.

    e. Select **Certificate** from the **Type of sign-in info** drop-down list.

    f. Do NOT enter a username or password.

    g. Uncheck the box next to **Remember my sign-in info** (see Figure 5-3).

    h. Click **Save**.

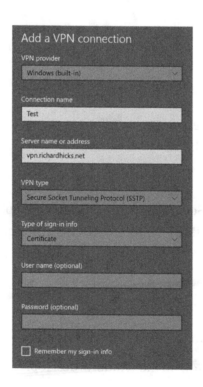

Figure 5-3. *VPN settings*

Authentication Settings

Once the VPN profile is created, the authentication settings must be updated to match those configured on the NPS server. Specifically, Protected EAP (PEAP) authentication using client certificates will be configured. To do this, begin by clicking **Change adapter options** on the VPN settings page (Figure 5-4).

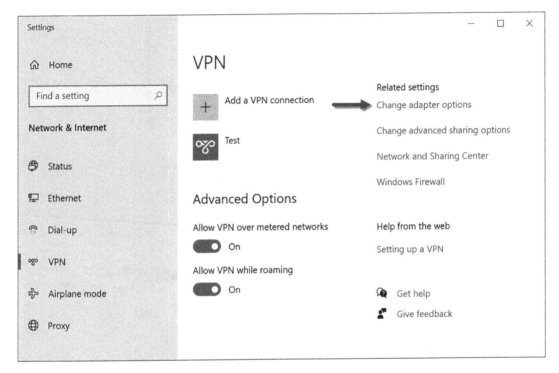

Figure 5-4. *Change adapter options*

Next, perform the following steps to configure PEAP authentication:

1. Right-click the **Test VPN profile** and choose **Properties**.

2. Select the **Security** tab.

3. In the **Authentication** section, select **Microsoft Protected EAP (PEAP) (encryption enabled)** from the **Use Extensible Authentication Protocol (EAP)** drop-down list (Figure 5-5).

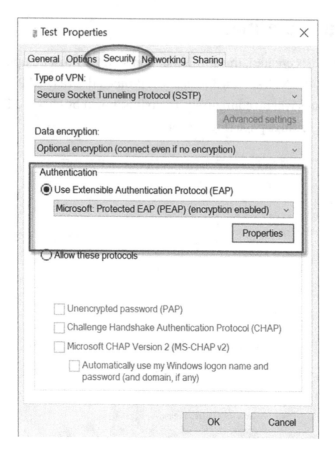

Figure 5-5. *VPN connection Security settings*

4. Click the **Properties** button.

   a. Enter the FQDN of the NPS server in the **Connect to these servers** field.

   b. Select the organization's root CA from the **Trusted Root Certification Authorities** list.

   c. Select **Don't ask user to authorize new servers or trusted CAs** from the **Notifications before connecting** drop-down list.

   d. Select **Smart Card or other certificate** from the **Select Authentication Method** drop-down list.

   e. Uncheck the box next to **Enable Fast Reconnect**.

   f. Check the box next to **Disconnect if server does not present Cryptobinding TLV** (Figure 5-6).

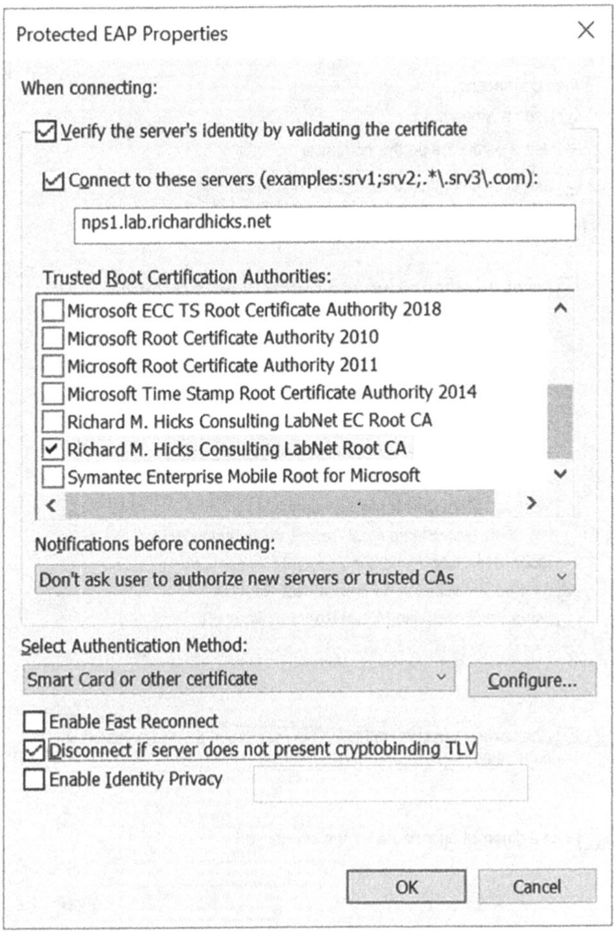

Figure 5-6. *VPN connection Protected EAP settings*

5. Click the **Configure** button.

   a. In the **When connecting** section, choose the option to **Use a certificate on this computer**.

   b. Enter the FQDN of the NPS server in the **Connect to these servers** field.

   c. Select the organization's root CA from the **Trusted Root Certification Authorities** list.

   d. Check the box next to **Don't prompt user to authorize new servers or trusted certification authorities** (Figure 5-7).

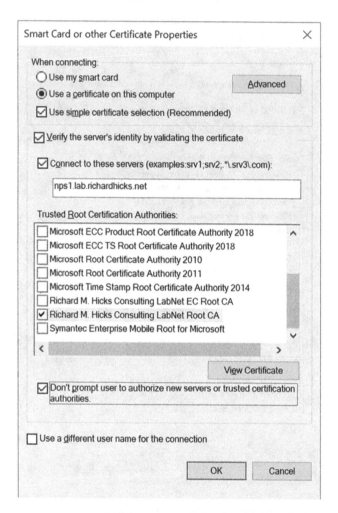

Figure 5-7. *VPN connection certificate settings*

6. Click the **Advanced** button.

   a. Check the box next to **Certificate Issuer**.

   b. Select the organization's root CA from the certification authorities list.

   c. Check the box next to **Extended Key Usage (EKU)**.

   d. Uncheck the box next to **All Purpose**.

   e. Uncheck the box next to **Any Purpose** (Figure 5-8).

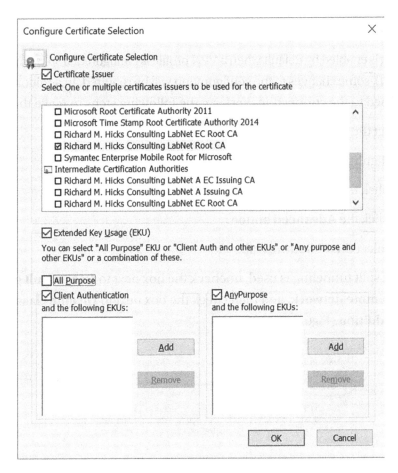

Figure 5-8. *VPN connection certificate selection settings*

7.   Click **Ok** three times to return to the VPN profile properties.

Note   PEAP configuration has numerous options for administrators to choose
from. The guidance previously provided aligns with current security best practices
and is recommended for most deployments. However, these settings may not be
applicable in all scenarios. A reference document for all Extensible Authentication
Protocol (EAP) settings can be found here: `https://docs.microsoft.com/en-`
`us/previous-versions/windows/it-pro/windows-server-2012-R2-`
`and-2012/hh945104(v=ws.11)`.

Network Settings

Force tunneling is enabled by default when a VPN profile is configured. If split tunneling is used (recommended), some changes to the configuration will be required. In addition, a DNS suffix must be assigned to the connection. Perform the following steps to make these changes:

1. Select the **Networking** tab.

   a. Highlight **Internet Protocol Version 4 (TCP/IPv4)**.

   b. Click the **Properties** button.

   c. Click the **Advanced** button.

   d. Select the **IP Settings** tab.

   e. If split tunneling is used, uncheck the box next to **Use default gateway on remote network**, and then check the box next to **Disable class based route addition** (Figure 5-9).

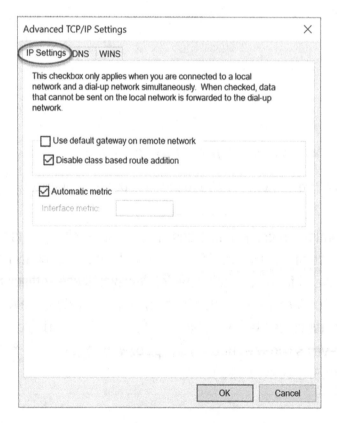

Figure 5-9. *VPN connection split tunneling settings*

Note   If force tunneling is required, leave the box next to **Use default gateway on remote network** checked.

f.   Select the **DNS** tab.

g.   Enter the DNS suffix for the internal network in the **DNS suffix for this connection** field (Figure 5-10).

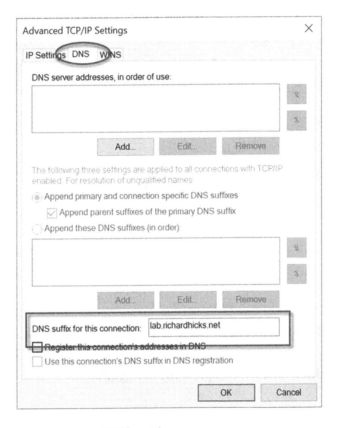

Figure 5-10. *VPN connection DNS settings*

2.   Click **Ok** twice to return to the VPN profile properties.

a. If IPv6 is required, highlight **Internet Protocol Version 6 (TCP/IPv6)**.

b. Click the **Properties** button.

c. Click the **Advanced** button.

   d. Select the **IP Settings** tab.

   e. If split tunneling is used, uncheck the box next to **Use default gateway on remote network** (Figure 5-11).

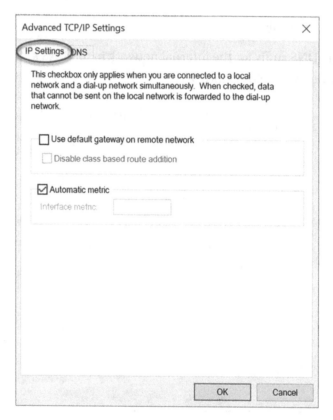

Figure 5-11. *VPN connection advanced TCP/IP settings*

   3. Click **Ok** three times to complete the configuration.

Routing

If split tunneling is configured, IP routes must be added to the VPN profile to ensure connectivity to on-premises resources over the tunnel. To do this, open an elevated PowerShell window and run the following commands. In the following example, routes are added to the VPN profile for the 172.16.0.0/16 IPv4 network and the 2001:470:f109::/64 network. Repeat these commands for any additional IP routes required.

```
Add-VpnConnectionRoute -ConnectionName Test -DestinationPrefix 172.16.0.0/16
Add-VpnConnectionRoute -ConnectionName Test -DestinationPrefix 2001:470:f109::/64
```

IPsec Policy

Finally, the test VPN profile must be configured with IPsec policy settings that match those configured on the VPN server. When connecting to a Windows VPN server running Windows Server 2019 and later, open an elevated PowerShell window and run the following command:

```
Set-VpnConnectionIPsecConfiguration -ConnectionName Test -Authentication
TransformConstants GCMAES128 -CipherTransformConstants GCMAES128 -DHGroup
Group14 -EncryptionMethod GCMAES128 -IntegrityCheckMethod SHA256 -PFSgroup
ECP256 -Force
```

When connecting to a Windows VPN server running Windows Server 2016 and earlier, run the following command:

```
Set-VpnConnectionIPsecConfiguration -ConnectionName $connection -Authentication
TransformConstants GCMAES128 -CipherTransformConstants GCMAES128 -DHGroup
Group14 -EncryptionMethod AES128 -IntegrityCheckMethod SHA256 -PFSgroup
PFS2048 -Force
```

To view the existing VPN connection IPsec policy configuration, run the following command:

```
Get-VpnConnection -Name 'Always On VPN' -AllUserConnection |
Select-Object -ExpandProperty IPSecCustomPolicy
```

To reset the VPN connection IPsec policy configuration, run the following command:

```
Set-VpnConnectionIPsecConfiguration -ConnectionName 'Test' -RevertToDefault -Force
```

Test Connection

The VPN infrastructure is configured to support both SSTP and IKEv2 VPN protocols. The test VPN connection is configured to use SSTP, so that will be tested first. After that, IKEv2 will be tested.

SSTP

To test the SSTP VPN connectivity, highlight the VPN connection and click **Connect** (Figure 5-12).

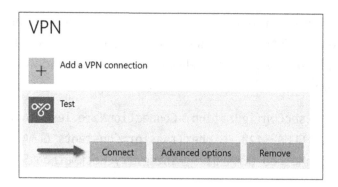

Figure 5-12. *Test the VPN connection*

If everything is configured correctly, the SSTP VPN connection will be successful (Figure 5-13).

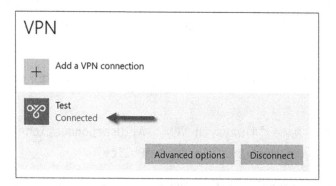

Figure 5-13. *VPN test connection successful*

Once the SSTP VPN connection is established, ensure all internal network resources are reachable over the VPN tunnel, including those that require authentication.

IKEv2

To test IKEv2 VPN connectivity, perform the following steps:

1. Click **Disconnect** on the VPN connection.

2. Click **Change adapter options** in the **Related settings** section.

3. Right-click the **Test VPN profile** and choose **Properties**.

4. Select the **Security** tab.

5. Select **IKEv2** from the **Type of VPN** drop-down list (Figure 5-14).

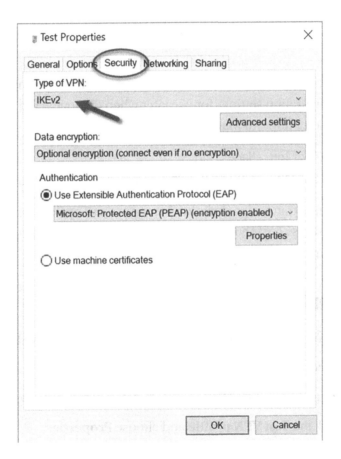

Figure 5-14. *VPN connection security settings*

6. Click **Ok**.

Once complete, click **Connect** on the Test VPN profile. Again, if everything is configured correctly, the IKEv2 VPN connection will be successful (Figure 5-15).

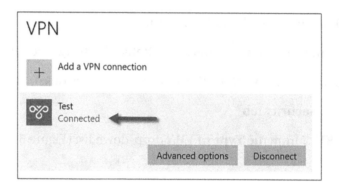

Figure 5-15. *VPN test connection successful*

Finally, open an elevated PowerShell window and run the following commands to export the EAP configuration settings for use later when deploying the Always On VPN profile using Microsoft Endpoint Manager or PowerShell:

```
$Vpn = Get-VpnConnection -Name Test
$Vpn.EapConfigXmlStream.InnerXml | Out-File .\eapconfig.txt
```

Optionally, administrators can download and run Get-EapConfiguration.ps1 from GitHub here: `https://github.com/richardhicks/aovpn/blob/master/Get-EapConfiguration.ps1`.

Device Authentication

To test IKEv2 VPN connectivity using device authentication, perform the following steps:

1. Click **Disconnect** on the VPN connection.

2. Click **Change adapter options** in the **Related settings** section.

3. Right-click the **Test VPN profile** and choose **Properties**.

4. Select the **Security** tab.

5. In the **Authentication** section, select the option to **Use machine certificates** (Figure 5-16).

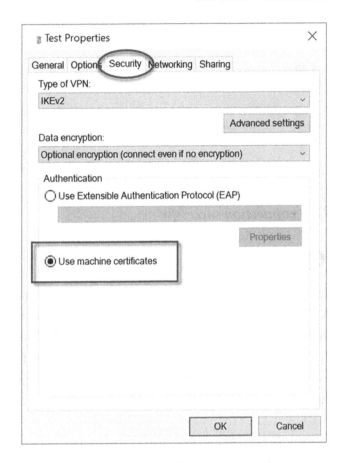

Figure 5-16. *VPN connection security settings*

    6.   Click **Ok**.

Once complete, click **Connect** on the Test VPN profile. Again, if everything is configured correctly, the IKEv2 VPN connection will be successful (Figure 5-17).

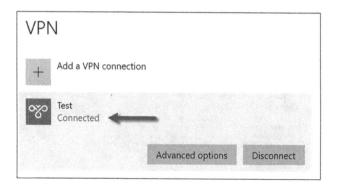

Figure 5-17. *VPN test connection successful*

Profile Deployment

Once the test VPN profile has been validated, Always On VPN profiles can be configured and deployed to Windows 10 clients. Microsoft Endpoint Manager is the preferred way to provision and deploy Always On VPN profiles to Windows 10 clients. However, Always On VPN profiles can be deployed using a PowerShell script and an XML configuration file. This script and XML file can then be deployed using System Center Configuration Manager (SCCM), Active Directory group policy startup scripts, or another third-party systems management tool.

Microsoft Endpoint Manager

As stated previously, Microsoft Endpoint Manager (MEM) is the preferred way to provision Always On VPN profiles to Windows 10 endpoints. Endpoint Manager includes a configuration wizard for Always On VPN that makes deployment much easier. In addition, any changes to the configuration are automatically pushed to client devices, which greatly simplifies administration and ongoing management.

Note   There are multiple configuration steps required to enable Windows device management using Azure Active Directory (AAD) and Microsoft Endpoint Manager (MEM). Configuring AAD and MEM is outside the scope of this book, however. For more information, consider reading *Learning Microsoft Endpoint Manager* (ISBN 978-0645127904) by Scott Duffey or *MDM: Fundamentals, Security, and the Modern Desktop* (ISBN 978-1119564324) by Jeremy Moskowitz.

Profile Configuration

To create and deploy an Always On VPN profile using Endpoint Manager, open a web browser, navigate to `https://endpoint.microsoft.com/`, and then perform the following steps:

1. In the navigation tree, click **Devices**.

2. Click **Configuration Profiles**.

User Tunnel

Perform the following steps to provision an Always On VPN user tunnel profile in Microsoft Endpoint Manager:

1. Click **Create profile**.

2. Select **Windows 10 and later** from the **Platform** drop-down list.

3. Select **Templates** from the **Profile type** drop-down list.

4. Click **VPN** in the **Template name** section.

5. Click **Create**.

Perform the following steps to configure the VPN profile:

1. Enter a descriptive name in the **Name** field. (*This is an administrative name only and is not displayed on the client.*)

2. Enter a description in the **Description** field (optional).

3. Click **Next** (Figure 5-18).

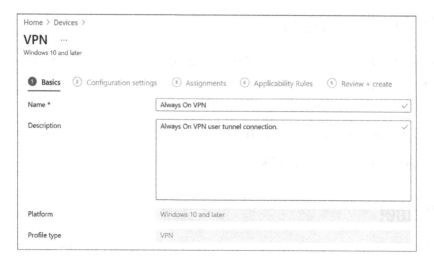

Figure 5-18. *VPN profile name*

4. Expand **Base VPN**.

   a. Enter a name for the connection in the **Connection name** field. (*This is the name of the VPN connection that will be displayed on the client.*)

   b. Enter a description of the server in the **Description** field.

   c. Enter the VPN server's public FQDN in the **VPN server address** field. Do NOT enter the public IP address of the VPN server here.

   d. Click **True** in the default server section.

   e. To register this VPN connection's IP address in internal DNS, click **Enable** in the **Register IP addresses with internal DNS** section.

Note   Registering the Always On VPN client's IP address in internal DNS is optional. When deploying both device tunnel and user tunnel connections, it is recommended to register the device tunnel connection in DNS, not the user tunnel.

---

   f. Select **Automatic** from the **Connection type** drop-down list.

Note   There is no option to explicitly choose SSTP as a connection type. However, selecting Automatic is effectively choosing SSTP, as the Automatic VPN type prioritizes SSTP over other VPN protocols.

g. Click **Enable** in the **Always On** section.

h. Click **Not configured** in the **Remember credentials at each logon** section.

i. Select **Certificates** from the **Authentication method** drop-down list.

j. Open the EAP configuration XML file exported previously and paste the contents of the file into the **EAP XML** field (Figure 5-19).

Figure 5-19. *VPN profile configuration settings*

5. Expand **DNS Settings**.

   a. Enter the internal DNS suffix in the **DNS suffixes** field (Figure 5-20).

Figure 5-20. *VPN profile DNS settings*

Note   DirectAccess administrators are likely familiar with the Name Resolution Policy Table (NRPT). There is an option to configure NRPT rules for Always On VPN, but it is recommended to avoid using them as much as possible. However, there may be some corner cases where NRPT configuration is required, for example, when VPN servers cannot be configured with DNS servers capable of resolving internal hostnames. NRPT configuration will be covered in more detail in the next chapter.

---

6. Expand **Split Tunneling**.

   a. If split tunneling is used, click **Enable**.

   b. Enter the IP network to route over the VPN connection in the **Destination Prefix** field.

   c. Enter the prefix size (IPv4 subnet mask bits) in the **Prefix size** field (Figure 5-21).

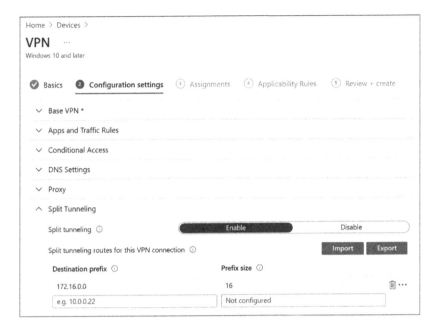

Figure 5-21. *VPN profile split tunneling settings*

Note   At the time of this writing, there is a bug in the Endpoint Manager interface that prevents administrators from adding IPv6 routes to the VPN connection. If IPv6 routing is required, it can be added later using PowerShell, or the VPN profile can be configured using the custom XML option discussed later in this chapter.

7.   Expand **Trusted Network Detection**.

    a.   Enter the DNS suffix of the internal network in the **Trusted network DNS suffixes field** (Figure 5-22).

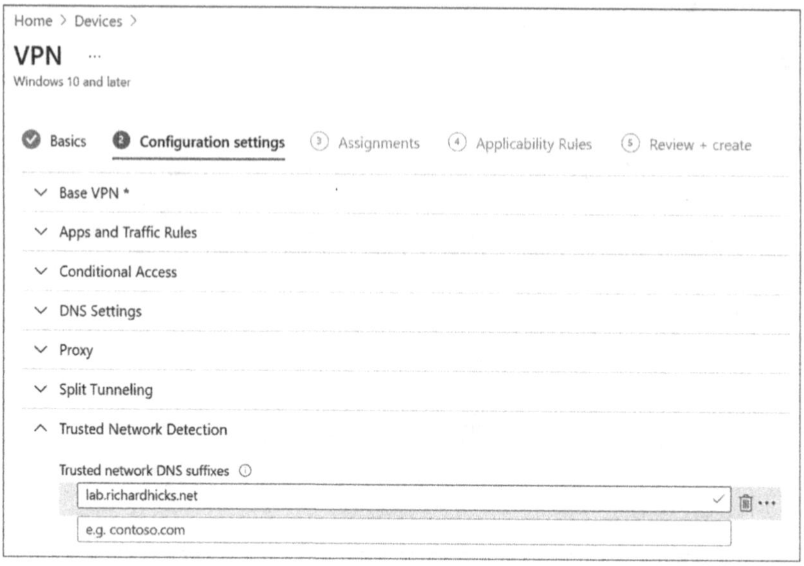

Figure 5-22. *VPN profile Trusted Network Detection settings*

8. Click **Next**.

9. Click **Add groups** and choose a user group to assign the VPN profile to.

10. Click **Next**.

11. Configure **Applicability Rules** as required (optional).

12. Click **Next**.

13. Review the configuration settings and click **Create**.

Once the device has synchronized with Microsoft Endpoint Manager, the Always On VPN user tunnel connect should appear in the network control panel and connect automatically when the device is outside the corporate network (Figure 5-23).

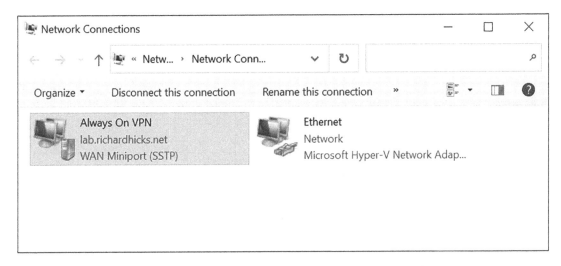

Figure 5-23. *VPN profile deployed and connection established*

Device Tunnel

Remember, the device tunnel is optional and only supported on Windows 10 Enterprise Edition clients that are joined to an Active Directory domain. If required, perform the following steps to provision an Always On VPN device tunnel profile in Microsoft Endpoint Manager:

1. Click **Create profile**.

2. Select **Windows 10 and later** from the **Platform** drop-down list.

3. Select **Templates** from the **Profile type** drop-down list.

4. Click **VPN** in the **Template name** section.

5. Click **Create**.

Perform the following steps to configure the VPN profile:

1. Enter a descriptive name in the **Name** field. (*This is an administrative name only and is not displayed on the client.*)

2. Enter a description in the **Description** field (optional).

3. Click **Next** (Figure 5-24).

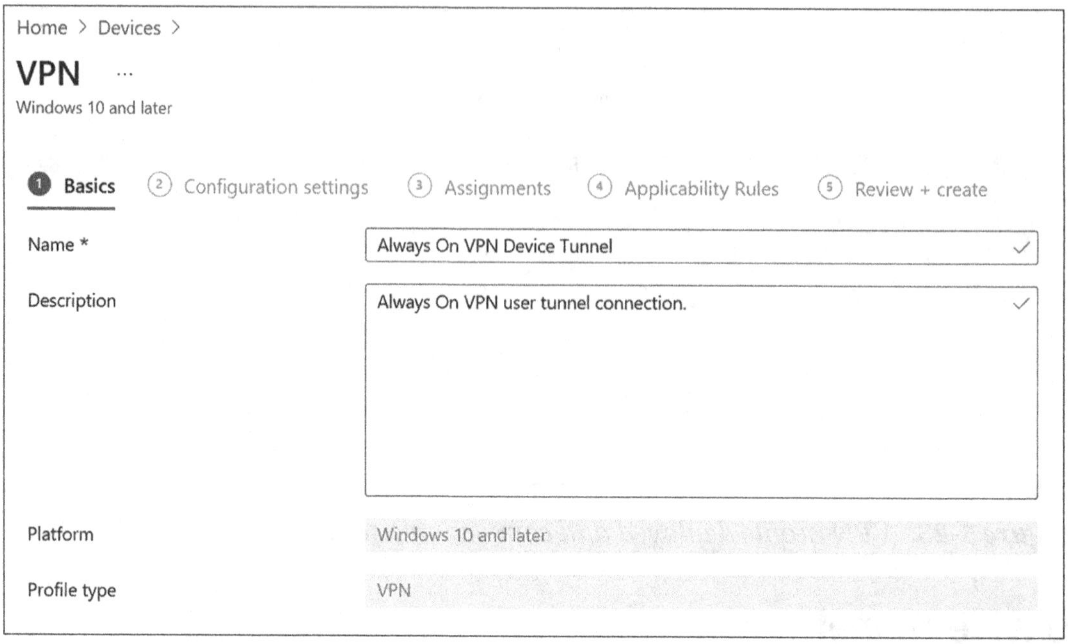

Home > Devices >

VPN ...
Windows 10 and later

1 Basics   ② Configuration settings   ③ Assignments   ④ Applicability Rules   ⑤ Review + create

Name *	Always On VPN Device Tunnel ✓
Description	Always On VPN user tunnel connection. ✓
Platform	Windows 10 and later
Profile type	VPN

Figure 5-24. *VPN profile name*

4. Expand **Base VPN**.

   a. Enter a name for the connection in the **Connection name** field. (*This is the name of the VPN connection that will be displayed on the client.*)

   b. Enter a description of the server in the **Description** field.

   c. Enter the VPN server's public FQDN in the **VPN server address** field. Do NOT enter the public IP address of the VPN server here.

   d. Click **True** in the default server section.

   e. To register this VPN connection's IP address in internal DNS, click **Enable** in the **Register IP addresses with internal DNS** section.

   f. Select **IKEv2** from the **Connection type** drop-down list.

   g. Click **Enable** in the **Always On** section.

   h. Click **Not configured** in the **Remember credentials at each logon** section.

   i. Select **Machine Certificates** in from the **Authentication method** drop-down list.

j. Click **Enable** in the **Device Tunnel** section.

k. In the **IKE Security Association Parameters** section, select the parameters that match those configured on the VPN server (Figure 5-25).

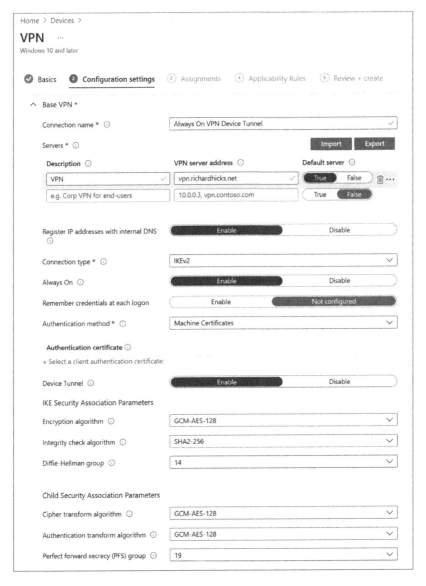

Figure 5-25. *VPN profile configuration settings*

5. Expand **DNS Settings**.

   a. Enter the internal DNS suffix in the **DNS suffixes** field (Figure 5-26).

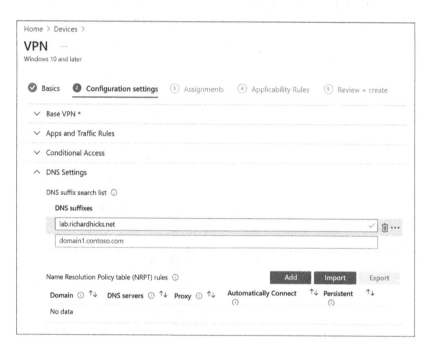

Figure 5-26. *VPN profile DNS settings*

Note   Although the Endpoint Manager UI includes an option to enable and configure the NRPT, Microsoft states explicitly the NRPT is not supported for use on the device tunnel. Details are here: `https://docs.microsoft.com/en-us/windows-server/remote/remote-access/vpn/vpn-device-tunnel-config`.

---

6. Expand **Split Tunneling**.

   a. Enter the IP network to route over the VPN connection in the **Destination Prefix** field.

   b. Enter the prefix size (IPv4 subnet mask bits) in the **Prefix size** field. It is recommended to configure host routes using /32 or /128 to individual servers accessible over the device tunnel (Figure 5-27).

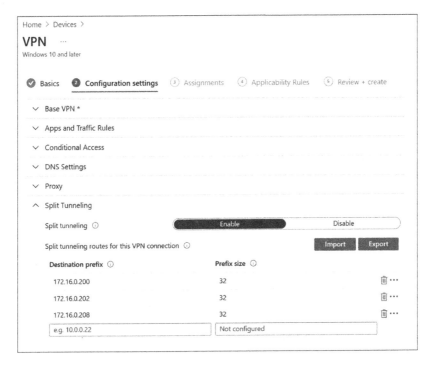

Figure 5-27. *VPN profile split tunneling settings*

7. Expand **Trusted Network Detection**.

    a. Enter the DNS suffix of the internal network in the **Trusted network DNS suffixes field** (Figure 5-28).

Figure 5-28. *VPN profile Trusted Network Detection settings*

8. Click **Next**.

9. Click **Add groups** and choose a device group to assign the VPN profile to.

10. Click **Next**.

11. Configure **Applicability Rules** as required (optional).

12. Click **Next**.

13. Review the configuration settings and click **Create**.

Once the device has synchronized with Microsoft Endpoint Manager, the Always On VPN device tunnel connect should appear in the network control panel and connect automatically when the device is outside the corporate network (Figure 5-29).

Figure 5-29. *VPN profile deployed and connection established*

Additional Configuration

When deploying Always On VPN profiles using Microsoft Endpoint Manager and configuring split tunneling, there is a known limitation with routing configuration that may need to be addressed. Specifically, Microsoft Endpoint Manager does not provide the ability to disable class-based route addition. This could yield unexpected results.

Administrators can disable this option after installation by editing the rasphone. pbk file (located in C:\Users\<username>\AppData\Roamin\Microsoft\Network\ Connections\Pbk\ or C:\ProgramData\Microsoft\Network\Connections\Pbk\) or by deploying Always On VPN profiles using custom XML (covered in the next chapter).

Note   More information regarding routing configuration limitations in Microsoft Endpoint Manager can be found here: `https://directaccess.` `richardhicks.com/2021/03/04/always-on-vpn-class-based-` `default-route-and-intune/`.

Custom XML

Although using the native Microsoft Endpoint Manager user interface for creating and provisioning Always On VPN profiles is preferred, it does have some limitations. Not all configuration settings and deployment scenarios are supported at the time of this writing. Here are a few examples of settings that are not configurable in Endpoint Manager:

- Disable class-based default routes

- Define exclusion routes

- Define IPv6 routes

- Deploy LockDown VPN profiles

As a workaround, a custom XML configuration file must be created that includes all the required settings.

XML Configuration

The following is a sample Always On VPN user tunnel XML configuration file for reference:

```
<VPNProfile>
    <AlwaysOn>true</AlwaysOn>
    <DnsSuffix>lab.richardhicks.net</DnsSuffix>
    <TrustedNetworkDetection>lab.richardhicks.net</TrustedNetworkDetection>
    <NativeProfile>
        <Servers>vpn.richardhicks.net</Servers>
        <NativeProtocolType>Automatic</NativeProtocolType>
        <Authentication>
            <UserMethod>Eap</UserMethod>
            <Eap>
                <Configuration>
                    <!-- Paste EAP configuration XML here -->
                </Configuration>
            </Eap>
        </Authentication>
        <RoutingPolicyType>SplitTunnel</RoutingPolicyType>
<DisableClassBasedDefaultRoute>true</DisableClassBasedDefaultRoute>
    </NativeProfile>
```

```
<Route>
    <Address>10.0.0.0</Address>
    <PrefixSize>8</PrefixSize>
</Route>
<Route>
    <Address>172.16.0.0</Address>
    <PrefixSize>12</PrefixSize>
</Route>
<Route>
    <Address>192.168.0.0</Address>
    <PrefixSize>16</PrefixSize>
</Route>
<Route>
    <Address>2001:db8:2112::</Address>
    <PrefixSize>48</PrefixSize>
</Route>
</VPNProfile>
```

Note   Example Always On VPN user tunnel and device tunnel XML configuration files can be downloaded here:

```
https://github.com/richardhicks/aovpn/blob/master/ProfileXML_
User.xml
```

```
https://github.com/richardhicks/aovpn/blob/master/ProfileXML_
Device.xml
```

In the previous example, the EAP configuration settings XML exported previously will be placed between the <Configuration> and </Configuration> tags. In addition, all RFC 1918 private IPv4 networks are included in the routing table. Make changes to this configuration file as necessary.

Note   There are myriad settings that can be included in the Always On VPN XML configuration file. The previous sample is a basic configuration file used to deploy a typical Always On VPN user tunnel profile. For a comprehensive list of all supported configuration settings, review the VPN v2 Configuration Service Provider (CSP) reference here: `https://docs.microsoft.com/en-us/windows/client-management/mdm/vpnv2-csp`.

Once the XML configuration file has been created, it can be deployed using Microsoft Endpoint Manager or PowerShell.

Endpoint Manager

Perform the following steps to create an Endpoint Manager configuration profile using the XML configuration file created previously:

1. Open a web browser and navigate to `https://endpoint.microsoft.com/`.

2. In the navigation tree, click **Devices**.

3. Click **Configuration Profiles**.

4. Click **Create profile**.

5. Select **Windows 10 and later** from the **Platform** drop-down list.

6. Select **Templates** from the **Profile type** drop-down list.

7. Click **Custom** in the **Template name** section.

8. Click **Create**.

Next, perform the following steps to configure the profile:

1. Enter a descriptive name in the **Name** field. (*This is an administrative name only and is not displayed on the client.*)

2. Enter a description in the **Description** field (optional).

3. Click **Next** (Figure 5-30).

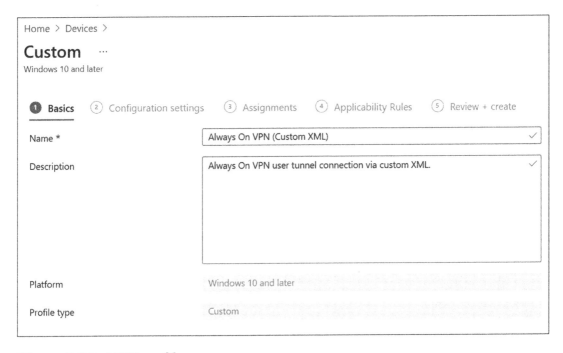

Figure 5-30. *VPN profile name*

4. Click **Add**.

5. Enter a descriptive name in the **Name** field (*This is an administrative name only and is not displayed on the client*).

6. Enter a description in the **Description** field (optional).

7. Enter the appropriate OMA-URI in the **OMA-URI** field.

   a. User tunnel OMA-URI: ./User/Vendor/MSFT/VPNv2/Always%20On%20 VPN/ProfileXML

   b. Device tunnel OMA-URI: ./Device/Vendor/MSFT/VPNv2/Always%20 On%20VPN%20Device%20Tunnel/ProfileXML

Note   Spaces in the OMA-URI are not supported and must be escaped using %20. Also, do not forget to include the leading "."

---

8. Select **String (XML file)** from the **Data type** drop-down list.

9. Click the folder icon next to the **Custom XML** field and select the XML configuration file.

10. Click **Save** (Figure 5-31).

Figure 5-31. *VPN profile OMA-URI settings*

11. Click **Next**.

12. Click **Add groups** and choose a user group to assign the VPN profile to.

13. Click **Next**.

14. Configure **Applicability Rules** as required (optional).

15. Click **Next**.

16. Review the configuration settings and click **Create**.

Note   If changes are required to be made to the VPN profile, administrators can update their XML configuration file and upload it to the previously created Endpoint Manager configuration profile. It is not necessary to configure a completely new profile in this scenario.

PowerShell Script

The custom XML configuration file can also be deployed using PowerShell. This is required when deploying Always On VPN profiles using System Center Configuration Manager (SCCM) or Active Directory group policy startup scripts.

Administrators may already be familiar with the MakeProfile.ps1 and VPN_Profile. ps1 scripts published by Microsoft. Although those scripts do work to provision an Always On VPN profile, they are rudimentary and do not follow some implementation best practices.

To address these limitations, an enhanced version of this script will be used. This updated script is robust and fine-tuned to align with current implementation best practices. It also provides better error handling and includes additional capabilities not present in the Microsoft scripts.

The enhanced Always On VPN provisioning script can be downloaded here:

```
https://github.com/richardhicks/aovpn/blob/master/New-AovpnConnection.ps1
```

User Tunnel

To provision an Always On VPN user tunnel, copy the preceding referenced PowerShell script along with the XML configuration file to the Windows 10 client. Next, open an elevated PowerShell window and run the following command:

```
.\New-AovpnConnection.ps1 -xmlFilePath .\ProfileXML_User.xml -ProfileName
'Always On VPN'
```

Note   The New-AovpnConnection.ps1 PowerShell script must be run with administrative privileges and in the context of the user. If the user does not have administrative rights, the profile will not be configured correctly. In this scenario, consider running the PowerShell script in the SYSTEM context (described later in this chapter) and using the -AllUserConnection switch to provision the Always On VPN profile in the All Users context.

Device Tunnel

Provisioning an Always On VPN device tunnel is similar to the user tunnel, with the exception that the script must be executed in the SYSTEM context. To do this, download the Sysinternals psexec.exe utility here:

```
https://docs.microsoft.com/en-us/sysinternals/downloads/psexec/
```

Copy psexec.exe to the Windows desktop, and then open an elevated PowerShell window and run the following command:

```
.\psexec.exe -i -s powershell.exe
```

This will open another PowerShell window running in the system context. In this window, run the following PowerShell command:

```
.\New-AovpnConnection.ps1 -xmlFilePath .\ProfileXML_Device.XML -ProfileName
'Always On VPN Device Tunnel' -DeviceTunnel
```

SCCM

Deploying Always On VPN profiles using SCCM is outside the scope of this book. However, administrators can refer to Microsoft's published guidance for this option here:

```
https://docs.microsoft.com/en-us/windows-server/remote/remote-access/vpn/
always-on-vpn/deploy/vpn-deploy-client-vpn-connections#configure-the-vpn-
client-by-using-configuration-manager.
```

Group Policy

Always On VPN profiles can also be provisioned using Active Directory group policy by assigning the deployment PowerShell script as a startup script and providing the path to the XML configuration file. To begin, copy the PowerShell script and XML configuration file to a network location accessible by Windows 10 clients. This can be the SYSVOL share on a domain controller or a file server.

Group Policy Object

Perform the following steps to create the Always On VPN deployment group policy object and assign it as required:

1. On a domain controller or administrator workstation, open the Group Policy Management console (gmpc.msc).

2. Expand the target domain, and then right-click **Group Policy Objects** and choose **New**.

3. Enter a descriptive name for the GPO and click **Ok**.

Policy Settings

Perform the following steps to deploy the Always On VPN PowerShell script as a startup script:

1. Right-click the **new GPO** and choose **Edit**.

2. Expand **Computer Configuration ➤ Policies ➤ Windows Settings**.

3. Highlight **Scripts (Startup/Shutdown)**, and then double-click **Startup**.

4. Select the **PowerShell Scripts** tab.

   a. Click **Add**.

   b. Enter the full path to the PowerShell script in the **Script Name** field.

   c. Enter "-xmlFilePath <full path to XML configuration file>" -AllUserConnection in the **Script Parameters** field (Figure 5-32).

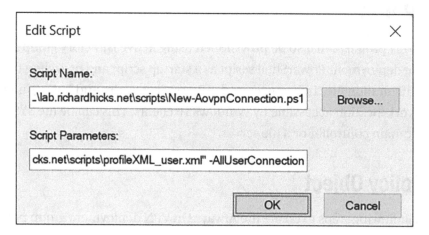

Figure 5-32. *Group Policy Object (GPO) startup script settings*

Note   It is crucial to use the -AllUserConnection parameter with the PowerShell provisioning script when deploying Always On VPN profiles using Active Directory group policy startup scripts. This is because startup scripts run in the SYSTEM context, not as the logged-on user.

---

   d. Click **Ok** twice, and then close the group policy management editor.

5. In the Group Policy Management console, highlight the **new GPO**.

6. In the **Security Filtering** section, click **Add**.

   a. Enter the name of the VPN Devices group in the **Enter the object name to select** field, and click **Check Names**.

    b. Click **Ok**.

    c. Highlight **Authenticated Users**, and click **Remove**.

    d. Click **Ok** and accept the warning message regarding the removal of Authenticated Users from the GPO.

7. Highlight the **Delegation** tab.

8. Click **Add**.

    a. Enter **Authenticated Users** in the **Enter the object name to select** field, and click **Check Names**.

    b. Click **Ok**.

    c. Select **Read** from the **Permissions** drop-down list.

    d. Click **Ok**.

Next, link the group policy object to the domain or an Organizational Unit (OU). Once complete, clients receiving the group policy will be provisioned with an Always On VPN user tunnel.

Note   The startup script will execute each time the device is booted. However, the PowerShell provisioning script includes logic to detect an existing profile of the same name and will not run if it exists. This prevents applying a configuration more than once, and it also ensures the profile is in place if it is deleted inadvertently.

The previously mentioned guidance demonstrates the provisioning of a Windows 10 Always On VPN user tunnel connection using Active Directory group policy startup scripts. The same procedure can be used to deploy a device tunnel as well. In this scenario, supply the device tunnel XML configuration file and use the -DeviceTunnel parameter for the PowerShell provisioning script instead.

Summary

At this point Always On VPN is fully implemented, albeit in a basic configuration. While this might meet the requirements for many deployment scenarios, there are additional configuration settings that might be required to provide the necessary access and user experience. In the next chapter, advanced configuration settings for Always On VPN configuration and deployment will be explored in detail.

CHAPTER 6

Advanced Configuration

In the previous chapter, Always On VPN user tunnel and device tunnel connections were deployed. However, the configurations included only the essential options to support Always On VPN connectivity.

Always On VPN has many different features and capabilities to meet a wide variety of deployment requirements. It may be necessary for administrators to make changes to the default DNS configuration to support split DNS scenarios, or a proxy server may be required to route Internet traffic to inspection devices.

Always On VPN supports traffic and application filters to meet Zero Trust Network Access (ZTNA) requirements as well. This allows administrators to control network access at a granular level to further improve the security and reduce the attack surface of the overall solution.

Finally, to prevent connection tampering and to ensure that no network access is possible without using the Always On VPN connection, administrators can deploy Always On VPN in LockDown mode.

Name Resolution Policy Table

DirectAccess administrators will be familiar with the Name Resolution Policy Table (NRPT). The NRPT enables policy-based name resolution request routing for Windows 10 clients. By configuring the NRPT, it is possible to direct selected name resolution requests to specific DNS servers instead of DNS servers configured on the client's network adapter.

© Richard M. Hicks 2022
R. M. Hicks, *Implementing Always On VPN*, https://doi.org/10.1007/978-1-4842-7741-6_6

The NRPT is optional and should be avoided as much as possible to simplify configuration and make troubleshooting easier. However, there are some use cases when configuring the NRPT will be required:

- VPN clients inherit the DNS servers from those configured on the VPN server. However, VPN servers may be configured with DNS servers that are not capable of resolving internal hostnames. In this scenario, NRPT must be configured to ensure Always On VPN clients resolve internal names using DNS servers other than those configured on the VPN interface.

- It may be required to resolve a public FQDN using internal DNS servers. This is common when split DNS is configured (same domain name internal and external).

Note   Enabling NRPT on the Always On VPN device tunnel is not supported. More details can be found here: `https://docs.microsoft.com/en-us/windows-server/remote/remote-access/vpn/vpn-device-tunnel-config#vpn-device-tunnel-configuration`.

Configure NRPT

Perform the following steps to configure the NRPT for Always On VPN user tunnel connections:

1. In the Microsoft Endpoint Manager management console, navigate to **Devices ➤ Configuration profiles** and click the Always On VPN profile.

2. Click **Properties**.

3. Click **Edit** next to **Configuration settings**.

4. Expand **DNS** settings.

5. Click **Add** next to **Name Resolution Policy table (NRPT) rules**.

    a. Enter the hostname or domain name in the **Domain** field.

    b. Enter the IP addresses of the internal DNS servers in the **DNS servers** field.

c. If a proxy server is required for this host or domain, enter the FQDN of the internal proxy in the **Proxy** field.

d. Leave the **Automatically Connect** and **Persistent** settings set to **Not configured** (Figure 6-1).

e. Click **Save**.

Figure 6-1. *Name Resolution Policy Table (NRPT) settings*

6. Click **Review + save**.

7. Click **Save**.

Note   To specify an entire namespace, include the leading "." for the domain (e.g., `.lab.richardhicks.net`). For an individual host, omit the leading "." (e.g., `www.richardhicks.net`).

Once the configuration has been synchronized on the client, open an elevated PowerShell window and run the following command to view the NRPT configuration:

```
Get-DnsClientNrptPolicy
```

The output of the command will show the NRPT settings, including the hostname or namespace, along with the DNS servers to use.

```
PS C:\> Get-DnsClientNrptPolicy

Namespace                          : .lab.richardhicks.net
QueryPolicy                        :
SecureNameQueryFallback            :
DirectAccessIPsecCARestriction     :
DirectAccessProxyName              :
DirectAccessDnsServers             :
DirectAccessEnabled                :
DirectAccessProxyType              : NoProxy
DirectAccessQueryIPsecEncryption   :
DirectAccessQueryIPsecRequired     : False
NameServers                        : {172.16.0.200, 172.16.0.201}
DnsSecIPsecCARestriction           :
DnsSecQueryIPsecEncryption         :
DnsSecQueryIPsecRequired           : False
DnsSecValidationRequired           : False
NameEncoding                       : Utf8WithoutMapping
```

It is important to note that the DNS servers on the VPN interface itself do not change when the NRPT is enabled. They are effectively overridden by the settings in the NRPT. Review the output of ipconfig.exe /all to confirm.

```
PS C:\> ipconfig.exe /all

Windows IP Configuration

    Host Name . . . . . . . . . . . . : CLIENT1
    Primary Dns Suffix  . . . . . . . : lab.richardhicks.net
    Node Type . . . . . . . . . . . . : Hybrid
    IP Routing Enabled. . . . . . . . : No
```

```
   WINS Proxy Enabled. . . . . . . . : No
   DNS Suffix Search List. . . . . . : lab.richardhicks.net

PPP adapter Always On VPN:

   Connection-specific DNS Suffix  . : lab.richardhicks.net
   Description . . . . . . . . . . . : Always On VPN
   Physical Address. . . . . . . . . :
   DHCP Enabled. . . . . . . . . . . : No
   Autoconfiguration Enabled . . . . : Yes
   IPv6 Address. . . . . . . . . . . : 2001:470:f109:1001:2cb0:7a3d:
                                       db26:eb42(Preferred)
   Link-local IPv6 Address . . . . . : fe80::2cb0:7a3d:db26:eb42%25(
                                       Preferred)
   IPv4 Address. . . . . . . . . . . : 172.16.101.10(Preferred)
   Subnet Mask . . . . . . . . . . . : 255.255.255.255
   Default Gateway . . . . . . . . . :
   DHCPv6 IAID . . . . . . . . . . . : 419435869
   DHCPv6 Client DUID. . . . . . . . : 00-01-00-01-28-55-4E-CE-00-15-5D-00-
                                       01-E0
   DNS Servers . . . . . . . . . . . : 2001:470:f109::ac15:65
                                       2001:470:f109::ac15:66
                                       172.21.12.101
                                       172.21.12.102
   NetBIOS over Tcpip. . . . . . . . : Enabled
```

Note   When testing name resolution with the NRPT configured, it is crucial to always use the Resolve-DnsName PowerShell command. Using DNS testing tools such as nslookup.exe will yield unexpected results since tools like this ignore the NRPT by design.

Proxy Server

For those organizations using an on-premises proxy server for Internet access, Always On VPN can be configured to route Internet traffic to them either globally or by individual host or domain. A proxy autoconfiguration file (PAC) can be used, or the proxy can be configured explicitly.

The global proxy configuration is supported only when Always On VPN is configured to use force tunneling. The global proxy is ignored on the Always On VPN client when split tunneling is enabled.

When split tunneling is in use, using a namespace proxy server is recommended. In both scenarios, the proxy server will only be enabled and used whenever the Always On VPN profile is active.

Global Explicit Proxy

Perform the following steps to configure an explicit global proxy server for an Always On VPN profile:

1. On the Always On VPN configuration profile, click **Edit** next to **Configuration settings**.

2. Expand the **Proxy** section.

3. Enter the IP address or FQDN of the proxy server in the **Address** field (only a single proxy server is supported at this time).

4. Enter the port number used by the proxy server in the **Port number** field.

5. Select **Enable** from the **Bypass proxy for local addresses** drop-down list (Figure 6-2).

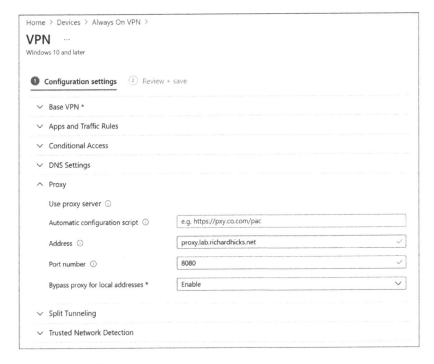

Figure 6-2. *VPN profile proxy server settings*

6. Click **Review + save**.

7. Click **Save**.

Global Proxy Autoconfiguration

Perform the following steps to configure a global proxy using a proxy autoconfiguration (PAC) file:

1. On the Always On VPN configuration profile, click **Edit** next to **Configuration settings**.

2. Expand the **Proxy** section.

3. Enter the URL for the proxy autoconfiguration file. Be sure to specify the port number when using nonstandard ports.

4. Select **Enable** from the **Bypass proxy for local addresses** drop-down list (Figure 6-3).

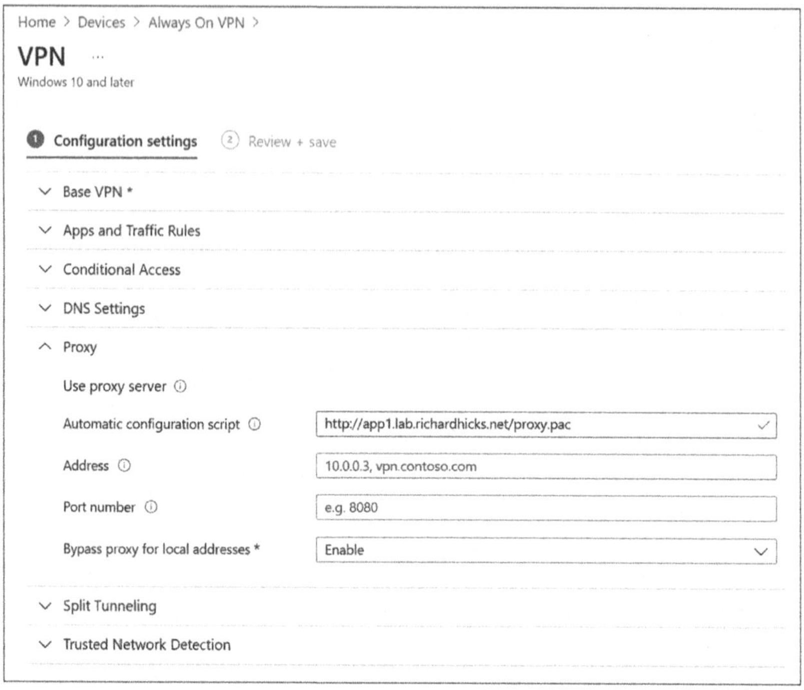

Figure 6-3. *VPN profile proxy server settings*

Note   Pay careful attention to the subtle differences in syntax between the explicit proxy and automatic configuration script settings. For explicit proxy, the address is entered as a hostname or FQDN. However, when specifying a proxy automatic configuration script, a URL must be provided.

To define an explicit global proxy using custom XML, include the following code between the `<VPNProfile>` and `</VPNProfile>` tags in the XML configuration file:

```
<Proxy>
    <Manual>
        <Server>proxy.corp.example.net:8080</Server>
    </Manual>
</Proxy>
```

To define a global proxy with an automatic configuration file using custom XML, include the following code between the `<VPNProfile>` and `</VPNProfile>` tags in the XML configuration file:

```
<Proxy>
   <AutoConfigURL>http://proxy.lab.richardhicks.net:8080/config.pac</
AutoConfiguURL>
</Proxy>
```

Namespace Proxy

Configuring a proxy server for a specific host or namespace is also supported. This can be helpful when split tunneling is configured, but access to a public website must come from the internal network. This is common when access to a public resource is restricted to the corporate network's public IP address, for example.

Microsoft Endpoint Manager does support configuration of proxy servers per host or namespace using NRPT rules, but as of this writing, there is a validation bug in the Endpoint Manager UI that prevents administrators from defining the proxy server correctly.

As a workaround, a namespace proxy can be defined using custom XML. The following is an example of defining a namespace proxy for the public domain richardhicks.com. Include the following code between the `<VPNProfile>` and `</VPNProfile>` tags in the XML configuration file:

```
<DomainNameInformation>
   <DomainName>.richardhicks.com</DomainName>
   <DnsServers>172.16.0.200,2001:470:f109::ac10:c8</DnsServers>
   <WebProxyServers>proxy.lab.richardhicks.net:8080</WebProxyServers>
</DomainNameInformation>
```

Proxy autoconfiguration files are not supported for namespace proxy scenarios.

Note   Be sure to include the leading "." to route the entire domain to the internal proxy server. It can be omitted for specific individual hosts (e.g., app.richardhicks.com).

Caveat

Administrators should understand that namespace proxy server configuration has some serious limitations. Specifically, namespace proxy servers are only supported by Internet Explorer. All other modern web browsers, including Microsoft Edge, ignore the namespace proxy server configuration. For obvious reasons, this severely limits this feature's usefulness in most organizations.

Traffic Filtering

Traffic filtering allows administrators to control network access over the Always On VPN connection at a granular level. Specifically, rules can be configured to control network access based on any combination of the following:

- Protocol (TCP, UDP, etc.)

- Source port (individual port or range of ports)

- Destination port (individual port or range of ports)

- Source IPv4 address (individual host, address range, or subnet)

- Destination IPv4 address (individual host, address range, or subnet)

Note   At the time of this writing, Microsoft Endpoint Manager does not support defining traffic rules using IPv6. Do not enable traffic rules at all when IPv6 is enabled for VPN. Doing so will result in a failed connection with error code 0x8000FFFF "catastrophic failure."

Multiple traffic filter rules can be configured to allow network access as required. Individual rules are evaluated using OR, and components within rules are evaluated using AND.

To create a traffic filter using Microsoft Endpoint Manager to restrict access to the Remote Desktop Protocol (RDP) to a specific server, perform the following steps:

1. On the Always On VPN configuration profile, click **Edit** next to **Configuration settings**.

2. Expand the **App and Traffic Rules** section.

3. Click **Add** next to **Network traffic rules for this VPN connection**.

4. Enter a descriptive name for the rule in the **Name** field.

5. Select **Split tunnel** from the **Rule type** drop-down list.

6. Enter **6** in the **Protocol** field (6=TCP, 17=UDP).

7. In the **Remote port ranges** section, enter **3389** in the **Lower port** and **Upper port** fields.

8. In the **Remote address ranges** section, enter the IPv4 address of the target server in the **Lower IPv4 address** and **Upper IPv4 address** fields (Figure 6-4).

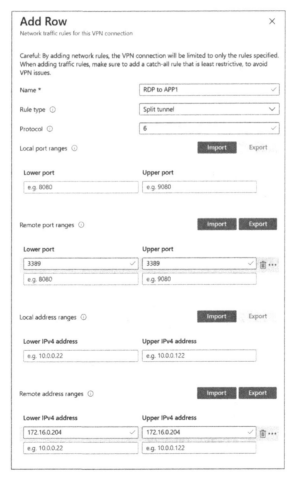

Figure 6-4. *VPN profile traffic filter settings*

9. Click **Save**.

10. Click **Review + save**.

11. Click **Save**.

To create a traffic filter rule using custom XML, include the following code between the <VPNProfile> and </VPNProfile> tags in the XML configuration file:

```
<TrafficFilter>
    <Protocol>6</Protocol>
    <RemotePortRanges>3389</RemotePortRanges>
    <RemoteAddressRanges>172.16.0.204</RemoteAddressRanges>
</TrafficFilter>
```

Once configured, the traffic filter defined in the previous example will restrict access to RDP to the IPv4 address 172.16.0.204. To confirm, open a PowerShell window and use the Test-NetConnection command to validate that RDP is reachable from the VPN client. Also, try connecting to a port other than 3389 to demonstrate the port is unreachable.

```
PS C:\> Test-NetConnection -Port 3389 app1

ComputerName     : app1
RemoteAddress    : 172.16.0.204
RemotePort       : 3389
InterfaceAlias   : Always On VPN
SourceAddress    : 172.16.101.5
TcpTestSucceeded : True


PS C:\> Test-NetConnection -Port 445 app1
WARNING: TCP connect to (172.16.0.204 : 445) failed
WARNING: Ping to 172.16.0.204 failed with status: 11050

ComputerName        : app1
RemoteAddress       : 172.16.0.204
RemotePort          : 445
InterfaceAlias      : Always On VPN
SourceAddress       : 172.16.101.5
```

```
PingSucceeded          : False
PingReplyDetails (RTT) : 0 ms
TcpTestSucceeded       : False
```

> **Note**   When a traffic filter is configured for Always On VPN, all other traffic is blocked unless explicitly allowed in a traffic filter rule. This includes unsolicited inbound traffic.

Direction

By default, traffic filters control traffic in the outbound direction (from the client to the internal network). Beginning with Windows 10 2004, Microsoft introduced support for inbound traffic filters. As of this writing, creating traffic filters with the inbound direction is not supported in the Microsoft Endpoint Manager user interface. This option is only available using custom XML.

To create an inbound traffic filter allowing traffic from the internal network using custom XML, include the following code between the <VPNProfile> and </VPNProfile> tags in the XML configuration file:

```
<TrafficFilter>
    <Protocol>6</Protocol>
    <LocalPortRanges>445</LocalPortRanges>
    <RemoteAddressRanges>172.16.0.0/16</RemoteAddressRanges>
    <Direction>Inbound</Direction>
</TrafficFilter>
```

In this example, hosts on-premises within the 172.16.0.0/16 network would have access to TCP port 445 (SMB) on the Always On VPN client. All other traffic will be denied.

Application Filtering

Application filters can be combined with traffic filters to further restrict access to on-premises resources. For example, an application filter might restrict access to the VPN to the mstsc.exe executable but then further restricted to using a specific protocol, port, and destination address to provide an additional layer of security.

Applications can be defined by the following:

- Package Family Name (PFN) – This is the unique name of a Microsoft Store application. The PFN for an application can be found using the Get-AppxPackage PowerShell command.

- File Path – This is the full path to any executable on the file system, for example, c:\Windows\System32\mstsc.exe.

- SYSTEM – This is used to allow Windows kernel-mode drivers (such as ping.exe and net.exe) to send traffic over the Always On VPN connection.

At the time of this writing, the Microsoft Endpoint Manager user interface does not provide the ability to configure application filtering. Custom XML configuration must be used to enable application filters.

Desktop Application Filter

To define a desktop application filter using custom XML, include the following code between the <VPNProfile> and </VPNProfile> tags in the XML configuration file:

```
<TrafficFilter>
    <App>
        <Id>c:\Windows\System32\mstsc.exe</Id>
    </App>
    <Protocol>6</Protocol>
    <RemotePortRanges>3389</RemotePortRanges>
    <RemoteAddressRanges>172.16.0.204</RemoteAddressRanges>
</TrafficFilter>
```

In this example, only the executable c:\Windows\System32\mstsc.exe will be able to access resources over the Always On VPN tunnel. All other applications and processes will be denied access.

Windows Store Application Filter

To define a Windows Store application filter using custom XML, include the following code between the <VPNProfile> and </VPNProfile> tags in the XML configuration file:

```
<TrafficFilter>
    <App>
        <Id>Microsoft.RemoteDesktop_8wekyb3d8bbwe</Id>
    </App>
    <Protocol>6</Protocol>
    <RemotePortRanges>3389</RemotePortRanges>
    <RemoteAddressRanges>172.16.0.0/16</RemoteAddressRanges>
</TrafficFilter>
```

In this example, only the Microsoft Windows Store Remote Desktop application will be able to access resources over the Always On VPN tunnel. All other applications and processes will be denied access.

SYSTEM Application Filter

To define a SYSTEM application filter using custom XML, include the following code between the <VPNProfile> and </VPNProfile> tags in the XML configuration file:

```
<TrafficFilter>
    <App>
        <Id>SYSTEM</Id>
    </App>
    <Protocol>1</Protocol>
    <RemoteAddressRanges>172.16.0.0/16</RemoteAddressRanges>
</TrafficFilter>
```

In this example, users will be able to ping all hosts on the 172.16.0.0/16 network. All other network traffic will be denied.

LockDown VPN

Users without administrative rights can make changes to the Always On VPN profile in Windows 10. Standard users can alter critical VPN settings and even add IP routes to the connection, which could result in unauthorized access. Users can even delete the Always On VPN connection entirely. To address this limitation, Microsoft allows administrators to deploy Always On VPN in "LockDown" mode.

When Always On VPN is configured in LockDown mode, the following conditions apply:

- The LockDown VPN connection is always on.

- The LockDown VPN connection is a device tunnel.

- The LockDown VPN connection cannot be disabled or disconnected.

- Users cannot make changes to or delete a LockDown Always On VPN connection, including those with administrative privileges.

- Force tunneling is enabled. Split tunneling is not supported with LockDown mode.

- If the VPN server is unreachable for any reason, all network access is blocked, including local network access. This applies to devices on the internal network as well.

- LockDown VPN connections must use IKEv2. SSTP is not supported with LockDown mode.

LockDown Limitations

Deploying Always On VPN in LockDown mode comes with some serious drawbacks. Since IKEv2 is the only supported protocol, VPN access may not be possible behind restrictive firewalls. Also, LockDown mode prevents clients from connecting to network resources from a network with a captive portal.

In addition, LockDown VPN is deployed as a device tunnel and uses only device certificate authentication. LockDown VPN does not support integration with Multifactor Authentication or Azure Conditional Access.

Configure LockDown VPN

At the time of this writing, the Microsoft Endpoint Manager UI does not support deploying Always On VPN in LockDown mode. It must be configured using custom XML.

To configure LockDown VPN, add the following code between the `<VPNProfile>` and `</VPNProfile>` tags in the XML configuration file:

```
<LockDown>true</LockDown>
```

A LockDown VPN profile is deployed as a device tunnel, which requires the following code to be included between the `<NativeProfile>` and `</NativeProfile>` tags in the XML configuration file:

```
<NativeProtocolType>IKEv2</NativeProtocolType>
<Authentication>
    <MachineMethod>Certificate</MachineMethod>
</Authentication>
```

Note   LockDown VPN is deployed as a device tunnel. Ensure the `./Device/Vendor/MSFT/VPNv2/<ProfileName>/ProfileXML` OMA-URI is specified when creating the configuration profile in Endpoint Manager. Also, as LockDown VPN is force tunneling by default, there is no need to define a RoutingPolicyType in the XML configuration file.

Deleting LockDown VPN

As stated previously, users cannot make changes to or delete a LockDown VPN connection. This presents a unique challenge for administrators when removing a LockDown VPN profile becomes necessary. Right-clicking the LockDown VPN connection and choosing **Delete** will result in an access denied message. Trying to remove the connection using PowerShell will result in the same error message.

To address this limitation, a PowerShell script to remove Always On VPN connections, including LockDown VPN connections, can be downloaded here:

```
https://github.com/richardhicks/aovpn/blob/master/Remove-AovpnConnection.ps1.
```

Summary

Always On VPN includes support for numerous features and functionalities, allowing administrators to tailor the solution to meet their specific requirements. Some of these features are exposed in the native Microsoft Endpoint Manager user interface, and others are not. In many cases, advanced settings are only configurable using the custom XML implementation option. Microsoft Endpoint Manager, as with most cloud-based services, is constantly changing. It is likely features described in this chapter as missing from the Endpoint Manager UI, and configurable only with custom XML will eventually be added in the future.

CHAPTER 7

Cloud Deployments

With many organizations moving applications and infrastructure to the cloud, often it is necessary to deploy VPN infrastructure there also. Administrators have several options to choose from when it comes to configuring VPN infrastructure in the cloud. In Azure, the native VPN options are Azure VPN gateway and Azure Virtual WAN. Windows Server Routing and Remote Access Service (RRAS) servers can be deployed on a Windows Server virtual machine hosted in Azure, with an important caveat. A Non-Microsoft Network Virtual Appliance (NVA) can also be provisioned to support Always On VPN connections in the cloud.

Azure VPN Gateway

The Azure VPN gateway is a popular solution for implementing VPN services in the cloud. The Azure VPN gateway is a fully managed solution that can be configured to support Always On VPN connections. Azure VPN gateway supports both SSTP and IKEv2 VPN protocols for client-based connections. There are a few important considerations to be made before choosing the Azure VPN gateway, however.

Advantages

Microsoft manages the VPN infrastructure in Azure, leaving administrators free to focus on other tasks. Also, updating the gateway SKU is all that's required to scale up or down, and this can be performed at any time. The Azure VPN gateway can support as many as 10,000 concurrent IKEv2 connections with an aggregate throughput of 10 Gbps.

175

© Richard M. Hicks 2022
R. M. Hicks, *Implementing Always On VPN*, https://doi.org/10.1007/978-1-4842-7741-6_7

Disadvantages

Support for the SSTP VPN protocol is limited to only 128 concurrent connections regardless of gateway SKU (256 concurrent in active-active configuration). This could present challenges for administrators, as IKEv2 has some operational limitations associated with it (see Chapter 2 for more details).

In addition, the Azure VPN gateway can only support Always On VPN user tunnel or device tunnel connections, but not both at the same time. This is due to a limitation with how authentication is configured on the Azure VPN gateway. Currently, only one authentication method is supported at a time, either RADIUS or device certificate. It does not support both on one gateway.

Finally, Always On VPN clients connecting to the Azure VPN gateway must be configured to use split tunneling. Force tunneling is not supported when using the Azure VPN gateway.

Requirements

To support point-to-site connections, the Azure VPN gateway must be configured as a route-based VPN gateway. Generation1 or Generation2 gateways both support client-based VPN connections.

Gateway SKUs

At the time of this writing, there are six Generation1 VPN gateway SKUs and eight Generation2 SKUs that support point-to-site connections in Azure. Select a gateway SKU that meets the concurrent connection and performance characteristics required for the individual deployment.

Note   A current list of Azure VPN gateway SKUs can be found here: `https://docs.microsoft.com/en-us/azure/vpn-gateway/vpn-gateway-about-vpngateways#gwsku`.

Site-to-Site Compatibility

The Azure VPN gateway can be configured to support both site-to-site and point-to-site VPN connections. These options are not mutually exclusive, either. It is common to deploy Azure VPN gateway to enable connectivity to and from an on-premises network, as well as provide VPN servers to support Always On VPN.

When using the Azure VPN gateway to support both site-to-site and point-to-site connections, be sure to take the additional site-to-site utilization into consideration when sizing and selecting a gateway SKU.

Azure VPN Gateway Configuration

Perform the following steps to create an Azure VPN gateway:

1. Open the Azure management console (`https://portal.azure. com/`) and navigate to the Resource Group where the gateway will be deployed.

2. In the Resource Group overview section, click **Create**.

3. In the **Search services and marketplace** field, enter "VPN gateway."

4. Click on **Virtual network gateway**.

5. Click **Create** (Figure 7-1).

Figure 7-1. *Create an Azure virtual network gateway*

Perform the following steps to define the configuration parameters for the Azure VPN gateway:

1. Select the appropriate subscription from the **Subscription** drop-down list.

2. Enter a descriptive name for the VPN gateway in the **Name** field.

3. Select an Azure region to deploy the resource into from the **Region** drop-down list.

4. Select **VPN** as the **Gateway type**.

5. Select **Route-based** as the **VPN type**.

6. Select an appropriate SKU for the gateway from the **SKU** drop-down list.

Note   The Azure VPN gateway is available in different sizes to meet the specific requirements for individual deployments. Detailed information about capabilities and throughput supported for individual SKUs can be found here: `https://docs.microsoft.com/en-us/azure/vpn-gateway/vpn-gateway-about-vpngateways#gwsku`.

---

7. Select **Generation2** from the **Generation** drop-down list.

8. Select a virtual network from the **Virtual network** drop-down list. Optionally, if no VNet exists, click **Create virtual network** and define a VNet.

9. Enter an address range to be dedicated to the VPN gateway. Specify the address prefix in CIDR notation. The subnet must be defined as /29 or larger.

10. Select **Create new** next to **Public IP address**. Optionally, select **Use existing** if a public IP address is already configured.

11. Enter a descriptive name in the **Public IP address name field**. This is not a public DNS name. This name is used to identify the resource in the Azure management console only.

12. If high availability is required, or if more than 1,000 concurrent IKEv2 connections are expected, select **Enabled** next to **Enable active-active mode**.

13. Click **Review + create** (Figure 7-2).

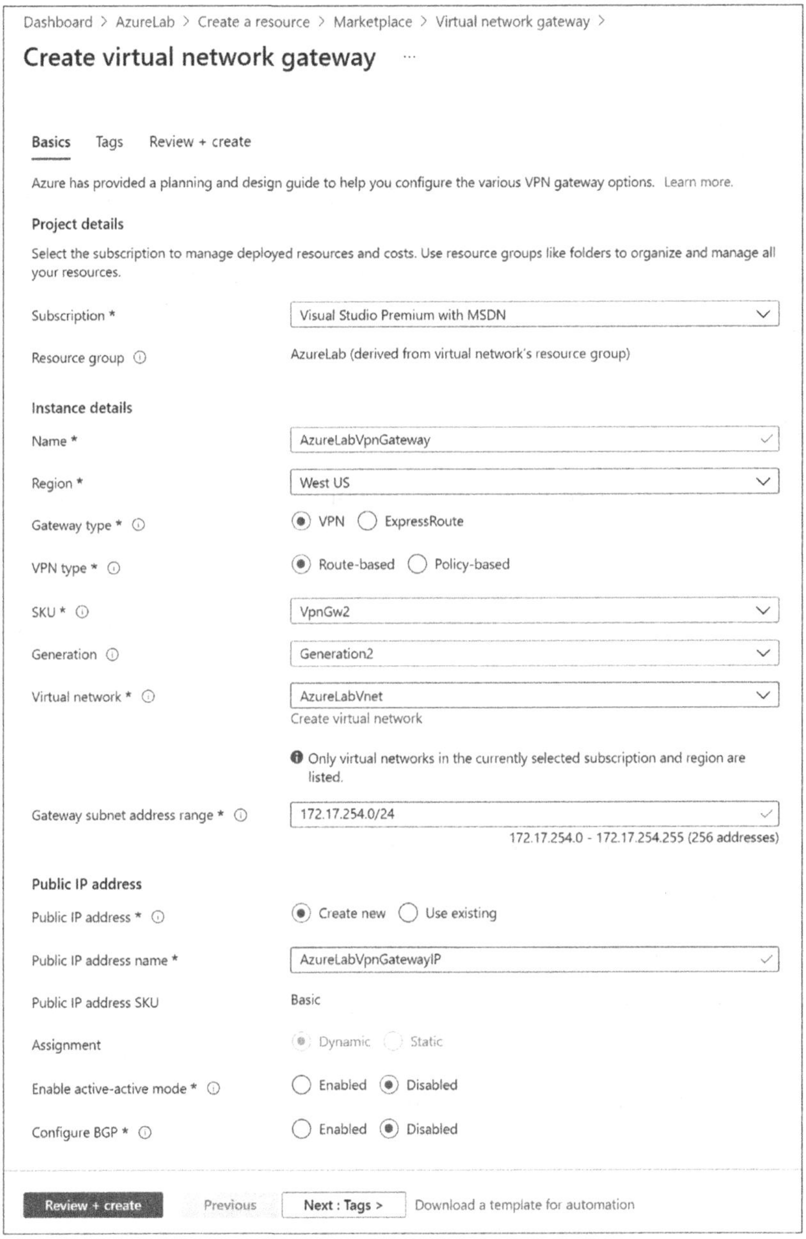

Figure 7-2. *Azure virtual network gateway settings*

Note   The Azure VPN gateway deployment process can take up to 30 minutes. Be patient!

Once Azure VPN gateway provisioning is complete, click the **Go To Resource** button to configure a point-to-site connection.

User Tunnel

The Always On VPN user tunnel is authenticated via RADIUS using Microsoft Network Policy Server (NPS) servers. NPS servers can be hosted in Azure, on-premises, or a combination of both. It is recommended that primary RADIUS servers be configured in Azure for optimal performance, however.

NPS Configuration

Before proceeding with the Azure VPN gateway configuration for Always On VPN user tunnels, the NPS server must be configured to accept authentication requests from the Azure VPN gateway. On the NPS server, open the NPS management console (nps.msc) and perform the following steps to configure the Azure VPN gateway as a RADIUS client on the NPS server:

1. Expand **RADIUS Clients and Servers**.

2. Right-click **RADIUS Clients** and choose **New**.

3. Check the box next to **Enable this RADIUS client**.

4. Enter a descriptive name in the **Friendly name** field.

5. Enter the **Azure VPN gateway subnet** in CIDR notation in the **Address (IP or DNS) field**.

Note   You can find the Azure VPN gateway subnet by looking at the subnets defined in the VNet where the gateway is deployed. The subnet will have the name "GatewaySubnet," as shown in Figure 7-3.

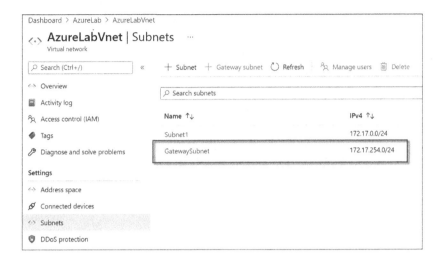

Figure 7-3. *Azure VNet gateway subnet*

6. Enter the shared secret to be used with the Azure VPN gateway in the Shared secret field. Select the **Generate** option to have a long, complex shared secret created automatically (Figure 7-4).

7. Click **Ok**.

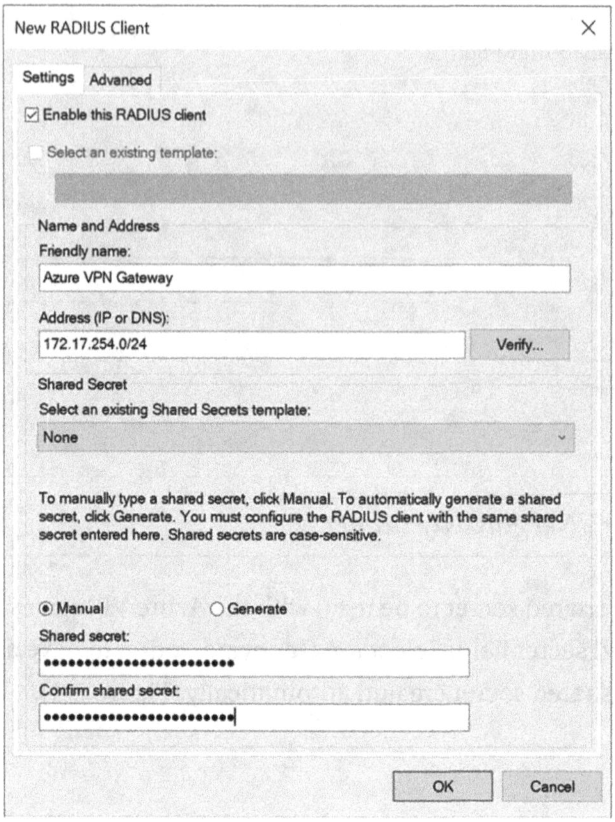

Figure 7-4. *RADIUS client settings*

Repeat the previously mentioned steps on the secondary RADIUS server if configured.

Gateway Configuration

Next, perform the following steps to configure the Azure VPN gateway to support Always On VPN user tunnel connections:

1. In the navigation pane, click **Point-to-site configuration**.

2. Click the **Configure now** link.

3. Enter an IP address range to assign to VPN clients in CIDR notation in the **Address pool** field.

> **Note**   The IPv4 address pool assigned to Always On VPN clients must be a unique network and not part of the address space of the Azure VNet. In addition, ensure the client IP address pool includes enough IP addresses to accommodate the maximum number of concurrent VPN clients expected. There is no need to configure Azure routing for this subnet. Routing for this subnet is handled by Azure automatically.

4. Select **IKEv2 and SSTP (SSL)** from the **Tunnel type** drop-down list.

5. Select **RADIUS authentication** from the **Authentication type** drop-down list.

6. Enter the IPv4 address of the primary RADIUS server in the **Primary Server IP address** field.

7. Enter the shared secret to be used with the primary RADIUS server in the **Primary Server secret** field.

8. Enter the IPv4 address of the secondary RADIUS server in the **Secondary Server IP address** field (optional).

9. Enter the shared secret to be used with the secondary RADIUS server in the **Secondary Server secret** field (optional, Figure 7-5).

10. Click **Save**.

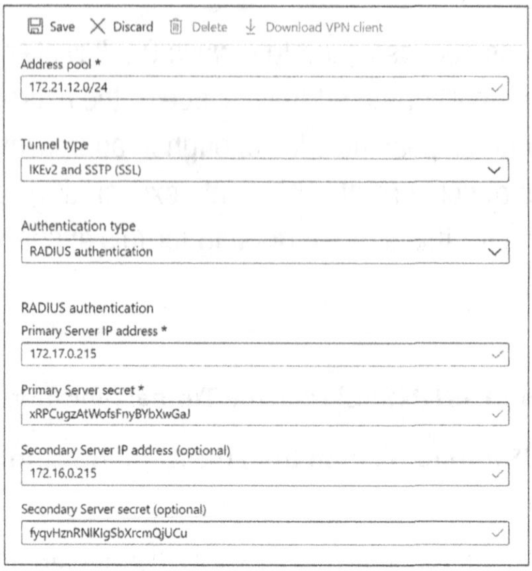

Save
Discard
Delete
Download VPN client
Address pool *
172.21.12.0/24
Tunnel type
IKEv2 and SSTP (SSL)
Authentication type
RADIUS authentication
RADIUS authentication
Primary Server IP address *
172.17.0.215
Primary Server secret *
xRPCugzAtWofsFnyBYbXwGaJ
Secondary Server IP address (optional)
172.16.0.215
Secondary Server secret (optional)
fyqvHznRNIKIgSbXrcmQjUCu

Figure 7-5. *Azure VPN gateway settings*

Once complete, perform the following steps to download the VPN client configuration files:

11. Click **Download VPN client.**
12. Select **EAPMSCHAPv2.**
13. Click **Download** (Figure 7-6).

Download VPN client
AzureLabVpnGateway
EAPMSCHAPv2
EAPTLS
Download

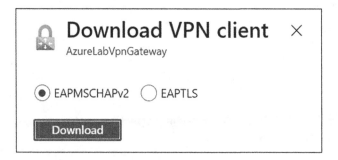

Figure 7-6. *Download VPN client configuration*

Note   Select EAPMSCHAPv2 when downloading the VPN client package, even if using another authentication scheme. The Azure VPN gateway client will not be used at all, in fact. However, the configuration files contain important information required to build the Always On VPN connection later.

Client Configuration

Configuring Always On VPN user tunnel connections to an Azure VPN gateway is identical to any other VPN gateway. However, Azure controls the hostname of the gateway as well as the certificate installed. This means the Azure-provided gateway hostname must be used in the client-side configuration.

To identify the Azure VPN gateway hostname, open the Azure VPN Client files downloaded previously. Open the zip file and navigate to the **Generic** folder. Open the VpnSettings.xml file in a text editor and copy the fully qualified domain name (FQDN) between the <VpnServer> and </VpnServer> tags, as shown in Figure 7-7.

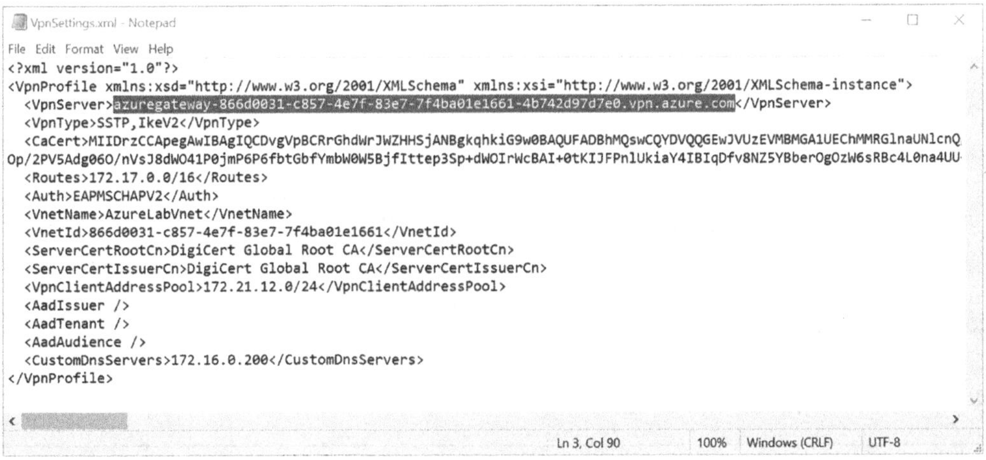

Figure 7-7.   Identify Azure VPN gateway hostname

Paste this FQDN in the **VPN server address** field in the **Base VPN** section of the Always On VPN device configuration profile in Microsoft Endpoint Manager, as shown in Figure 7-8.

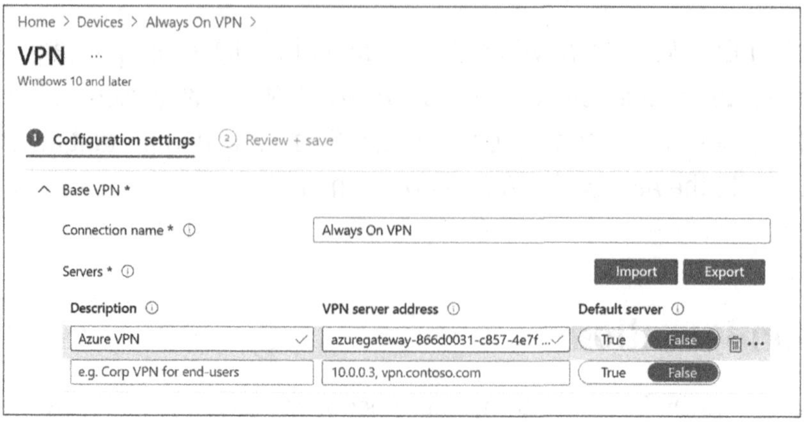

Figure 7-8. *VPN profile settings*

When configuring Always On VPN with custom XML, paste the FQDN of the Azure VPN gateway between the <VpnServer> and </VpnServer> tags in the XML configuration file, as shown in Figure 7-9.

Figure 7-9. *VPN profile settings*

Note   Updating default cryptography settings is recommended if using IKEv2 for the Always On VPN user tunnel with Azure VPN gateway. Details on making those changes on the Azure VPN gateway are covered later in this chapter.

Device Tunnel

The Always On VPN device tunnel is authenticated using a device certificate issued to the endpoint by the organization's internal Certification Authority (CA). The internal root CA certificate (certificate only, no private key!) must be uploaded to the Azure VPN gateway to support device certificate authentication.

Root Certificate

Before proceeding with the Azure VPN gateway configuration for Always On VPN device tunnel, the root certificate must be exported in Base-64 format. On an issuing CA server, open the Enterprise PKI management console (pkiview.msc) and perform the following steps:

1. Highlight the root CA server in the navigation pane.

2. Right-click CA Certificate and choose **View Certificate**.

3. Select the **Details** tab and click **Copy to File**.

4. Click **Next**.

5. Choose **Base-64 encoded X.509 (.CER)** (Figure 7-10).

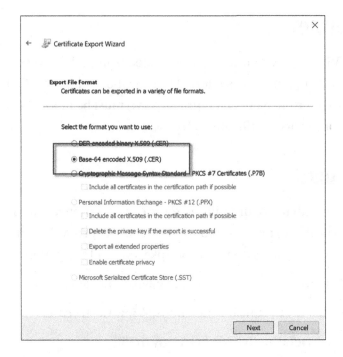

Figure 7-10. *Export CA certificate*

6.   Click **Next**.

7.   Enter a location to save the file to.

8.   Click **Next**.

9.   Click **Finish**.

10.   Click **Ok**.

Next, open the file in Notepad or another text editor and copy the contents of the certificate file between (but not including) the **BEGIN CERTIFICATE** and **END CERTIFICATE** tags, as shown in Figure 7-11.

Figure 7-11. *Root CA certificate*

Gateway Configuration

Perform the following steps to configure the Azure VPN gateway to support Always On VPN device tunnel connections:

1. In the navigation pane, click **Point-to-site configuration**.

2. Click the **Configure now** link.

3. Enter an IP address range to assign to VPN clients in CIDR notation in the **Address pool** field.

4. Select **IKEv2 and SSTP (SSL)** from the **Tunnel type** drop-down list.

5. Select **Azure certificate** from the **Authentication type** drop-down list.

6. In the **Root certificates** section, enter a descriptive name for the root certificate in the **Name** field, and then paste the certificate data copied previously into the **Public certificate data** field (Figure 7-12).

7. Click **Save**.

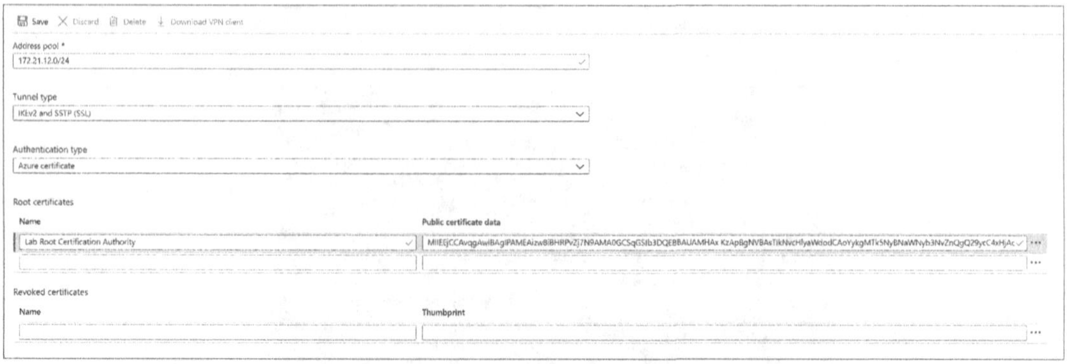

Figure 7-12. *Azure VPN gateway root certificate settings*

Client Configuration

The process for configuring Always On VPN device tunnel connections to Azure VPN
gateway is the same as the user tunnel, described previously in this chapter. Paste the
FQDN of the Azure VPN gateway in the **VPN server address** field in the **Base VPN**
section of the Always On VPN device configuration profile in Microsoft Endpoint
Manager, as shown in Figure 7-13.

Figure 7-13. *VPN profile settings*

IKEv2 Cryptography

It is recommended to update the default IPsec policy settings used by the Azure VPN gateway to improve both security and performance. By default, the Azure VPN gateway is configured to use AES-256 encryption. In addition, the default settings use DH2 (1024-bit RSA key). Best practice is to use GCM ciphers and to use 128-bit AES to improve performance. Also, 2048-bit keys should be used.

Changes to the Azure VPN gateway IPsec policy are not exposed in the Microsoft Endpoint Manager UI. Administrators must use PowerShell to make these changes.

Update Azure VPN IPsec Policy

Install the Azure PowerShell module on an administrative workstation by running the following command:

```
Install-Module -Name Az -Scope CurrentUser -Repository PSGallery -Force
```

Next, open an elevated PowerShell window and run the following command:

```
Connect-AzAccount
```

The administrator will be prompted to enter their credentials to authenticate to Azure. Once complete, run the following command to select the appropriate Azure subscription. In this example, the "Visual Studio Premium with MSDN" subscription is selected:

```
Select-AzSubscription -SubscriptionName 'Visual Studio Premium with MSDN'
```

Now create variables that hold the Azure VPN gateway name and the Resource Group name where the Azure VPN gateway is provisioned.

```
$Gateway = 'AzureLabVPNGateway'
$ResourceGroup = 'AzureLab'
```

Note   It may be necessary to import the Az.Network PowerShell module before running the previous commands. If an error occurs, run the Import-Module Az.Network command and continue.

Next, define a new IPsec policy using best practice settings.

```
$IPsecPolicy = New-AzVpnClientIpsecParameter -IpsecEncryption
GCMAES128 -IpsecIntegrity GCMAES128 -SALifeTime 28800 -SADataSize
102400000 -IkeEncryption GCMAES128 -IkeIntegrity SHA256 -DhGroup
DHGroup14 -PfsGroup ECP256
```

Now apply the new IPsec policy by running the following command:

```
Set-AzVpnClientIpsecParameter -VirtualNetworkGatewayName
$Gateway -ResourceGroupName $ResourceGroup -VpnClientIPsecParameter $IPsecPolicy
```

Once complete, the IPsec policy settings can be confirmed using the following command:

```
Get-AzVpnClientIpsecParameter -Name $Gateway -ResourceGroupName
$ResourceGroup
```

Update Client Policy

It is crucial that the IPsec policy on the Always On VPN client match the settings configured on the Azure VPN gateway exactly.

When configuring Always On VPN with Microsoft Endpoint Manager, select the configuration options shown in Figure 7-14 in the **IKE Security Association Parameters** and **Child Security Association Parameters** in the **Base VPN** section of the Always On VPN device tunnel configuration profile in Microsoft Endpoint Manager.

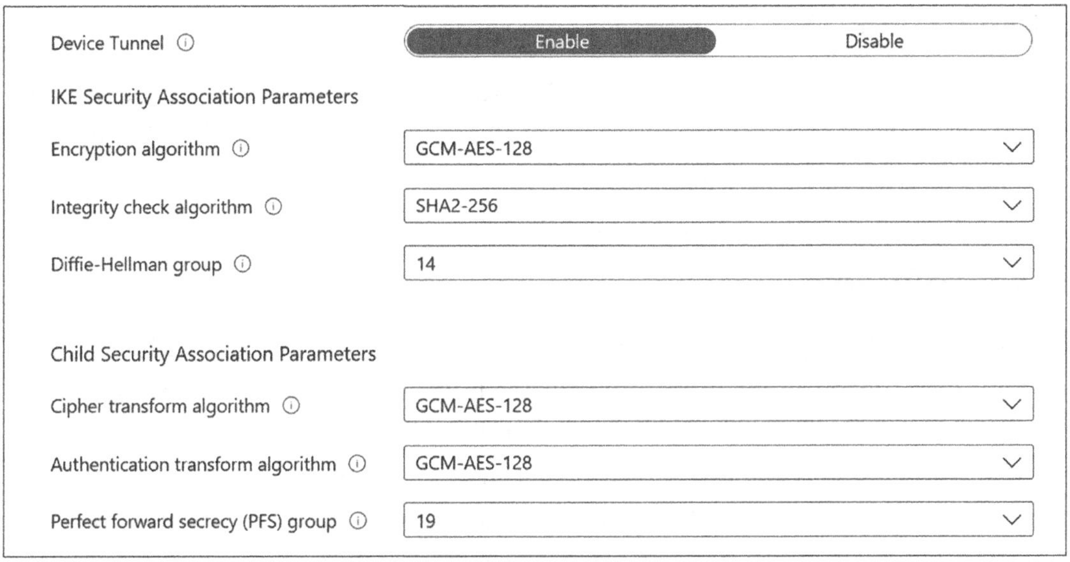

Figure 7-14. *VPN profile cryptography settings*

When configuring Always On VPN with custom XML, add the following code to the XML configuration between the

```
<CryptographySuite>    <AuthenticationTransformConstants>GCMAES128</
AuthenticationTransformConstants>
    <CipherTransformConstants>GCMAES128</CipherTransformConstants>
    <EncryptionMethod>AES_GCM_128</EncryptionMethod>
    <IntegrityCheckMethod>SHA256</IntegrityCheckMethod>
    <DHGroup>Group14</DHGroup>
    <PfsGroup>ECP256</PfsGroup>
</CryptographySuite>
```

Azure Virtual WAN

Azure Virtual WAN is another option for administrators to consider when choosing a fully managed VPN service in the cloud. Azure Virtual WAN is an advanced network service that provides a variety of connectivity options, including point-to-site connectivity options that offer some important advantages over the Azure VPN gateway. However, it is not without some crucial limitations.

Advantages

Azure Virtual WAN can scale much higher than Azure VPN gateway, supporting as many as 100,000 concurrent IKEv2 client VPN connections with an aggregate throughput of 200 Gbps at the time of this writing.

Disadvantages

Azure Virtual WAN supports only IKEv2 for client-based VPN connections. This may present some challenges for client connectivity under certain circumstances. Details on the limitations of the IKEv2 VPN protocol are outlined in Chapter 2.

Like the Azure VPN gateway, Azure Virtual WAN supports Always On VPN user tunnel or device tunnel connections, but not at the same time. Azure Virtual WAN suffers from the same limitation as Azure VPN gateway, namely, that it supports only one authentication scheme at a time, either RADIUS or device certificate authentication. It does not support both on the same gateway.

Also, Always On VPN clients connecting to the Azure Virtual WAN must be configured to use split tunneling. Force tunneling is not supported using Azure Virtual WAN.

Requirements

Azure Virtual WAN must be deployed using the Standard configuration option. Point-to-site connections are not supported using the basic configuration option.

Azure Virtual WAN Configuration

Perform the following steps to create an Azure Virtual WAN:

1. Open the Azure management console (`https://portal.azure.com/`), and navigate to the Resource Group where the Virtual WAN will be deployed.

2. In the Resource Group overview section, click **Create**.

3. In the **Search services and marketplace** field, enter "Virtual WAN."

4. Click **Virtual WAN**.

5. Click **Create** (Figure 7-15).

Figure 7-15. *Create an Azure Virtual WAN*

Perform the following steps to define the configuration parameters for the Azure Virtual WAN:

1. Select the appropriate subscription from the **Subscription** drop-down list.

2. Select the resource group where the Virtual WAN will be deployed from the **Resource group** drop-down list.

3. Select an Azure region to deploy the resource into from the **Region** drop-down list.

4. Enter a descriptive name for the Virtual WAN in the **Name** field.

5. Select **Standard** from the **Type** drop-down list.

6. Click **Review + create** (Figure 7-16).

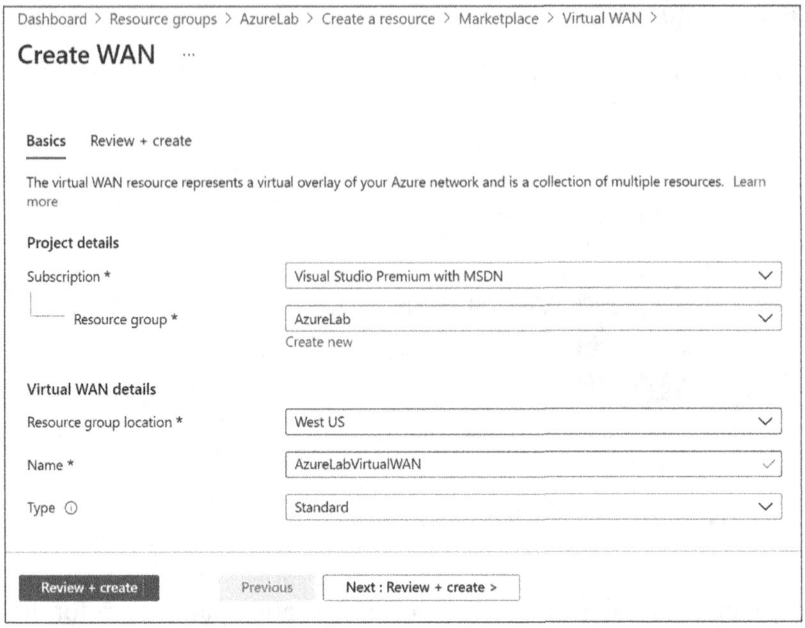

Figure 7-16. Azure Virtual WAN settings

Once Azure Virtual WAN provisioning is complete, click the **Go to resource** button to continue to provision an Azure Virtual WAN hub.

Virtual WAN Hub

Perform the following steps to provision a new Virtual WAN hub:

1. In the **Connectivity** section of the navigation pane, click **Hubs**.

2. Click **New Hub**.

3. Select an Azure region from the **Region** drop-down list.

4. Enter a descriptive name in the **Name** field.

5. Enter an IPv4 address space in CIDR notation in the **Hub private address space field**.

6. Click **Review + create** (Figure 7-17).

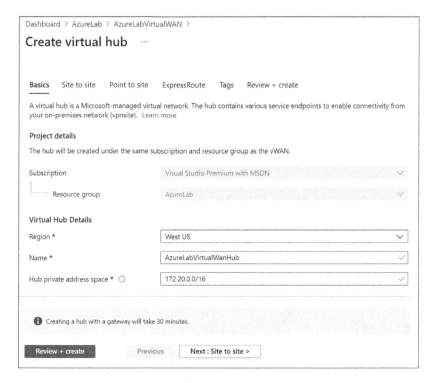

Figure 7-17. *Azure Virtual WAN hub settings*

Note The Azure Virtual WAN hub deployment process can take up to 30 minutes. Be patient!

Once Azure Virtual WAN hub provisioning is complete, navigate to the Azure Virtual WAN and perform the following steps to create a user VPN connection:

1. In the **Connectivity** section of the navigation pane, click **User VPN configurations**.

2. Click **Create user VPN config**.

3. Enter a descriptive name for the VPN configuration in the **Name** field.

4. Select **IKEv2 VPN** from the **Tunnel type** drop-down list.

5. Click **Custom** in the **IPsec** section.

6. For the **IKE Phase 1** settings, choose **GCMAES128**, **SHA256**, and **DHGroup14**.

7. For the **IKE Phase 2 (IPsec)** settings, choose **GCMAES128**, **GCMAES128**, and **ECP256**, as shown in Figure 7-18.

8. Click **Next**.

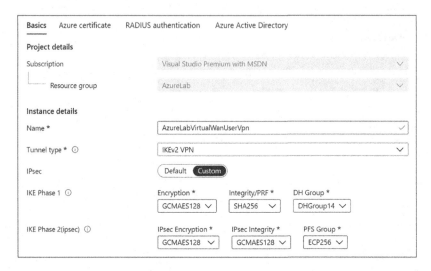

Figure 7-18. *Azure Virtual WAN cryptography settings*

The remaining steps vary depending on whether Always On VPN user tunnels or device tunnels are to be supported.

Certificate Authentication

If configuring Azure Virtual WAN to support Always On VPN *device tunnel* connections, perform the following steps. If configuring Azure Virtual WAN to support Always On VPN *user tunnel* connections, skip this section and proceed to RADIUS authentication:

1. Click **Yes** next to **Azure certificate**.

2. Enter a descriptive name for the root certificate in the **Root Certificate Name** field, and then paste the certificate data copied previously into the **Public Certificate Data** field (Figure 7-19). The process for gathering the certificate data is described earlier in this chapter.

3. Click **Next**.

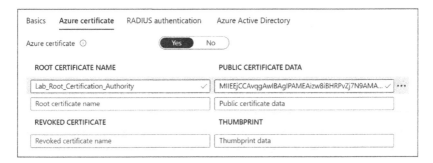

Figure 7-19. *Azure Virtual WAN certificate authentication settings*

RADIUS Authentication

If configuring Azure Virtual WAN to support Always On VPN user tunnel connections, perform the following steps. Do NOT configure RADIUS authentication if Always On VPN device tunnel connections are required:

1. Click **Yes** next to **RADIUS authentication**.

2. Enter the shared secret to be used with the primary RADIUS server in the **Primary Server secret** field.

3. Enter the IPv4 address of the primary RADIUS server in the **Primary Server IP address** field.

4. Enter the shared secret to be used with the secondary RADIUS server in the **Secondary Server secret** field (optional, Figure 7-20).

5. Enter the IPv4 address of the secondary RADIUS server in the **Secondary Server IP address** field (optional).

6. Click **Review + create** (Figure 7-20).

Figure 7-20. *Azure Virtual WAN RADIUS authentication settings*

Point-to-Site Connection

Next, perform the following steps to configure a point-to-site connection to Azure Virtual WAN:

1. Navigate to the Azure Virtual WAN, and click **Hubs** in the **Connectivity** section of the navigation pane.

2. Click the hub created previously.

3. In the navigation pane, click **User VPN (Point to site)** in the **Connectivity** section.

4. Click **Create VPN gateway**.

5. Select an appropriate number of scale units to provide the required throughput for the deployment from the **Gateway scale units** drop-down list.

6. Select the point-to-site configuration created previously from the **Point-to-site configuration** drop-down list.

7. Select **Microsoft network** below **Routing preference**.

8. Enter an IP address range in CIDR notation in the **Client address pool** field. Ensure the client IP address pool includes enough IP addresses to accommodate the maximum number of concurrent VPN clients expected.

9. Enter the IP addresses of the DNS servers to be used by Always On VPN clients in the **Custom DNS Servers** field.

10. Click **Create** (Figure 7-21).

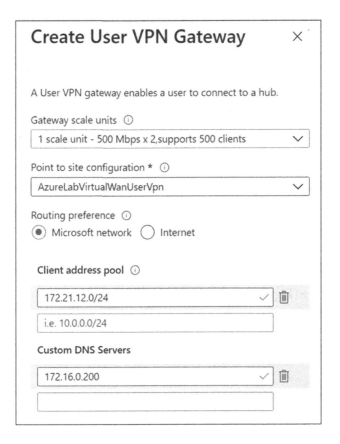

Figure 7-21. *Azure Virtual WAN settings*

Note   The Azure Virtual WAN gateway deployment process can take up to 30 minutes. Be patient!

VNet Connection

Before continuing, any Azure VNets must first be connected to the Azure Virtual WAN hub to be reachable by Always On VPN clients. Perform the following steps to connect an existing Azure VNet to Azure Virtual WAN:

1. In the Azure Virtual WAN, click **Virtual Network Connections** in the **Connectivity** section of the navigation pane.

2. Click **Add Connection**.

3. Enter a descriptive name for the virtual network connection in the **Connection name** field.

4. Select the hub created previously from the **Hubs** drop-down list.

5. Select the Azure subscription where the resource will be deployed from the **Subscription** drop-down list.

6. Select the Azure resource group where the resource will be deployed from the **Resource group** drop-down list.

7. Select the Azure VNet to connect to the hub from the **Virtual network** drop-down list.

8. Select **Default** from the **Associate Route Table** drop-down list.

9. Click **Create** (Figure 7-22).

Figure 7-22. *Azure Virtual WAN connection settings*

Client Configuration

In the Azure Virtual WAN configuration, click **User VPN configurations** in the
Connectivity section of the navigation pane, and then perform the following steps to
create an Always On VPN user tunnel or device tunnel connection:

1. Click **Download virtual WAN user VPN profile**.

2. Select **EAPTLS** below **Authentication type**.

3. Click **Generate and download profile** (Figure 7-23).

Download virtual WAN user V...   ×

↓ Generate and download profile

Authentication type *
  ⦿ EAPTLS   ○ EAPMSCHAPv2

Figure 7-23. *Download Azure Virtual WAN configuration profile*

Open the downloaded zip file and navigate to the **Generic** folder. Open the
VpnSettings.xml file in a text editor, and copy the FQDN between the <VpnServer> and
</VpnServer> tags, as shown in Figure 7-24.

Figure 7-24. *Azure Virtual WAN hostname*

Paste this FQDN in the **VPN server address** field in the **Base VPN** section of the Always On VPN device configuration profile in Microsoft Endpoint Manager, as shown in Figure 7-25.

Figure 7-25. *Azure Virtual WAN settings*

When configuring Always On VPN with custom XML, paste the FQDN of the Azure VPN gateway between the `<VpnServer>` and `</VpnServer>` tags in the XML configuration file, as shown in Figure 7-26.

Figure 7-26. *Azure Virtual WAN hostname*

Windows Server RRAS

In addition to the Azure native infrastructure options like Azure VPN gateway and Azure Virtual WAN, it is also possible to provision a Windows Server 2022 virtual machine in Azure and configure it to accept Always On VPN connections.

Supportability

While implementing Windows Server with Routing and Remote Access Service (RRAS) in Azure might seem intuitive, it is interesting to note that RRAS is not a formally supported workload on Windows Server in Azure[1] (Figure 7-27).

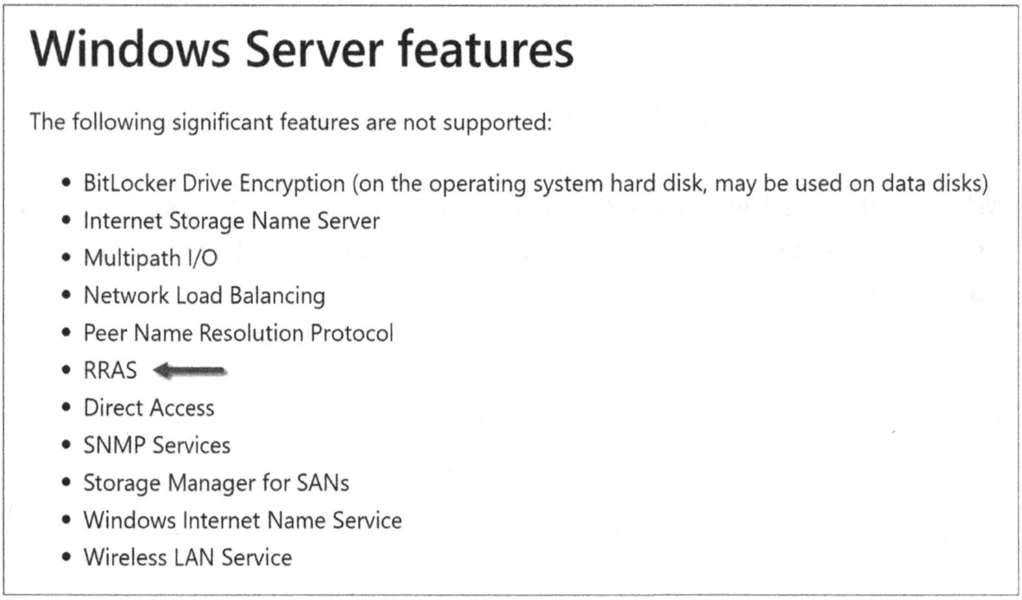

Windows Server features

The following significant features are not supported:

- BitLocker Drive Encryption (on the operating system hard disk, may be used on data disks)
- Internet Storage Name Server
- Multipath I/O
- Network Load Balancing
- Peer Name Resolution Protocol
- RRAS ◄━━━━
- Direct Access
- SNMP Services
- Storage Manager for SANs
- Windows Internet Name Service
- Wireless LAN Service

Figure 7-27. *Unsupported Windows Server features in Azure*

However, "not supported" is different than "doesn't work." In fact, implementing RRAS on Windows Server in Azure works quite well. If organizations are willing to accept the support limitation, it can be an effective solution to overcome some of the drawbacks associated with the native Azure VPN infrastructure options described previously in this chapter.

---

[1] https://docs.microsoft.com/en-US/troubleshoot/azure/virtual-machines/
server-software-support#windows-server-features

Azure RRAS Configuration

Configuring RRAS on a Windows Server virtual machine in Azure is nearly identical to deploying on-premises. The server can be deployed with one or two network interfaces, and joining the server to a domain is optional.

Public IP Address

A public IP address must be assigned to the VPN server's external network interface or the internal interface if the VPN server is configured with a single network adapter. Perform the following steps to associate a public IP address to the VPN server:

1. Open the properties page for the RRAS virtual machine, and click **Networking** in the **Settings** section of the navigation pane.

2. Click the link next to **Network Interface**.

3. Click **IP configurations** in the **Settings** section of the navigation pane.

4. Click the IP address listed in **ipconfig1**.

5. Click **Associate** below **Public IP address**.

6. Click **Create new**.

7. Enter a descriptive name for the public IP address.

8. Select a **SKU** and optionally an **Assignment** method (Figure 7-28).

9. Click **Save**.

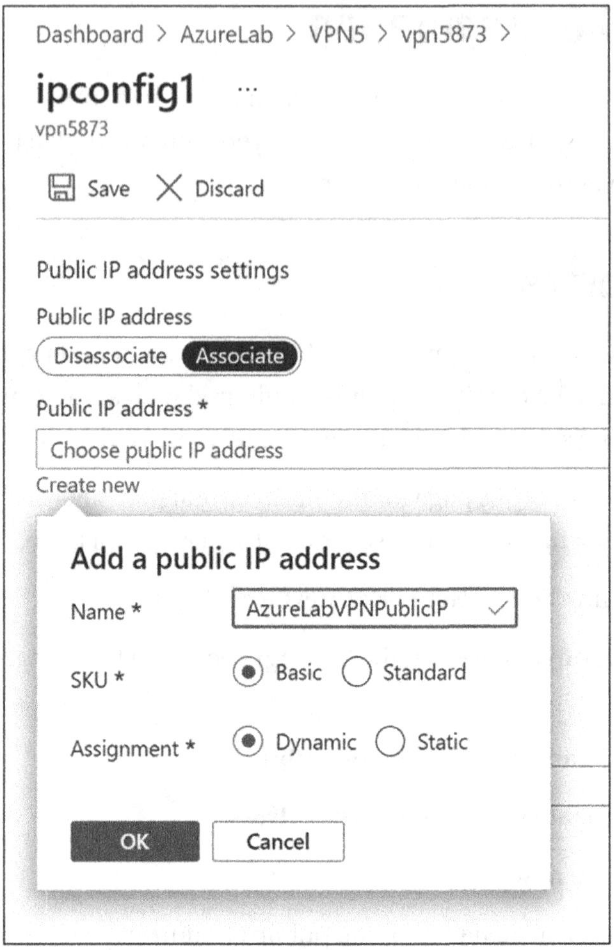

Figure 7-28. *Azure public IP address settings*

When using a dynamic public IP address, create a DNS name for the IP by performing the following steps:

1. Open the properties page for the public IP address created previously and click **Configuration** in the **Settings** section of the navigation pane.

2. Enter a name in the **DNS name label (optional)** field (Figure 7-29).

3. Click **Save**.

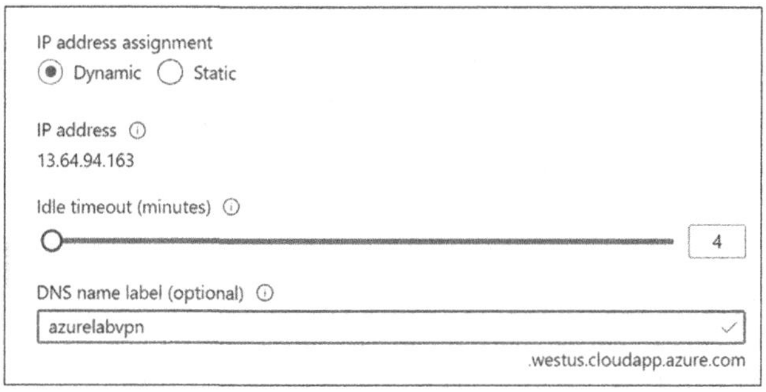

Figure 7-29. *Azure public IP address settings*

Once complete, create a CNAME record in public DNS that maps a hostname to be used by Always On VPN clients to the hostname defined for the public IP. In this example, azurelabvpn.richardhicks.net is mapped to azurelabvpn.westus.cloudapp. azure.com.

```
PS C:\> Resolve-DnsName -Name azurelabvpn.richardhicks.net

Name                              Type   TTL   Section    NameHost
----                              ----   ---   -------    --------
azurelabvpn.richardhicks.net      CNAME  300   Answer     azurelabvpn.westus.
cloudapp.azure.com

Name       : azurelabvpn.westus.cloudapp.azure.com
QueryType  : A
TTL        : 10
Section    : Answer
IP4Address : 13.64.94.163

Name                     : westus.cloudapp.azure.com
QueryType                : SOA
TTL                      : 60
Section                  : Authority
NameAdministrator        : msnhst.microsoft.com
SerialNumber             : 10001
TimeToZoneRefresh        : 900
TimeToZoneFailureRetry   : 300
TimeToExpiration         : 604800
DefaultTTL               : 60
```

Note   If a static IP address is configured for the Azure public IP address, an A host record can be configured pointing directly to the IP address itself.

Inbound Traffic

Network Security Groups (NSGs) and firewalls may be configured in the path between the public IP address and the VPN server. Ensure any NSGs or firewall's inline is updated to allow the following protocols and ports inbound to the VPN server.

- TCP port 443 (SSTP)
- UDP port 500 (IKEv2)
- UDP port 4500 (IKEv2 NAT traversal)

Client IP Subnet

Static IP address pool assignment must be used with RRAS hosted in Azure. Using DHCP for VPN client IP address assignment on RRAS in Azure is not supported and will not work. The IP subnet assigned to VPN clients by RRAS must be unique and not overlap with any existing subnets in the Azure VNet. If more than one VPN server is deployed, each server should be configured to assign a unique subnet for its clients.

IP Forwarding

IP forwarding must be enabled on the VPN server's internal network interface. Perform the following steps to enable IP forwarding on the RRAS virtual machine in Azure:

1. Open the properties page for the internal network interface assigned to the VPN server and click **IP configurations** in the **Settings** section of the navigation pane.

2. Click **Enabled** next to **IP forwarding** (Figure 7-30).

3. Click **Save**.

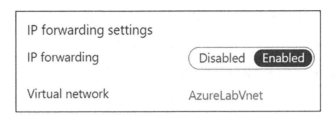

IP forwarding settings

IP forwarding   Disabled **Enabled**

Virtual network   AzureLabVnet

Figure 7-30. *Azure IP forwarding settings*

Routing

Azure must be configured to route the VPN client IP subnet back to the VPN server virtual machine. Perform the following steps to create and assign a route table in Azure:

1. Open the Resource Group in Azure where the virtual machine is provisioned and click **Create**.

2. Enter "route table" in the **Search services and marketplace field**.

3. Click on **Route table**.

4. Click **Create** (Figure 7-31).

Figure 7-31. *Create an Azure route table*

5. Select the appropriate subscription from the **Subscription** drop-down list.

6. Select the appropriate resource group from the **Resource group** drop-down list.

7. Select an appropriate region from the **Region** drop-down list.

8. Enter a descriptive name for the route table in the **Name** field.

9. Select **Yes** next to **Propagate gateway routes**.

10. Click **Review + Create** (Figure 7-32).

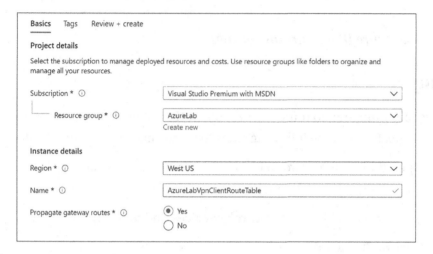

Figure 7-32. *Azure route table settings*

Once provisioning is complete, click the **Go to resource** button and perform the following steps to configure the routing table:

1. Click **Routes** in the **Settings** section of the navigation pane.

2. Click **Add**.

3. Enter a descriptive name in the **Route name** field.

4. Enter the IP address prefix assigned to VPN clients by the VPN server in the **Address prefix** field.

5. Select **Virtual appliance** from the **Next hop type** drop-down list.

6. Enter the IP address of the VPN server's internal network interface in the **Next hop address** field (Figure 7-33).

7. Click **Create**.

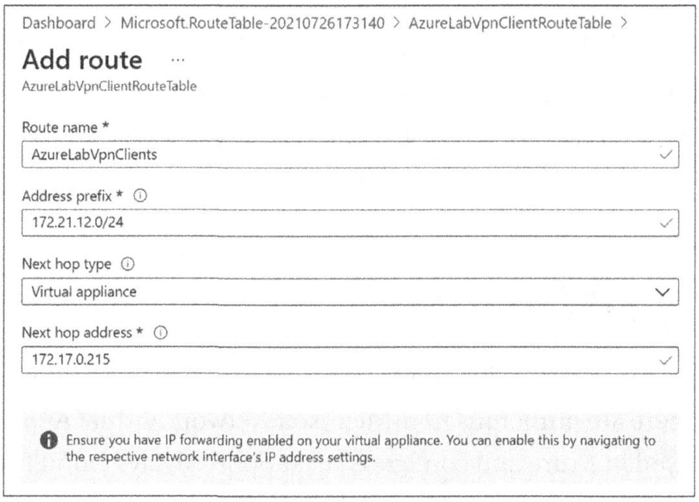

Figure 7-33. *Add routes to the Azure route table*

Next, perform the following steps to associate the route table with an Azure VNet:

1. Click **Subnets** in the **Settings** section of the navigation pane.

2. Click **Associate**.

3. Select a VNet that must be accessed by VPN clients from the
    Virtual network drop-down list.

4. Select a subnet that must be accessed by VPN clients from the
    Subnet drop-down list.

5. Click **Ok** (Figure 7-34).

6. Repeat the steps previously mentioned for each subnet that must
    be access by VPN clients.

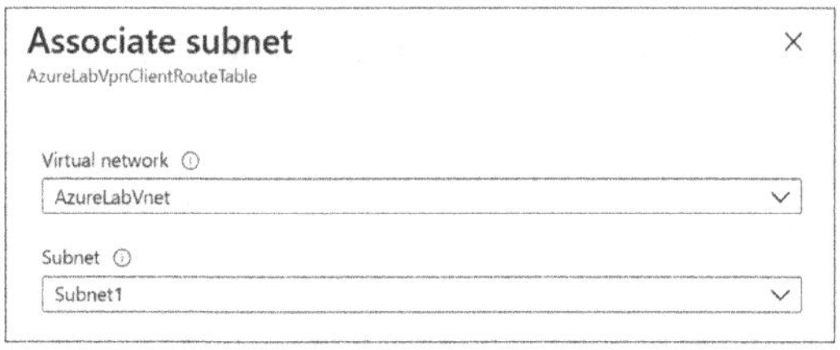

Figure 7-34. *Associate a subnet with the Azure route table*

Note   If Always On VPN clients connecting to the RRAS server in Azure need access to on-premises resources over a site-to-site VPN connection, assign the route table to the GatewaySubnet also using the previous steps.

Third-Party VPN in Azure

Administrators are by no means limited to using the Azure native VPN gateway or RRAS options. In fact, there are numerous non-Microsoft Network Virtual Appliances (NVAs) that can be deployed in Azure and configured to support Always On VPN connections. Many popular security vendors like Cisco, Palo Alto, Checkpoint, and many others offer Azure NVAs that can be configured to support client-based VPN.

Unfortunately, documenting those options is outside the scope of this book. However, many of the principles outlined in this chapter are applicable also to third-party VPN appliances deployed in Azure.

Summary

Administrators have many options to choose from when deciding to host VPN services in Microsoft Azure. The Azure VPN gateway is not difficult to configure and offers good support. The Azure Virtual WAN offers more scalability and throughput but is more limited in its support of Always On VPN. Deploying Windows Server with the RRAS role configured is another alternative although it comes with some support limitations. Finally, administrators are not limited to deploy VPN servers for Always On VPN in Azure alone. Windows Servers with RRAS installed can also be deployed in Amazon Web Services (AWS), Google Cloud Platform (GCP), and, no doubt, many others. Configuring VPN on those services is outside the scope of this book, unfortunately.

## CHAPTER 8

Deploy Certificates with Intune

Certificates used for Always On VPN are most commonly deployed using on-premises Active Directory and certificate autoenrollment. Of course, this assumes the endpoint is on the internal network and is joined to the domain.

However, some deployment scenarios such as hybrid Azure AD join with Autopilot provisioning and native Azure AD join necessitate the provisioning of certificates without being domain-joined or first having access to the internal network.

Fortunately, Microsoft Endpoint Manager/Intune provides support for provisioning certificates in this way. Specifically, the Certificate Connector for Microsoft Intune can be deployed on-premises and configured to connect Intune to the on-premises PKI, enabling certificate provisioning when endpoints require certificates before connecting to the internal network and for enrolling users or devices for certificates that are not joined to the domain.

Deployment Options

When deploying certificates using Microsoft Endpoint Manager/Intune, administrators have two choices. The recommended solution is using PKCS (Public Key Cryptography Standards) certificates. Alternatively, SCEP (Simple Certificate Enrollment Protocol) certificates can be used.

PKCS

Using PKCS certificates is recommended for deploying certificates with Endpoint Manager/Intune to support Always On VPN. When using PKCS certificates, the on-premises configuration is much simpler, making the solution easier to implement

© Richard M. Hicks 2022
R. M. Hicks, *Implementing Always On VPN*, https://doi.org/10.1007/978-1-4842-7741-6_8

and support. In addition, using PKCS certificates requires no inbound access at all. The Certificate Connector for Microsoft Intune requires outbound access only when using PKCS, which significantly simplifies the configuration and improves security overall.

SCEP

SCEP certificates are optional but may be required to support other types of certificate enrollment[1] using Intune. The main advantage to using SCEP is that certificate private keys never leave the endpoint. However, implementing and supporting SCEP is much more difficult. SCEP is quite complex and has many critical dependencies. The Network Device Enrollment Service (NDES) role must be configured on a Windows Server to support SCEP (NDES is Microsoft's implementation of SCEP). It also requires inbound access from the Internet, which requires opening the edge firewall to allow access or implementing an application delivery controller (ADC) or another reverse proxy to facilitate this communication. Overall, SCEP is much more challenging to manage and troubleshoot compared to PKCS. As such, it is recommended that PKCS be used whenever possible.

PKCS Certificates

To deploy PKCS certificates with Microsoft Endpoint Manager/Intune, permissions must be configured on the issuing CA for the Certificate Connector for Intune computer account to allow it to issue and manage certificates. In addition, a certificate template must be created for use by Intune when enrolling users and devices for a certificate. Once complete, the Certificate Connector for Microsoft Intune can be installed, and configuration profiles can be created in Intune to provision user and device certificates as required.

---

[1] https://docs.microsoft.com/en-us/mem/intune/protect/certificates-configure# supported-platforms-and-certificate-profiles

CA Permissions

To configure permissions on the CA to allow the computer where the Certificate Connector for Intune is installed to issue and manage certificates, open the Certification Authority management console (certsrv.msc) on an issuing CA or an administrative workstation with the remote administration tools installed and perform the following steps:

1. Right-click the issuing CA and choose **Properties**.

2. Select the **Security** tab.

3. Click **Add**.

4. Click **Object Types**.

5. Check the box next to **Computers**.

6. Click **Ok**.

7. Enter the name of the computer where the Certificate Connector for Intune will be installed.

8. Click **Ok**.

9. Grant the **Allow** permission for **Request Certificates** and **Issue and Manage certificates** (Figure 8-1).

10. Click **Ok**.

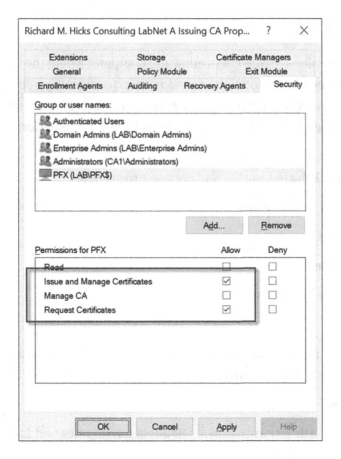

Figure 8-1.   *Configure CA permissions*

Certificate Template

To create and publish a PKCS certificate template to be used by the Certificate Connector for Intune, open the Certificate Templates management console (certtmpl.msc) on an issuing CA or an administrative workstation with the remote management tools installed and perform the following steps:

1. Right-click the **User** template and choose **Duplicate**.

2. Select the **Compatibility** tab.

   a. Select **Windows Server 2008 R2** from the **Certification Authority** drop-down list.

   b. Select **Windows 7/Server 2008 R2** from the **Certificate recipient** drop-down list (Figure 8-2).

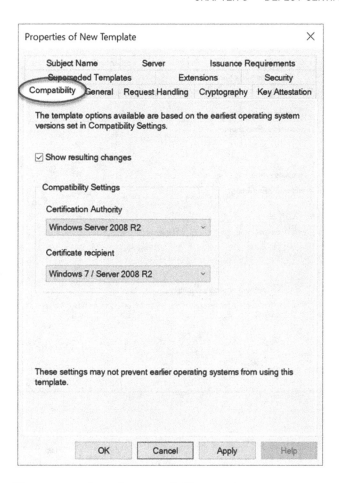

Figure 8-2. *Certificate template Compatibility settings*

3. Select the **General** tab.

    a. Enter a descriptive name in the **Template display name** field.

    b. Uncheck the box next to **Publish certificate in Active Directory** (Figure 8-3).

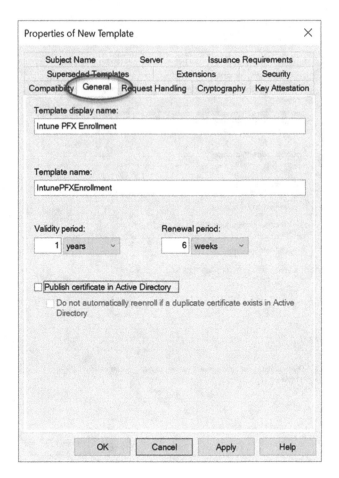

Figure 8-3. *Certificate template General settings*

4. Select the **Request Handling** tab.

    a. Check the box next to **Allow private key to be exported** (Figure 8-4).

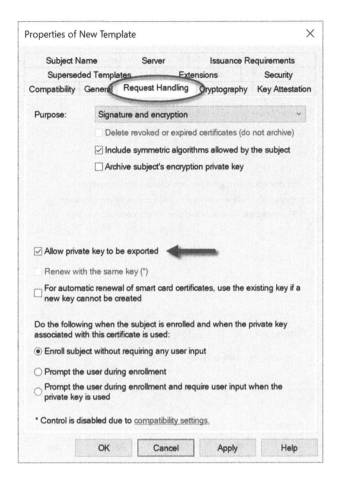

Figure 8-4. Certificate template Request Handling settings

5. Select the **Cryptography** tab.

    a. Select **Key Storage Provider** from the **Provider Category** drop-down list.

    b. Select **RSA** from the **Algorithm name** drop-down list.

    c. Enter **2048** in the **Minimum key size** field.

    d. Select **Requests can use any provider available on the subject's computer**.

    e. Select **SHA256** from the **Request hash** drop-down list (Figure 8-5).

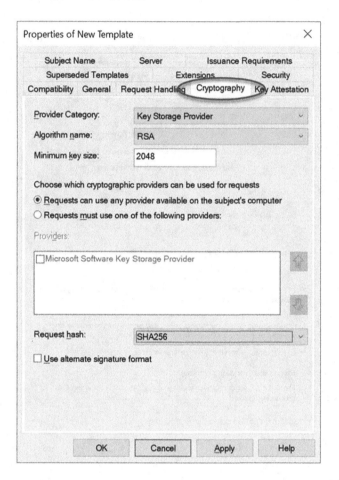

Figure 8-5. *Certificate template Cryptography settings*

6. Select the **Subject Name** tab.

   a. Select **Supply in the request** (Figure 8-6).

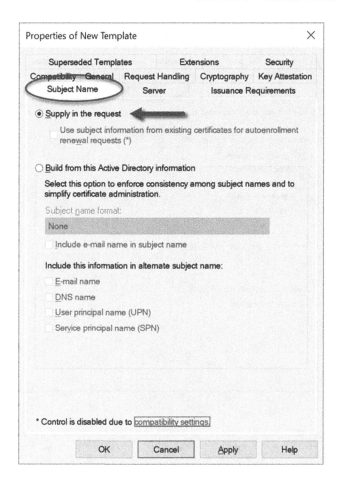

Figure 8-6. *Certificate template Subject Name settings*

7. Select the **Extensions** tab.

   a. Highlight **Application Policies** and click **Edit**.

   b. Highlight **Secure Email** and click **Remove**.

   c. Highlight **Encrypting File System** and click **Remove**.

   d. Click **Ok** (Figure 8-7).

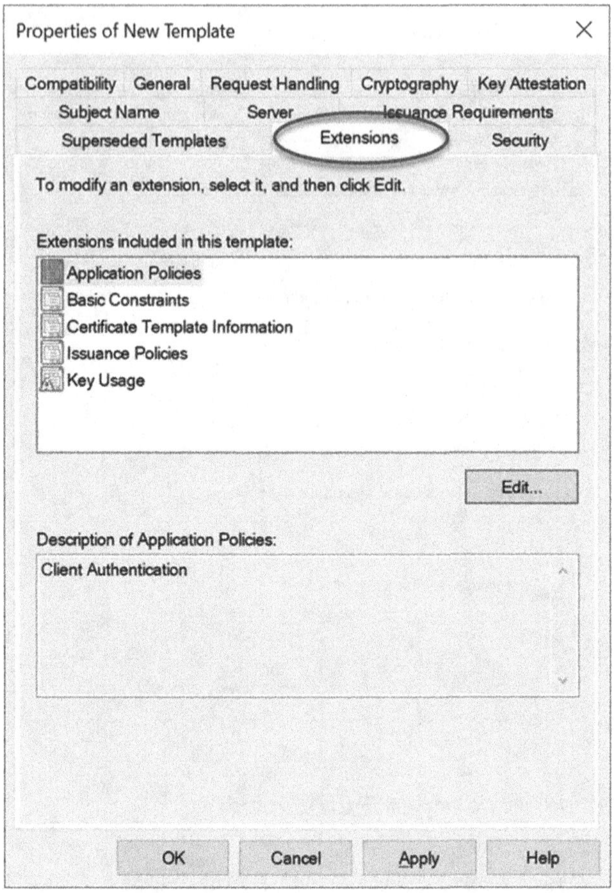

Figure 8-7. *Certificate template Extensions settings*

8. Select the **Security** tab.

   a. Click **Add**.

   b. Click **Object Types**.

   c. Check the box next to **Computers**.

   d. Click **Ok**.

   e. Enter the name of the computer where the Certificate Connector for Intune is installed.

   f. Click **Ok**.

g. Grant the **Allow** permission for **Read** and **Enroll** (Figure 8-8).

h. Click **Ok**.

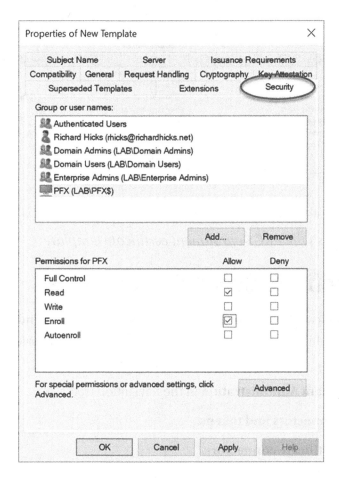

Figure 8-8. *Certificate template Security settings*

Next, open the Certification Authority management console (certsrv.msc) and perform the following steps to publish the certificate template:

1. Expand **Certification Authority**, and then right-click **Certificate Templates** and choose **New ➤ Certificate Template to Issue**.

2. Highlight the certificate template created previously and click **Ok** (Figure 8-9).

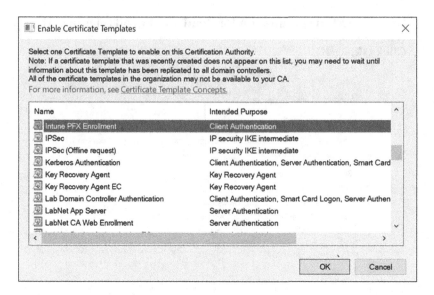

Figure 8-9. *Publish the PKCS enrollment certificate template*

Install Certificate Connector for Intune

To install the Certificate Connector for Intune, open the Microsoft Endpoint Manager management console (`https://endpoint.microsoft.com/`) and perform the following steps:

1. Click **Tenant Administration** in the navigation tree.

2. Click **Connectors and tokens**.

3. Click **Certificate connectors**.

4. Click **Add**.

5. Click the Certificate Connector link to download the installer.

6. Click **Save File** (Figure 8-10).

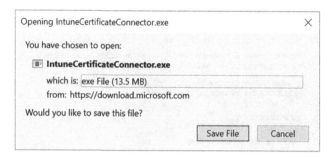

Figure 8-10. *Download the Certificate Connector for Intune*

After the download completes, copy the file to the computer where the Certificate Connector for Intune will be installed and perform the following steps:

Note   It is recommended to install the Certificate Connector for Intune on a dedicated server. It should not be installed on the CA server itself. Also, the Certificate Connector for Intune does not support installation on Server Core. It must be installed on Windows Server with Desktop Experience (GUI).

---

1. Open the Server Manager (servermanager.exe) and highlight **Local Server** in the navigation tree.

2. Click **On** next to **IE Enhanced Security Configuration**.

3. Click **Off** in the **Administrators** section (Figure 8-11).

4. Click **Ok**.

Figure 8-11. *Disable Internet Explorer Enhanced Security configuration*

Next, launch the Certificate Connector for Intune installer executable
(IntuneCertificateConnector.exe) and perform the following steps:

1. Check the box next to **I agree to the license terms and
    conditions**.

2. Click **Install**.

3. Click **Configure Now**.

4. Click **Next** on the **Welcome** screen.

5.   Uncheck the box next to **PKCS imported certificates**
     (Figure 8-12) and click **Next**.

Figure 8-12. *Select Certificate Connector for Intune features*

6.   Select **SYSTEM account** and click **Next** (Figure 8-13).

Figure 8-13. *Select Certificate Connector for Intune service account*

7.   If required, enter proxy server information, and click **Next** (Figure 8-14).

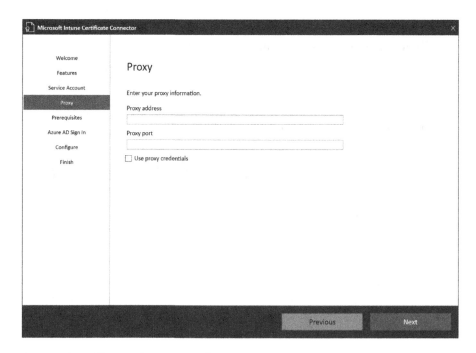

Figure 8-14. *Certificate Connector for Intune proxy settings*

8. Click **Next** on the **Prerequisites** screen (Figure 8-15).

Figure 8-15. *Certificate Connector for Intune prerequisites check*

9. Select the appropriate Azure cloud infrastructure from the **Environment** drop-down list and click **Sign In**.

10. Enter the credentials for an Azure global administrator when prompted.

11. Click **Next** after sign-in is complete (Figure 8-16).

Figure 8-16. *Certificate Connector for Intune Azure AD sign in*

12. Click **Exit** when the configuration is complete (Figure 8-17).

Figure 8-17. *Certificate Connector for Intune configuration completed*

Once the installation of the Certificate Connector for Intune is complete, administrators can view the status of the connector in Intune by navigating to **Tenant administration ➤ Connectors and tokens ➤ Certificate connectors** (Figure 8-18).

Figure 8-18. *Certificate Connector for Intune status*

In addition, administrators can change the name of the Certificate Connector by clicking the connector and entering a friendly name in the **Name** field and clicking **Save** (Figure 8-19).

Figure 8-19. *Rename the Certificate Connector for Intune*

PKCS Intune Configuration

Once the on-premises infrastructure is in place, Intune device configuration profiles can be created to provision user and/or device certificates. Before proceeding, the certification authority's root and intermediate certificates must be configured for deployment by Intune.

Export CA Certificates

On an issuing CA server, or an administrative workstation with the remote management tools installed, open the Enterprise PKI management console (pkiview.msc) and perform the following steps to deploy the root and intermediate certificates using Intune:

1. Highlight the root CA in the navigation tree.

2. Right-click **CA Certificate** and choose **View Certificate**.

3. Select the **Details** tab and click **Copy to File**.

4. Click **Next**.

5. Select **DER encoded binary X.509 (.CER)** and click **Next**.

6. Enter a location to save the file to.

7. Click **Next**.

8. Click **Finish**.

9. Click **Ok**.

Repeat the previous steps for any intermediate or issuing CAs in the organization.

Deploy CA Certificates

To deploy the organization's root and intermediate certificates with Intune, open the Microsoft Endpoint Manager management console (`https://endpoint.microsoft.com/`) and perform the following steps:

1. Click **Devices** in the navigation tree.

2. Click **Configuration profiles**.

3. Click **Create profile**.

4. Select **Windows 10 and later** from the **Platform** drop-down list.

5. Select **Templates** from the **Profile** type drop-down list.

6. Click **Trusted certificate**.

7. Click **Create** (Figure 8-20).

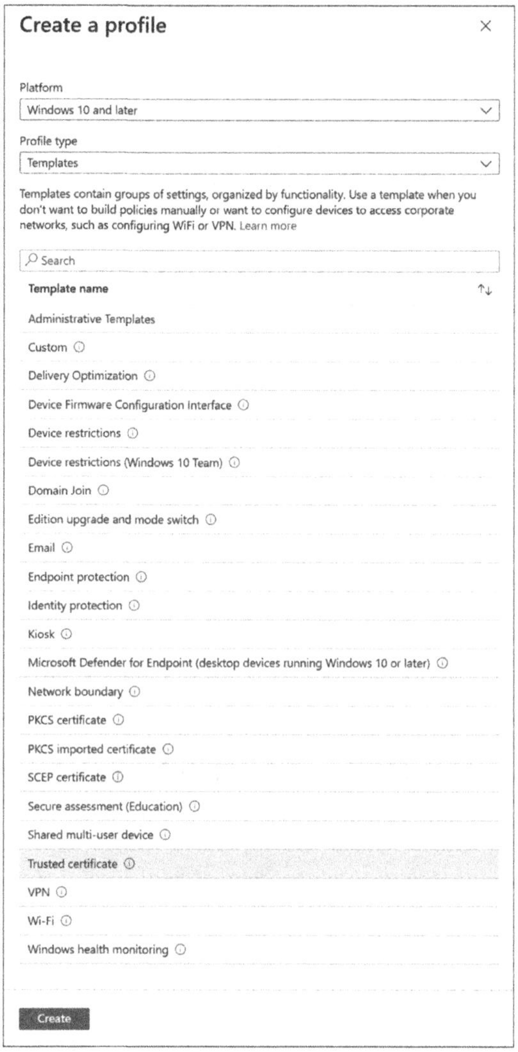

Figure 8-20. *Create an Trusted Certificate profile*

Perform the following steps to configure the Trusted Certificate profile:

1. Enter a descriptive name for the profile in the **Name** field.

2. Enter a description in the **Description** field (optional).

3. Click **Next** (Figure 8-21).

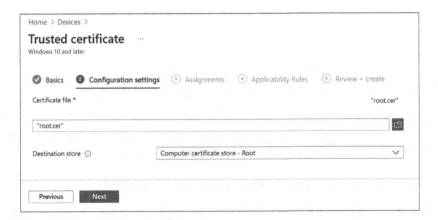

Figure 8-21. *Trusted certificate profile name*

4. Click the folder icon and select the root certificate file exported
    previously.

5. Select **Computer certificate store – Root** from the **Destination
    store** drop-down list (Figure 8-22).

6. Click **Next**.

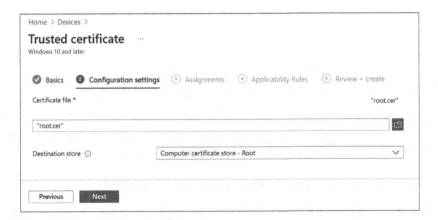

Figure 8-22. *Trusted certificate profile root certificate settings*

7. Click **Add groups** and choose an appropriate group to include.

8. Click **Select**.

9. Click **Next**.

10. Click **Next**.

11. Click **Create**.

Repeat the previous steps to deploy any intermediate CA certificates, if required. When publishing an intermediate certificate, be sure to select **Computer certificate store – Intermediate** from the **Destination store** drop-down list, as shown in Figure 8-23.

Figure 8-23. *Trusted certificate profile intermediate CA certificate settings*

PKCS User Certificate

Perform the following steps to deploy a PKCS user authentication certificate using Intune:

1. Click **Devices** in the navigation tree.

2. Click **Configuration profiles**.

3. Click **Create profile**.

4. Select **Windows 10 and later** from the **Platform** drop-down list.

5. Select **Templates** from the **Profile type** drop-down list.

6. Click **PKCS certificate**.

7. Click **Create** (Figure 8-24).

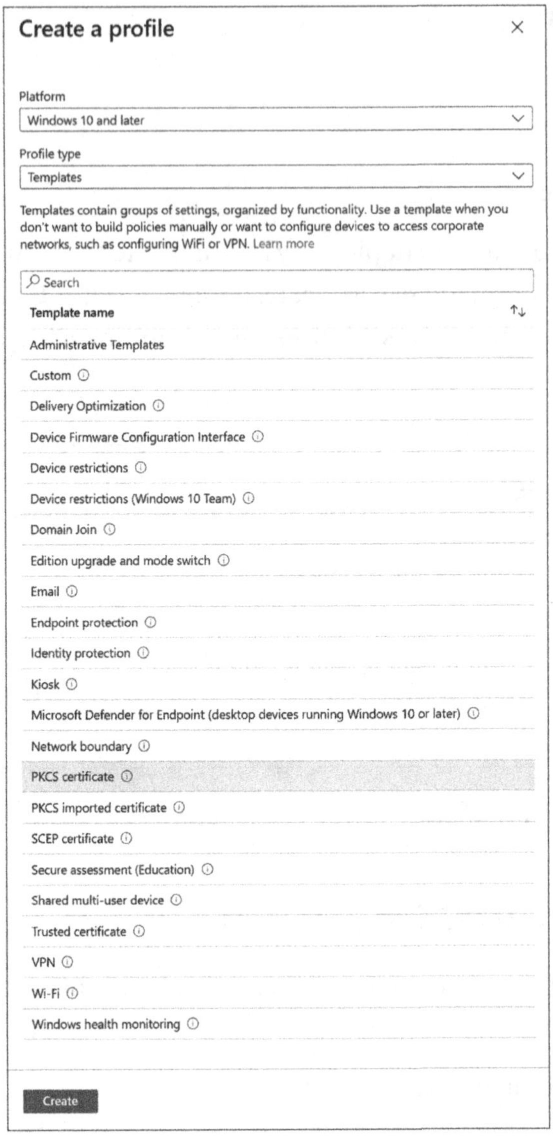

Figure 8-24. *Create a PKCS user certificate profile*

Perform the following steps to configure the PKCS user authentication certificate profile:

1. Enter a descriptive name for the profile in the **Name** field.

2. Enter a description in the **Description** field (optional).

3. Click **Next** (Figure 8-25).

Figure 8-25. *PKCS certificate profile name*

4. Adjust the **Renewal threshold** and **Certificate validity period**
    values, if necessary. Otherwise, accept the defaults.

5. Select **Enroll to Trusted Platform Module (TPM) KSP, otherwise
    fail** from the **Key Storage Provider (KSP)** drop-down list.

Note   If devices without TPM must be supported, or if fallback to software KSP
is required (not recommended), select **Enroll to Trusted Platform Module (TPM)
KSP if present, otherwise Software KSP**.

---

6. Enter the hostname (FQDN) of the issuing CA server in the
    Certification authority field.

7. Enter the common name of the Certification Authority in the
    Certification authority name field. The common name of the CA
    can be found by running certuil.exe -dump on any domain-joined
    workstation or server.

8. Enter the name of the certificate template created previously in the **Certificate template name** field. Be sure to enter the Template Name and not the Template Display Name here (the Template Name is just the Template Display Name without the spaces).

9. Select **User** from the **Certificate type** drop-down list.

10. Enter **CN={{UserName}}** in the **Subject name format** field.

11. In the **Subject alternative name** section, select **User principal name (UPN)** from the **Attribute** drop-down list and enter **{{UserPrincipalName}}** in the **Value** field.

12. In the **Extended key usage** section, select **Client Authentication (1.3.6.1.5.5.7.3.2)** from the **Predefined values** drop-down list.

13. Click **Next** (Figure 8-26).

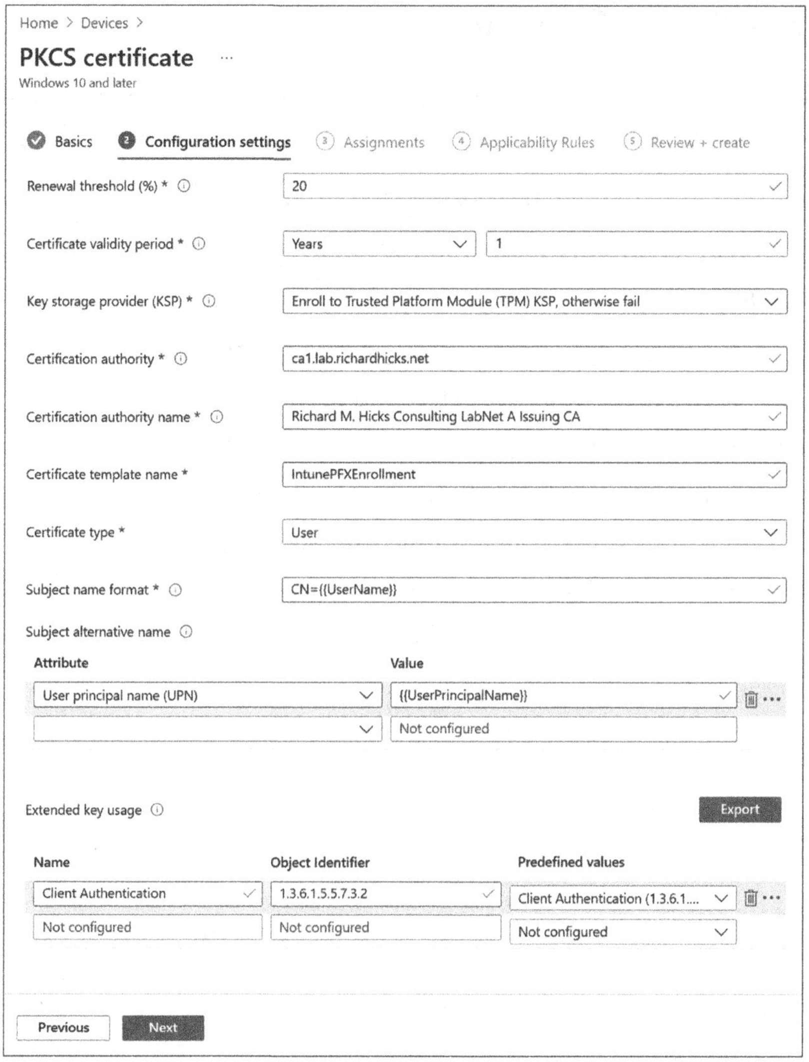

Home > Devices >

PKCS certificate ...
Windows 10 and later

✅ Basics   ② **Configuration settings**   ③ Assignments   ④ Applicability Rules   ⑤ Review + create

Renewal threshold (%) * ⓘ

| 20 | ✓ |

Certificate validity period * ⓘ

| Years | ⌄ | 1 | ✓ |

Key storage provider (KSP) * ⓘ

| Enroll to Trusted Platform Module (TPM) KSP, otherwise fail | ⌄ |

Certification authority * ⓘ

| ca1.lab.richardhicks.net | ✓ |

Certification authority name * ⓘ

| Richard M. Hicks Consulting LabNet A Issuing CA | ✓ |

Certificate template name *

| IntunePFXEnrollment | ✓ |

Certificate type *

| User | ⌄ |

Subject name format * ⓘ

| CN={{UserName}} | ✓ |

Subject alternative name ⓘ

Attribute	Value	
User principal name (UPN) ⌄	{{UserPrincipalName}} ⌄	🗑 ···
⌄	Not configured	

Extended key usage ⓘ   [Export]

Name	Object Identifier	Predefined values	
Client Authentication ✓	1.3.6.1.5.5.7.3.2 ✓	Client Authentication (1.3.6.1.... ⌄	🗑 ···
Not configured	Not configured	Not configured ⌄	

[Previous] [Next]

Figure 8-26. *PKCS user certificate profile settings*

14. Click **Add groups** and choose an appropriate user group to include.

15. Click **Select**.

16. Click **Next**.

17. Click **Next**.

18. Click **Create**.

PKCS Device Certificate

The procedure for deploying a PKCS device authentication certificate using Intune is nearly identical to the user authentication certificate with the following exceptions:

1. Select **Device** from the **Certificate type** drop-down list.

2. Enter **CN={{FullyQualifiedDomainName}}** in the **Subject name format** field.

3. In the **Subject alternative name** section, select **DNS** from the **Attribute** drop-down list, and then enter **{{FullyQualifiedDomainName}}** in the **Value** field.

4. The **Extended key usage** is **Client Authentication (1.3.6.1.5.5.7.3.2)** just as it is for the user authentication certificate (Figure 8-27).

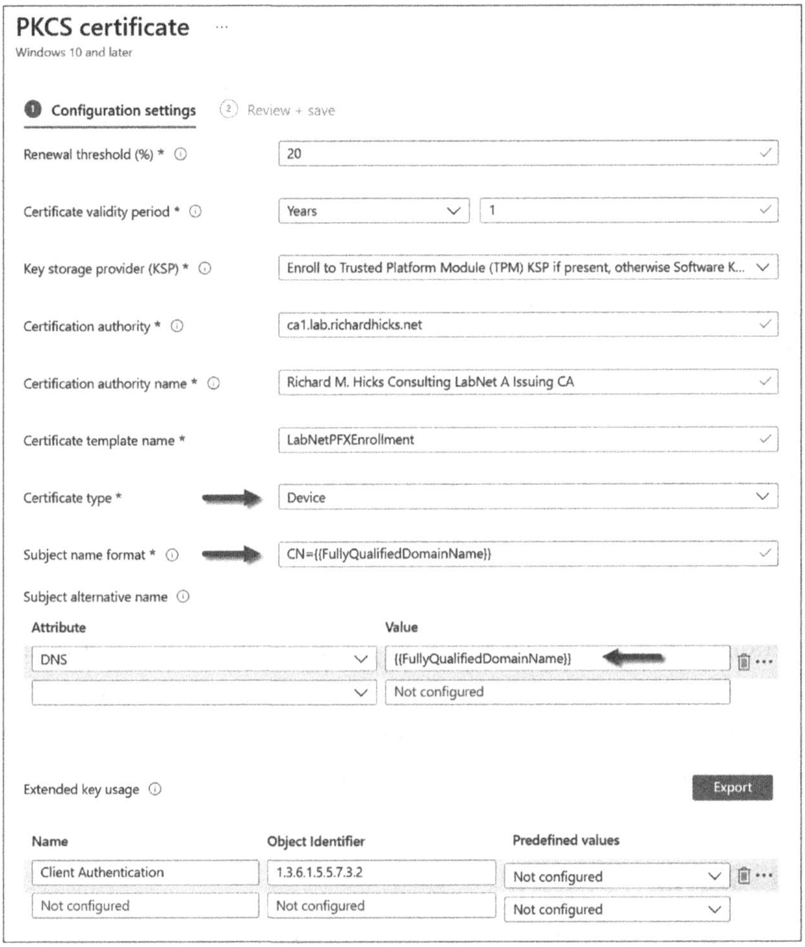

PKCS certificate   ...
Windows 10 and later

① Configuration settings   **②** Review + save

Renewal threshold (%) * ⓘ   20

Certificate validity period * ⓘ   Years   ⌄   1

Key storage provider (KSP) * ⓘ   Enroll to Trusted Platform Module (TPM) KSP if present, otherwise Software K... ⌄

Certification authority * ⓘ   ca1.lab.richardhicks.net

Certification authority name * ⓘ   Richard M. Hicks Consulting LabNet A Issuing CA

Certificate template name *   LabNetPFXEnrollment

Certificate type *   Device   ⌄

Subject name format * ⓘ   CN={{FullyQualifiedDomainName}}   ⌄

Subject alternative name ⓘ

Attribute   **Value**

DNS   ⌄   {{FullyQualifiedDomainName}}   🗑 ...

                                    ⌄   Not configured

Extended key usage ⓘ   [Export]

Name   **Object Identifier**   **Predefined values**

Client Authentication   1.3.6.1.5.5.7.3.2   Not configured   ⌄ 🗑 ...

Not configured   Not configured   Not configured   ⌄

Figure 8-27. *PKCS device certificate profile settings*

Once the configuration is complete, the user and/or device authentication certificates should appear in the users or devices certificate store, respectively, once the endpoint synchronizes with Intune.

Note   Details about issued certificates can be found in the C:\Program Files\ Microsoft Intune\PFXCertificateConnector\PfxRequest\Succeed\ folder on the Intune Certificate Connector server. A PowerShell script to output issued certificate details can be found here: `https://github.com/richardhicks/aovpn/blob/` `master/Get-IssuedPfxCertificates.ps1`.

SCEP Certificates

An alternative to deploying PKCS certificates with Microsoft Endpoint Manager/Intune is to use SCEP certificates. As stated previously, it is recommended to use PKCS certificates whenever possible. However, there may be some deployment scenarios that require SCEP.

It is recommended to install NDES on a dedicated server. It should not be installed on the CA server itself. The Certificate Connector for Intune must be installed in the NDES server, however.

Although the NDES role is supported on Windows Server Core, the Intune Certificate Connector is not. With that, NDES must be installed on a Windows Server with Desktop Experience (GUI) installed.

Service Account

It is recommended to configure NDES to use a service account for access to the issuing CA. The service account is a standard user account in Active Directory with no special permissions required. The service account only requires membership in the Domain Users group and the logon as a service right on the NDES server.

CA Permissions

Once the NDES service account has been provisioned, open the Certification Authority management console (certsrv.msc) on an issuing CA or an administrative workstation with the remote administration tools installed and perform the following steps:

1. Right-click the issuing CA and choose **Properties**.

2. Select the **Security** tab.

3. Click **Add**.

4. Enter the name of the NDES service account.

5. Click **Ok**.

6. Grant the **Allow** permission for **Request Certificates** and **Issue and Manage certificates** (Figure 8-28).

7. Click **Ok**.

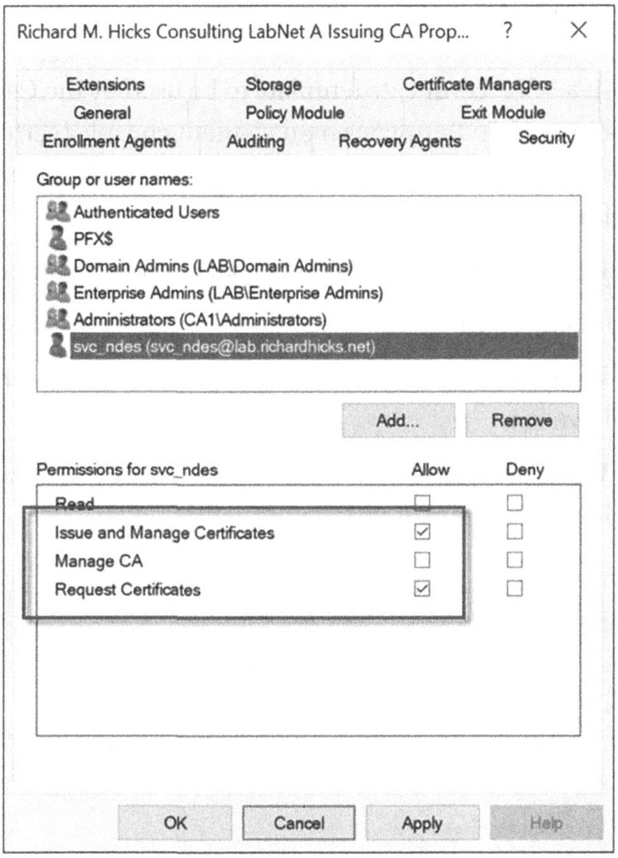

Figure 8-28. *CA permissions*

A configuration change on the issuing CA is required to allow Intune to specify the validity period of the certificate. To do this, open an elevated PowerShell window on the issuing CA and run the following commands:

```
certutil.exe -setreg Policy\EditFlags +EDITF_ATTRIBUTEENDDATE
```

Restart the Active Directory Certificate Services service (CertSvc) on the issuing CA for the change to take effect by running the following PowerShell command:

```
Restart-Service CertSvc -Passthru
```

Certificate Template

To create and publish a SCEP certificate template to be used by the Certificate Connector for Intune, open the Certificate Templates management console (certtmpl.msc) on an issuing CA or an administrative workstation with the remote management tools installed and perform the following steps:

1. Right-click the **User** certificate template and choose **Duplicate**.

2. Select the **Compatibility** tab.

   a. Select **Windows Server 2003** from the **Certification Authority** drop-down list.

   b. Select **Windows XP/Server 2003** from the **Certificate recipient** drop-down list (Figure 8-29).

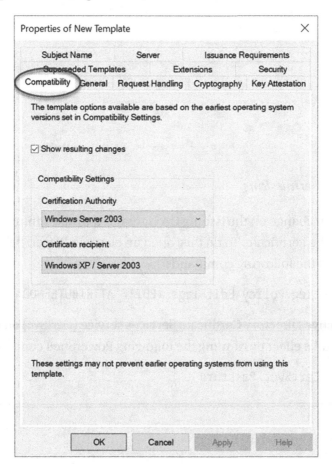

Figure 8-29. *Certificate template compatibility settings*

3. Select the **General** tab.

   a. Enter a descriptive name in the **Template display name** field.

   b. Uncheck the box next to **Publish certificate in Active Directory** (Figure 8-30).

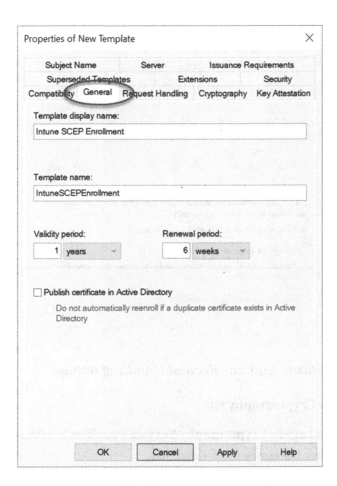

Figure 8-30. *Certificate template General settings*

4. Select the **Request Handling** tab.

   a. Uncheck the box next to **Allow private key to be exported** (Figure 8-31).

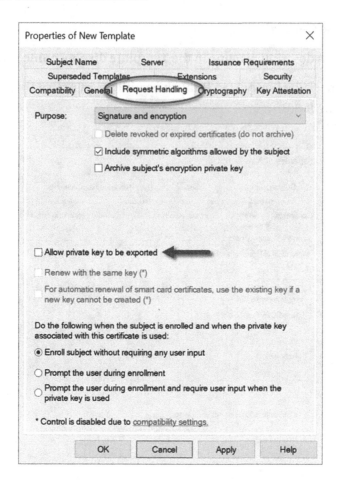

Figure 8-31. *Certificate template Request Handling settings*

5. Select the **Cryptography** tab.

    a. Ensure **Legacy Cryptography Service Provider** is listed in the **Provider Category** drop-down list.

    b. Enter **2048** in the **Minimum key size field** (Figure 8-32).

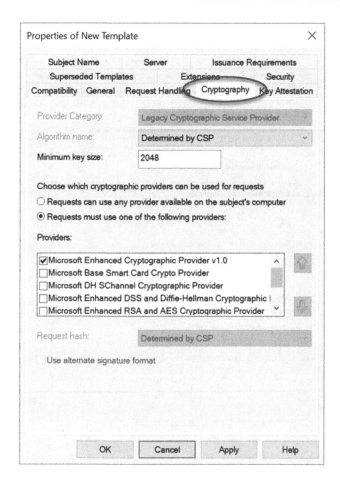

Figure 8-32. *Certificate template Cryptography settings*

6. Select the **Subject Name** tab.

    a. Select **Supply in the request** (Figure 8-33).

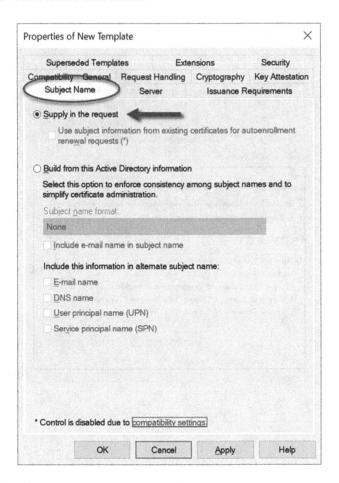

Figure 8-33. *Certificate template Subject Name settings*

7. Select the **Extensions** tab.

    a. Highlight **Application Policies** and click **Edit**.

    b. Highlight **Secure Email** and click **Remove**.

    c. Highlight **Encrypting File System** and click **Remove**.

    d. Click **Ok** (Figure 8-34).

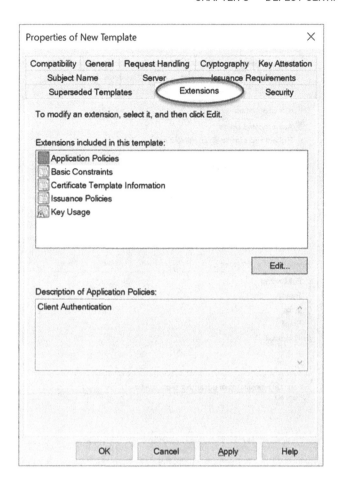

Figure 8-34. *Certificate template Extensions settings*

8. Select the **Security** tab.

   a. Click **Add**.

   b. Enter the name of the NDES service account and click **Ok**.

   c. Grant the **Allow** permission for **Read** and **Enroll** (Figure 8-35).

   d. Click **Ok**.

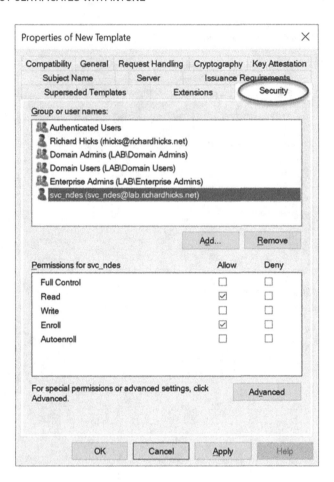

Figure 8-35. *Certificate template Security settings*

Next, open the Certification Authority management console (certsrv.msc) and perform the following steps to publish the certificate template:

1. Expand **Certification Authority**, and then right-click **Certificate Templates** and choose **New ➤ Certificate Template to Issue**.

2. Highlight the certificate template created previously and click **Ok** (Figure 8-36).

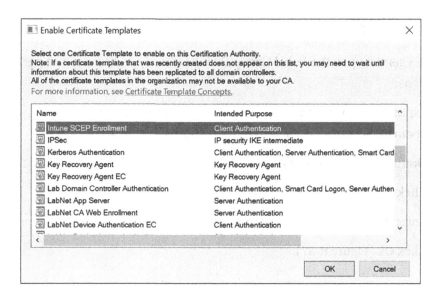

Figure 8-36. *Publish the SCEP enrollment certificate template*

Install NDES

Next, install the NDES role by opening an elevated PowerShell window on the NDES server and running the following commands:

```
Install-WindowsFeature ADCS-Device-Enrollment -IncludeManagementTools
Install-WindowsFeature -Name @("Web-Filtering", "Web-ASP-Net", "Web-ASP-
Net45", "Web-WMI", "NET-HTTP-Activation", "NET-WCF-HTTP-Activation45")
```

Once complete, add the NDES service account to the IIS_IUSRS local group on the NDES server by running the following PowerShell command:

```
Add-LocalGroupMember -Group IIS_IUSRS -Member 'lab\svc_ndes'
```

Finally, register a Service Principal Name (SPN) in Active Directory for the NDES service account by running the following commands. The command syntax is `setspn.exe -s http/<servername> <domain\accountname>`. Run the command to register both the server's hostname and FQDN, as shown in this example:

```
setspn.exe -s http/ndes lab\svc_ndes
setspn.exe -s http/ndes.lab.richardhicks.net lab\svc_ndes
```

Configure NDES

On the NDES server, open the Local Group Policy Editor (gpedit.msc) and perform the following steps:

1. Expand **Computer Configuration ➤ Windows Settings ➤ Security Settings** and highlight **User Rights Assignment**.

2. Double-click **Log on as a service**.

3. Click **Add User or Group**.

4. Enter the NDES service account and click **Ok**.

5. Click **Ok** (Figure 8-37).

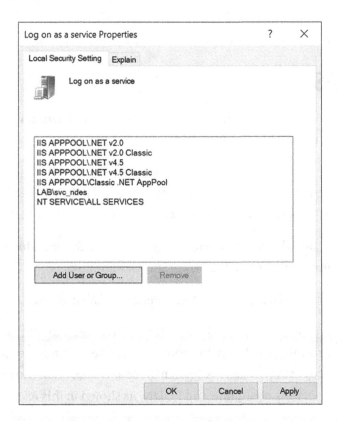

Figure 8-37. *Local user rights assignment settings*

Next, configure the NDES role by running the following PowerShell commands. Replace the password, the NDES service account name, and the CA common name accordingly.

```
$pwdtext = 'sUPerSecReTp@sSw0rd'
$pwd = ConvertTo-SecureString -String $pwdtext -AsPlainText -Force
Install-AdcsNetworkDeviceEnrollmentService -ServiceAccountName lab\svc_ndes
-ServiceAccountPassword $pwd -caconfig 'CA1.lab.richardhicks.net\Richard
M. Hicks Consulting LabNet A Issuing CA' -Force
```

Note   The CA common name can be found by running certutil.exe -dump on any domain-joined server or workstation.

Next, run the following PowerShell commands to configure NDES to use the certificate template created previously. Be sure to use the Template Name in the following commands and not the Template Display Name.

```
$Template = 'IntuneSCEPEnrollment'
Set-ItemProperty -Path HKLM:\SOFTWARE\Microsoft\Cryptography\MSCEP\
-Name  EncryptionTemplate -Value $Template -Force
Set-ItemProperty -Path HKLM:\SOFTWARE\Microsoft\Cryptography\MSCEP\
-Name  GeneralPurposeTemplate -Value $Template -Force
Set-ItemProperty -Path HKLM:\SOFTWARE\Microsoft\Cryptography\MSCEP\
-Name  SignatureTemplate -Value $Template -Force
```

Run the following PowerShell commands to enable long URL support in IIS:

```
New-ItemProperty -Path 'HKLM:\SYSTEM\CurrentControlSet\Services\HTTP\
Parameters\' -Name MaxFieldLength -Type DWORD -Value 65534
New-ItemProperty -Path 'HKLM:\SYSTEM\CurrentControlSet\Services\HTTP\
Parameters\' -Name MaxRequestBytes -Type DWORD -Value 65534
```

Run the following commands to update the max URL length and max query string request filtering values in IIS:

```
c:\windows\system32\inetsrv\appcmd.exe set config /section:requestfiltering
/requestlimits.maxurl:65534
c:\windows\system32\inetsrv\appcmd.exe set config /section:requestfiltering
/requestlimits.maxquerystring:65534
```

Once complete, restart the computer. Do not simply run iisreset.exe. A full restart is required for the changes to take effect.

Publish NDES

The NDES server must be published on the Internet to allow endpoints to enroll for certificates. This can be accomplished in several different ways.

Edge firewall – Administrators can configure the enterprise edge firewall to allow inbound TCP port 443 to the NDES server.

Reverse proxy – A reverse proxy appliance or application delivery controller (ADC) can be configured to publish HTTPS to the public Internet. If choosing this option, do not configure preauthentication.

Web Application Proxy – The Web Application Proxy (WAP) role of Windows Server can be configured to proxy NDES to the public Internet. For more information about configuring WAP, visit `https://docs.microsoft.com/en-us/previous-versions/windows/it-pro/windows-server-2012-R2-and-2012/dn383662(v=ws.11)`.

Azure AD Application Proxy – The Azure AD Application Proxy can also be configured to publish NDES to the public Internet. For more information regarding Azure AD Application Proxy, visit `https://docs.microsoft.com/en-us/azure/active-directory/app-proxy/application-proxy`.

NDES TLS Certificate

Regardless of which solution is configured to allow public Internet traffic to reach the NDES server, a TLS certificate must be installed to provide secure communication. It is recommended that a public TLS certificate be used for this purpose. If the NDES server is published directly to the Internet, a public TLS certificate should be used. If the NDES server is published to the Internet using a reverse proxy (load balancer or application proxy) a certificate issued by the internal PKI can be used.

The process of generating a certificate request for a public TLS certificate is the same as the SSTP certificate, which is outlined in Chapter 4. The Subject Name on the certificate must match the public FQDN of the NDES server.

Once the public TLS certificate has been installed on the NDES server, open an elevated PowerShell window and run the following commands. Be sure to replace the thumbprint value in the following example with the thumbprint of the actual certificate to be used.

```
$Thumbprint = '6EBF08D01EB207DC9B5DF2F4FCCAA92DAB7BE4F1'
$Cert = Get-ChildItem -Path cert:\localmachine\my\$thumbprint
New-WebBinding -Name "Default Web Site" -IP "*" -Port 443 -Protocol https

Set-Location IIS:\sslbindings
$Cert | new-item 0.0.0.0!443
Set-Location C:\
iisreset.exe
```

Install Intune Certificate Connector

Installing and configuring the Intune Certificate Connector for SCEP is similar to PKCS. Follow the steps listed earlier in this chapter for installing the connector with the following exceptions.

1. When prompted to select **Features**, choose **SCEP** and **Certificate revocation** only (Figure 8-38).

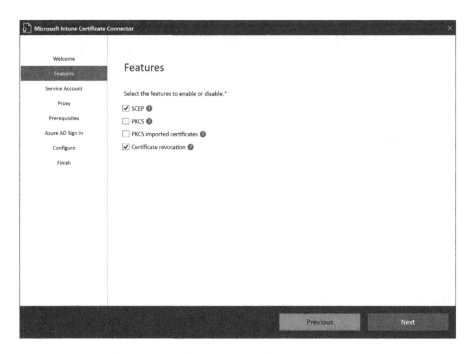

Figure 8-38. *Select Certificate Connector for Intune features*

2. When prompted for the **Service Account**, select **Domain account**. Enter the account name and password for the NDES service account (Figure 8-39).

Figure 8-39. *Configure Certificate Connector for Intune service account*

SCEP User Certificate

The process for deploying SCEP user and device authentication certificates is similar to PKCS. Follow the steps outlined previously in this chapter to upload and provision the root and any intermediate CA certificates, and then perform the following steps to deploy a SCEP user authentication certificate using Intune:

1. Click **Devices** in the navigation tree.

2. Click **Configuration profiles**.

3. Click **Create profile**.

4. Select **Windows 10 and later** from the **Platform** drop-down list.

5. Select **Templates** from the **Profile type** drop-down list.

6. Click **SCEP certificate**.

7. Click **Create** (Figure 8-40).

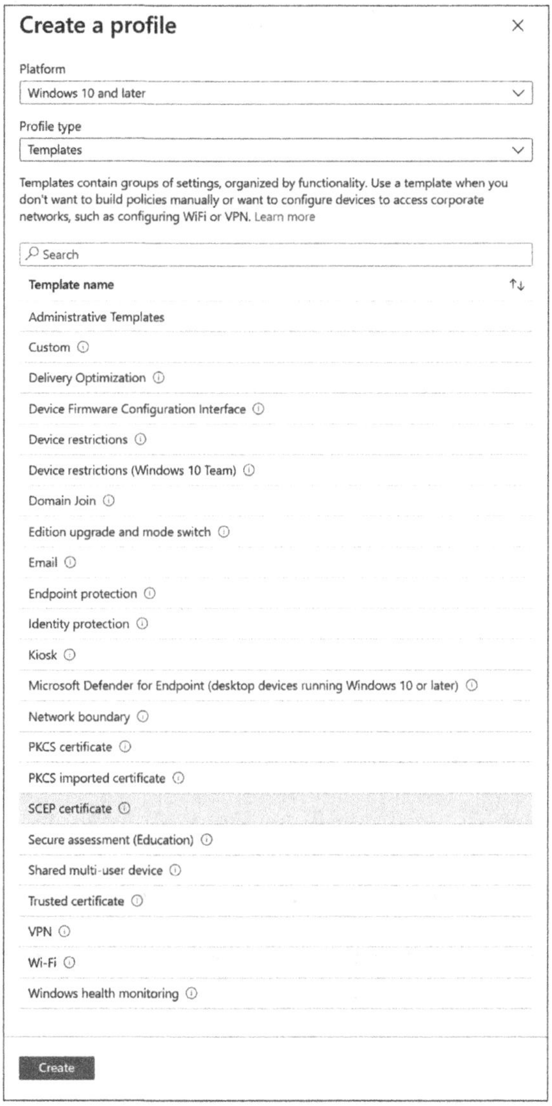

Figure 8-40. *Create a SCEP certificate profile*

Perform the following steps to configure the SCEP user authentication certificate profile:

1. Enter a descriptive name for the profile in the **Name** field.

2. Enter a description in the **Description** field (optional).

3. Click **Next** (Figure 8-41).

Figure 8-41. *SCEP certificate profile name*

4. Select **User** from the **Certificate type** drop-down list.

5. Enter **CN={{UserName}}** in the **Subject name format** field.

6. In the **Subject alternative name** section, select **User principal name (UPN)** from the **Attribute** drop-down list and enter **{{UserPrincipalName}}** in the **Value** field.

7. Adjust the **Certificate validity period** value, if necessary. Otherwise accept the defaults.

8. Select **Enroll to Trusted Platform Module (TPM) KSP, otherwise fail** from the **Key Storage Provider (KSP)** drop-down list.

Note   If devices without TPM must be supported, or if fallback to software KSP is required (not recommended), select **Enroll to Trusted Platform Module (TPM) KSP if present, otherwise Software KSP**.

9.   Check the boxes next to **Digital Signature** and **Key encipherment** in the **Key usage** drop-down list.

10. Select **2048** from the **Key size (bits)** drop-down list.

11. Check the box next to **SHA-2** in the **Hash algorithm** drop-down list.

12. Click **Root Certificate** and choose the appropriate root certificate.

13. Click **Ok**.

14. In the **Extended key usage** section, select **Client Authentication (1.3.6.1.5.5.7.3.2)** from the **Predefined values** drop-down list.

15. Enter the public FQDN for the NDES server. The format is https://<publicfqdn>/certsrv/mscep/mscep.dll (Figure 8-42).

16. Click **Next**.

Figure 8-42. *SCEP certificate profile settings*

17. Click **Add groups** and choose an appropriate user group to include.

18. Click **Select**.

19. Click **Next**.

20. Click **Next**.

21. Click **Create**.

SCEP Device Certificate

The procedure for deploying a PKCS device authentication certificate using Intune is nearly identical to the user authentication certificate with the following exceptions.

1. Select **Device** from the **Certificate type** drop-down list.

2. In the **Subject name format field**, enter **CN={{FullyQualified DomainName}}**.

3. In the **Subject alternative name** section, select **DNS** from the **Attribute** drop-down list, and then enter **{{FullyQualifiedDomainName}}** in the **Value** field (Figure 8-43).

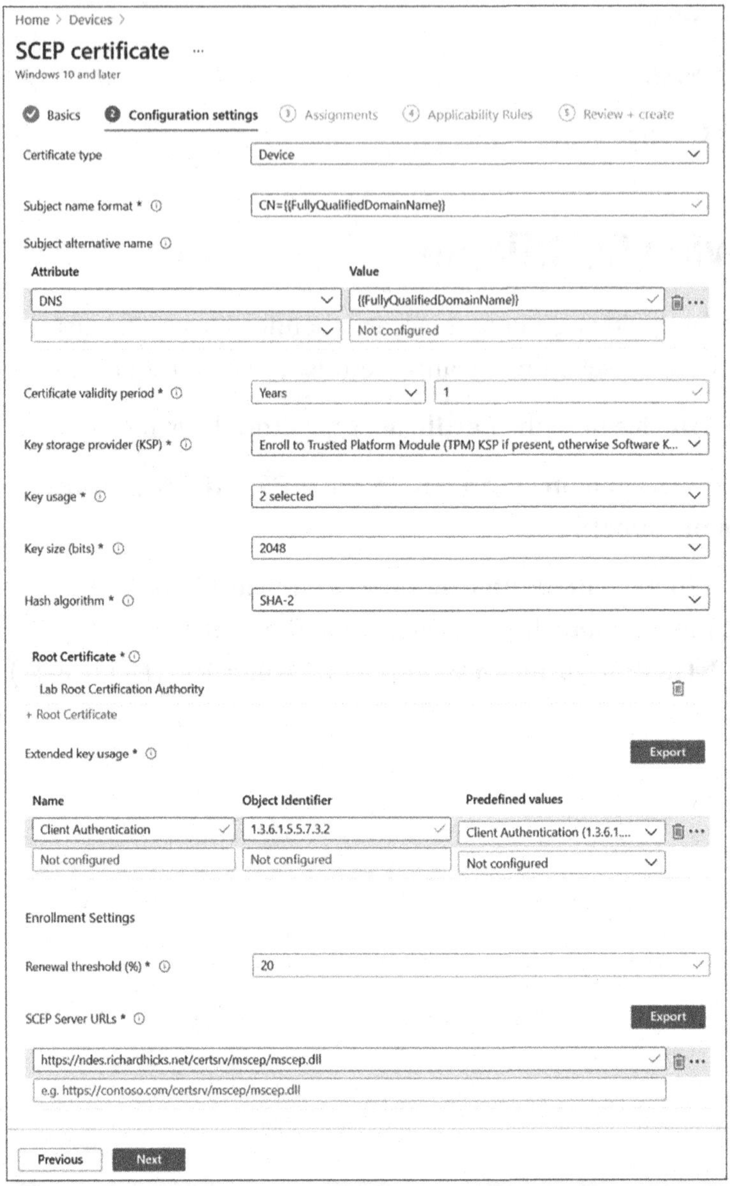

Figure 8-43. *SCEP certificate profile settings*

Once the configuration is complete, the user and/or device authentication certificates should appear in the users or devices certificate store, respectively, once the endpoint synchronizes with Intune.

Summary

Microsoft Endpoint Manager/Intune and the Certificate Connector for Microsoft Intune can be a powerful tool, allowing administrators to provision certificates to endpoint before the device or user connects to the internal network. This is most helpful when supporting endpoints that are Azure AD joined only and especially useful for remote hybrid Azure AD join using Autopilot.

While Intune supports both PKCS and SCEP certificates, administrators are encouraged to use PKCS whenever possible, as it is much easier to configure and operate. SCEP might offer slightly better security, but that doesn't mean PKCS is inherently *insecure*. SCEP is complex with many more moving parts, while PKCS is more straightforward and works much more reliably.

CHAPTER 9

Azure MFA Integration

Allowing users to access the network remotely is inherently risky. Administrators must be certain that users connecting from the Internet are indeed who they claim to be. Traditionally, supplying a username and password was acceptable. However, authentication credentials are easily lost or stolen, allowing attackers to easily gain access to resources without being detected.

Multifactor authentication is the most common method used to reduce this risk and prevent a rogue user from accessing the network using stolen credentials. When MFA is configured, users must provide another form of authentication in addition to their username and password. Commonly this is implemented in the form of a phone-based application that challenges the user to authorize their login.

There are many ways in which MFA can be integrated with Always On VPN. The most common is to use Azure MFA, which is easily configured and deployed. Azure MFA can be integrated with Windows Server Network Policy Server (NPS) or be enabled using Azure Conditional Access.

Azure MFA

Azure Multifactor Authentication (MFA) is a powerful tool used to greatly improve security and assurance for users accessing on-premises resources using Always On VPN. Azure MFA can be implemented with Always On VPN by integrating directly with the Network Policy Server (NPS) server or by defining an MFA policy using Azure Conditional Access.

© Richard M. Hicks 2022
R. M. Hicks, *Implementing Always On VPN*, https://doi.org/10.1007/978-1-4842-7741-6_9

Is MFA Necessary?

Without a doubt, MFA is a positive way to improve security and assurance for user authentication, especially for remote access. However, it is important to consider the risk MFA is designed to mitigate and the potential negative side effects of using MFA with Always On VPN specifically.

Risk Mitigation

MFA is designed to mitigate the risk of an attacker using stolen credentials to gain unauthorized access to the network. Typically, this occurs when a user's credentials are compromised in some form, either by a successful phishing attack, keylogging, etc. Enforcing MFA ensures that even if an attacker has stolen valid credentials, they will not be able to authenticate successfully without also accepting the MFA challenge.

Certificate Authentication

The recommended authentication method for Always On VPN is Protected Extensible Authentication Protocol (PEAP), using client authentication certificates issued by the organization's internal PKI. In this configuration, users are not entering usernames/passwords. Instead, they can only connect to Always On VPN if they have the correct user authentication certificate present on their device. In addition, if security best practices are followed, the client authentication certificate is protected by the Trusted Platform Module (TPM), which is a hardware security device on the endpoint that provides excellent protection for the certificate's private key. This ensures an attacker with access to the device, even with administrative rights, cannot compromise the certificate's private key.

In this scenario, a TPM-backed user authentication certificate serves as a de facto MFA. The "something you know" is the credentials to access the device, and the "something you have" is the device provisioned with the user authentication certificate. Even if an attacker had access to valid user credentials, they would not be able to establish a VPN connection using those credentials alone. They will still need the certificate to authenticate successfully.

Additional Considerations

Always On VPN presents another unique challenge for MFA in that Always On VPN connections are not user-initiated. Always On VPN connections are transparent to the user, and they may not necessarily occur immediately when the user logs on. Also, an Always On VPN connection may drop or otherwise terminate in the background and later reconnect automatically without user intervention. In these scenarios, users may receive MFA challenges without having performed any explicit action.

This has the negative side effect of training users to accept MFA challenges for which they might not have initiated. The MFA challenge lacks context, so the user will be unable to determine if the challenge was their Always On VPN device establishing a connection or if an attacker has compromised their password and is attempting to access resources using those stolen credentials.

Recommendation

Considering the risks associated with enabling MFA for Always On VPN specifically, it is recommended that MFA not be used when Always On VPN is configured to use PEAP with client certificates for authentication. However, if MSCHAPv2 is used for authentication instead, MFA should be considered a requirement.

Azure MFA with NPS

The quickest way to enable Azure MFA for Always On VPN is to install the NPS Extension for Azure MFA on the NPS server(s) configured for VPN authentication. Once configured, authentication requests processed by the NPS server will also be validated using Azure MFA.

Note   Once the NPS Extension for Azure MFA is installed on the NPS server, ALL authentication requests processed by the server will require Azure MFA. If the NPS server is a shared resource and used to provide authentication for other services in the environment (e.g., routers, switches, Wi-Fi, etc.), then a separate NPS server should be deployed that is dedicated to provided authentication for Always On VPN connections.

Requirements

To use the Azure MFA with Windows Server NPS, users must have a valid Azure MFA license assigned to their account. Azure MFA is included with Azure AD Premium P1 and P2, as well as Enterprise Mobility + Security. It is important to note, however, that the NPS Extension for Azure MFA does not support consumption-based licenses.

Note   A complete list of Azure MFA NPS Extension prerequisites can be found here: `https://docs.microsoft.com/en-us/azure/active-directory/ authentication/howto-mfa-nps-extension#prerequisites`.

Install NPS Extension

To begin, download the NPS Extension for Azure MFA from Microsoft here:

`www.microsoft.com/en-us/download/details.aspx?id=54688`

Note   It is strongly recommended to ensure Always On VPN is working correctly before installing the NPS extension.

Next, Internet Explorer (IE) Enhanced Security Configuration (ESC) must be disabled before continuing. On the NPS server, perform the following steps to disable IE ESC:

1. Open Server Manager and select **Local Server** in the navigation tree.

2. Click the link next to **IE Enhanced Security Configuration**.

3. In the **Administrators** section, select **Off** (Figure 9-1).

4. Click **Ok**.

Figure 9-1. *Disable Internet Explorer Enhanced Security configuration*

Once complete, run the NPS Extension for Azure MFA installer and click **Install**. Click **Close** once the installer completes.

To finalize the configuration, open an elevated PowerShell window and perform the following steps:

1. Navigate to the **C:\Program Files\Microsoft\AzureMfa\Config** folder.

2. Run the **AzureMfaNpsExtnConfigSetup.ps1** PowerShell script.

3. Enter "Y" if prompted to install the NuGet provider.

4. Enter the credentials for an Azure global administrator when prompted.

5. Enter the **Tenant ID** when prompted by the PowerShell script.

6. Press **Enter** to complete the configuration.

For deployments with more than one NPS server, repeat the previously mentioned steps to install the NPS Extension for Azure MFA on each NPS server providing authentication for Always On VPN connections.

Update RRAS Authentication

By default, Windows Server RRAS is configured with a RADIUS timeout value of 5 seconds. This is obviously not enough time for a user to accept the authentication challenge, so it must be modified to allow more time to complete the authentication request. To do this, perform the following steps on each VPN server used for Always On VPN:

1. Open the Routing and Remote Access Service (RRAS) management console.

2. Right-click the VPN server and choose **Properties**.

3. Select the **Security** tab.

4. Click **Configure** next to **RADIUS Authentication**.

5. Highlight the first NPS server in the list and click **Edit**.

6. Enter **120** in the **Time-out (seconds)** field (Figure 9-2).

7. Click **Ok**.

8. Repeat the previous steps for any additional NPS servers configured on the RRAS server.

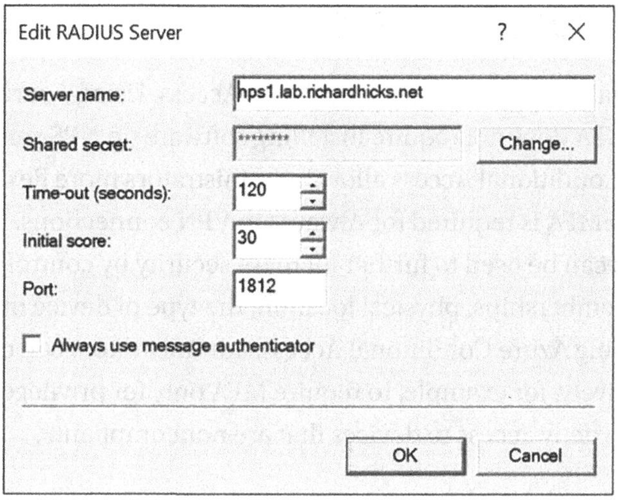

Figure 9-2. *RADIUS server settings*

Certificate Management

During the installation process, a self-signed certificate was created and uploaded to Azure by the installer. As with any certificate, it will eventually expire. The certificate lifetime for the Azure MFA certificate is two years. This means administrators must renew this certificate again prior to the expiration date. This can be done by running the AzureMfaNpsExtnConfigSetup.ps1 script again.

Note   The NPS Extension for Azure MFA supports certificate rollover beginning with release 1.0.1.32. This allows administrators to renew certificates prior to expiration, if necessary.

Troubleshooting Script

To aid in troubleshooting authentication requests using NPS Extension for Azure MFA, Microsoft has provided a script that can be used to test and evaluate the configuration. The script can be downloaded here:

https://docs.microsoft.com/en-us/samples/azure-samples/azure-mfa-nps-extension-health-check/azure-mfa-nps-extension-health-check/.

Azure Conditional Access

MFA can also be enabled using Azure Conditional Access. Using Azure Conditional Access to enforce MFA does not require installing software on NPS servers. In addition, configuring Azure Conditional Access allows administrators more flexibility and control over how and when MFA is required for Always On VPN connections. In addition, Azure Conditional Access can be used to further increase security by controlling access based on user or group memberships, physical location, the type of device or application being used, and more. Using Azure Conditional Access, administrators can create policies that enforce MFA selectively, for example, to require MFA only for privileged users but not standard users or to deny access to devices that are noncompliant.

Requirements

Azure Conditional Access requires Azure AD Premium P1 or Microsoft 365 Premium.

Configure Azure Conditional Access

Azure Conditional Access issues a short-lived certificate to a user who meets the requirements of the defined Conditional Access policy. This certificate is then used for authentication to Always On VPN. There are several steps required to prepare the infrastructure to support authentication using Azure Conditional Access certificates.

VPN Root Certificate

Open the Azure Active Directory portal (https://aad.portal.azure.com/) and perform the following steps to create an Azure Conditional Access VPN root certificate:

1. Click **Azure Active Directory** in the navigation tree.

2. Click **Conditional Access**.

3. In the navigation tree, click **VPN connectivity**.

4. Click **New certificate**.

5. Choose a suitable certificate lifetime from the **Select duration** drop-down list.

6. Click **Create** (Figure 9-3).

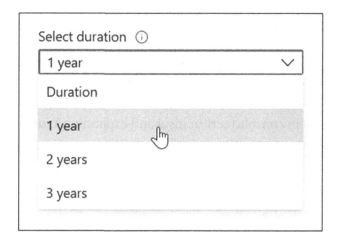

Figure 9-3. *Azure VPN certificate settings*

Once complete, the new VPN root certificate will appear in the management console. Click **Download certificate** to download and save the certificate file.

Publish Certificate

To support using Azure Conditional Access certificates for Always On VPN authentication, the Azure Conditional Access VPN root certificate must be published in the on-premises Active Directory. Specifically, the Azure VPN root certificate must be published to the Trusted Root Certification Authorities container on all domain-joined systems. In addition, the Azure Conditional Access VPN root certificate must be published to the Enterprise NTAuth store to support authentication.

Copy the Azure Conditional Access VPN root certificate file to a domain-joined computer, and then open an elevated command window and run the following commands to publish the certificate:

```
certutil.exe -dspublish -f VpnCert.cer RootCA
certutil.exe -dspublish -f VpnCert.cer NTAuthCA
```

Note   The Azure Conditional Access VPN root certificate has a lifetime of one year. Be sure to repeat these steps before the certificate expires.

Verify Certificates

Once Active Directory replication is complete, update group policy (gpupdate.exe) and confirm the new Azure Conditional Access VPN root certificate appears in the Trusted Root Certification Authorities certificate store by opening the Local Computer Certificates management console (certlm.msc) and expanding **Trusted Root Certification Authorities ➤ Certificates**. (Figure 9-3).

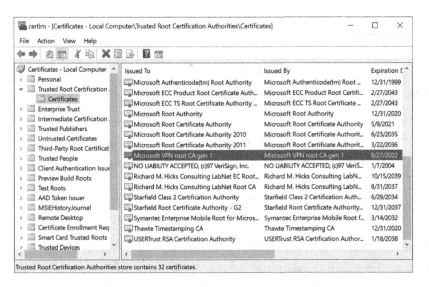

Figure 9-4. *Azure VPN root certificate*

On Windows Server Core, confirm the new Azure Conditional Access VPN root certificate appears in the Trusted Root Certification Authorities certificate store by running the following command:

```
Get-ChildItem -Path Cert:\LocalMachine\Root\ | Where-Object Subject -Match 'VPN'
```

Next, confirm the new Azure Conditional Access VPN root certificate appears in the Enterprise NTAuth certificate store by opening an elevated command window and running the following command (Figure 9-5).

```
certutil.exe -viewstore -enterprise NTAuth
```

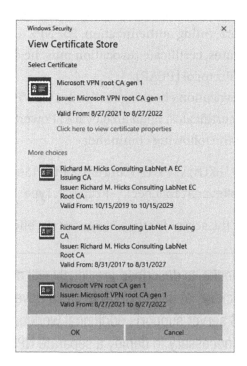

Figure 9-5. *Azure VPN certificate in NTAuth store*

On Windows Server Core, confirm the new Azure Conditional Access VPN root certificate appears in the Enterprise NTAuth certificate store by running the following command:

```
certutil.exe -store -enterprise NTAuth
```

NPS Configuration

Azure Conditional Access issues short-lived certificates that are used to authenticate to the VPN server. These certificates have a lifetime of one hour and, as such, do not need to be checked for revocation. In fact, the certificates themselves do not include a revocation URL. However, by default, Windows Server NPS performs certificate revocation checks when performing authentication. For NPS to work with Azure Conditional Access certificates, certificate revocation must be disabled for Protected Extensible Authentication Protocol (PEAP).

To disable certificate revocation checking for Always On VPN clients using PEAP with client authentication certificates, open an elevated PowerShell command window on the NPS server and run the following command:

```
New-ItemProperty -Path 'HKLM:\SYSTEM\CurrentControlSet\Services\RasMan\PPP\
EAP\13\' -Name IgnoreNoRevocationCheck -PropertyType DWORD -Value 1 -Force
```

Once complete, restart the server for the change to take effect.

Note   Disabling CRL checks as described previously will disable revocation checking for all NPS policies that use PEAP. This could have unintended consequences if the NPS server supports additional workloads that also use PEAP, such as Wi-Fi. It may be necessary to deploy a separate NPS server dedicated to VPN in these scenarios.

Update NPS Policy

Next, perform the following steps to update the existing Always On VPN Network Policy to only accept a certificate issued by Azure Conditional Access:

1. On the NPS server, open the NPS management console (nps.msc).

2. In the navigation tree, expand **Policies** and **Network Policies**.

3. Double-click the Network Policy used for Always On VPN.

4. Select the **Settings** tab.

5. Select **Vendor Specific** in the **RADIUS Attributes** section in the navigation tree.

6. Click **Add**.

    a. Select **Allowed-Certificate-OID** from the **Attributes** list.

    b. Click **Add**.

    c. Click **Add**.

    d. Enter **"1.3.6.1.4.1.311.87"** in the **Attribute value** field.

    e. Click **Ok**.

    f. Click **Ok**.

7. Click **Close**.

8. Click **Ok** (Figure 9-6).

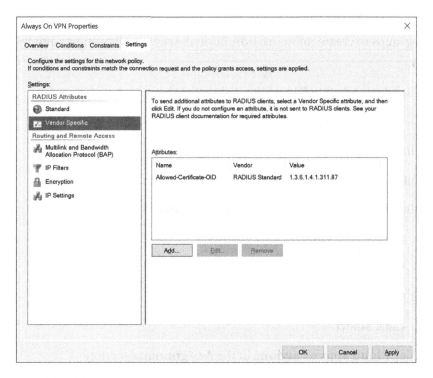

Figure 9-6. *RADIUS server settings*

> **Note**   After the Allowed-Certificate-OID Vendor Specific attribute has been
> configured and saved, it will subsequently be displayed in the Standard section of
> the RADIUS attributes section and will not appear in the Vendor Specific section.
> This is expected behavior.

Conditional Access Policy

Once the on-premises infrastructure is configured to support Azure Conditional Access, the next step is to create the Conditional Access policy and define the appropriate actions and conditions to enforce MFA as required.

Create Policy

Open the Azure Active Directory portal (`https://aad.portal.azure.com/`) and perform the following steps to create an Azure Conditional Access policy and assign it to the VPN Users group:

1. Click **Azure Active Directory** in the navigation tree.

2. Click **Conditional Access**.

3. Click **New policy**.

4. Enter a descriptive name in the **Name** field.

5. Click **Users and groups** in the **Assignments** section.

    a. Choose **Select users and groups**.

    b. Check the box next to **Users and groups**.

    c. Click the VPN Users group.

    d. Click **Select**.

6. Click **Cloud apps or actions** in the **Assignments** section.

    a. Click **Select apps**.

    b. Check the box next to **VPN Server**.

    c. Click **Select**.

7. Click **Conditions** in the **Assignments** section.

   a. Click **Device platforms**.

   b. Click **Yes** in the **Configure** section.

   c. Click **Done**.

8. Click **Grant** in the **Access controls** section.

   a. Select **Grant access**.

   b. Check the box next to **Require multi-factor authentication**.

   c. Click **Select**.

9. Click **On** below **Enable policy**.

10. Click **Create** (Figure 9-7).

Figure 9-7. *Create Conditional Access policy*

Client Configuration

Once the infrastructure has been configured to support Azure Conditional Access, the client configuration must be updated to enable access.

Endpoint Manager UI

To enable Azure Conditional Access and SSO when using the native Microsoft Endpoint Manager UI to configure Always On VPN, edit the Always On VPN device configuration profile and perform the following steps:

1. Expand **Conditional Access**.

2. Click **Enable** next to **Conditional access for this VPN connection**.

3. Click **Enable** next to **Single sign-on (SSO) with alternate certificate**.

4. Enter **Client Authentication** in the **Name** field.

5. Enter **1.3.6.1.5.5.7.3.2** in the **Object Identifier** field.

6. Enter the hash of the issuing CA server's certificate in the **Issuer hash** field. This is the CA that issued the client authentication certificate to be used for SSO authentication.

7. Click **Review + Save**.

8. Click **Save** (Figure 9-8).

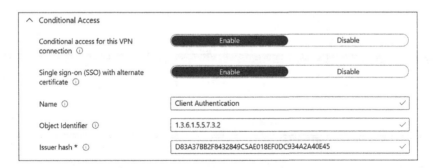

Figure 9-8. *VPN profile Conditional Access settings*

EAP Configuration

The Always On VPN client configuration must be updated to use the short-lived Azure Conditional Access certificate to authenticate to the VPN server. To do this, open the Microsoft Endpoint Manager management console (`https://endpoint.microsoft.com/`) and navigate to the Always On VPN device configuration profile, and then perform the following steps:

1. Expand **Base VPN**.

2. Copy the contents of the EAP XML section to a new text document.

3. If any **TLS extensions** are defined, remove them. These are elements in the XML that begin with <TLSExtensions> and end with </TLSExtensions>.

4. Add the following XML code block to the EAP XML after </AcceptServerName> and before </EapType>:

```
<TLSExtensions xmlns="http://www.microsoft.com/provisioning/
EapTlsConnectionPropertiesV2">
                <FilteringInfo xmlns="http://www.microsoft.com/
                provisioning/EapTlsConnectionPropertiesV3">
                    <EKUMapping>
                        <EKUMap>
                            <EKUName>AAD Conditional Access</EKUName>
                            <EKUOID>1.3.6.1.4.1.311.87</EKUOID>
                        </EKUMap>
                    </EKUMapping>
                    <ClientAuthEKUList Enabled="true">
                        <EKUMapInList>
                            <EKUName>AAD Conditional Access</EKUName>
                        </EKUMapInList>
                    </ClientAuthEKUList>
                </FilteringInfo>
            </TLSExtensions>
```

Once complete, copy the updated XML into the EAP XML field and click **Review + save**; then click **Save**.

Custom XML

To enable Azure Conditional Access and SSO when using the custom XML deployment method, add the following code block to the XML configuration file between the <VPNProfile> and </VPNProfile> elements:

```
<VPNProfile>
    <DeviceCompliance>
        <Enabled>true</Enabled>
        <Sso>
            <Enabled>true</Enabled>
            <Eku>1.3.6.1.5.5.7.3.2</Eku>
            <IssuerHash> D83A37BB2F8432849C5AE018EF0DC934A2A40E45
            </IssuerHash>
        </Sso>
    </DeviceCompliance>
</VPNProfile>
```

Note   Be sure to enter the hash of the issuing CA server's certificate in the Issuer hash section of the earlier XML. This is the CA that issued the client authentication certificate to be used for SSO authentication.

Third-Party MFA

Always On VPN also supports integration with various third-party MFA platforms. Documenting all of them is outside the scope of this book, unfortunately. Most MFA providers have published guidance for integrating with Microsoft VPN. Consult the vendor's documentation library for implementation guidance.

Summary

Authenticating users remotely presents some unique challenges for administrators. Allowing users to connect using usernames and passwords alone is incredibly risky, as user credentials are easily stolen by attackers. Integrating Microsoft Azure Multifactor Authentication is an excellent way to mitigate this risk.

Of course, moving away from usernames/passwords for authentication in favor of certificate-based authentication is ideal, effectively eliminating the necessity for additional MFA as certificates are a type of MFA themselves.

Regardless, administrators may still want to enforce MFA to mitigate the risk of stolen devices, or they may wish to control access based on any number of factors, including endpoint health, device type, behavior, or even location. Integrating Azure Conditional Access with Always On VPN can address those needs easily.

CHAPTER 10

High Availability

Until now, this book focused on deploying a single Windows Server Routing and Remote Access Service (RRAS) server for VPN and a single Windows Server Network Policy Server (NPS) server for authentication. While this may work just fine for small deployments, there are many times where additional VPN or NPS servers are required to meet the capacity requirements to support the expected number of concurrent users.

In addition, organizations may choose to implement additional VPN and/or NPS servers to eliminate single points of failure to improve reliability and increase service uptime. Also, VPN and NPS servers may be deployed in different datacenters or geographies for disaster recovery or to provide geographic redundancy.

VPN High Availability

High availability for VPN servers can be configured using either the native Windows Server Network Load Balancing (NLB) feature or an external load balancer.

Prerequisites

Before enabling high availability for RRAS VPN, it will be necessary to deploy additional VPN servers using the same configuration. The only difference will be that the IP address space assigned to VPN clients must be unique per server. Using DHCP is not recommended when configuring VPN server high availability. In addition, ensure the server is configured with the necessary certificates for IKEv2 and SSTP, as required. Also, don't forget to add the new VPN server as a RADIUS client on existing NPS servers.

© Richard M. Hicks 2022
R. M. Hicks, *Implementing Always On VPN*, https://doi.org/10.1007/978-1-4842-7741-6_10

Windows NLB

NLB can be configured to provide load balancing for VPN services by installing and configuring the NLB role on the VPN servers. The advantage to using NLB is that it requires no additional hardware or software and adds no additional costs. However, NLB has some serious drawbacks that limit its usefulness in many environments.

Limitations

Although NLB works reasonably well, it suffers from a few limitations. First, NLB is broadcast-based and is quite noisy on the network. Specifically, each NLB node issues broadcast heartbeat messages on the network segment every second. As the number of nodes increases, so does the amount of broadcast traffic. This can be mitigated somewhat by placing the VPN servers in a dedicated and isolated network segment or VLAN.

The Microsoft documentation indicates the maximum number of nodes in an NLB cluster is 32[1]. However, in practice, the maximum number of nodes is closer to eight, with a maximum of four nodes based on experience. After this, the broadcast traffic generated results in diminishing returns. If NLB is used and more than four nodes are required, it is recommended that a separate NLB cluster on a different network segment be provisioned. Ideally, an external load balancer should be deployed for optimum performance.

Also, NLB can be problematic in some virtual environments. Specifically, there are known issues and limitations with using NLB in VMware environments. NLB must be configured to use multicast operation mode[2]. In addition, changes may be required to border routers to ensure proper functionality in virtual environments.

Note   NLB is not supported on Windows Server deployed in Microsoft Azure and other cloud environments. When deploying RRAS in a cloud-hosted environment, using the cloud provider's native load balancing infrastructure or a third-party load balancing appliance will be required.

---

[1] https://docs.microsoft.com/en-us/windows-server/networking/technologies/network-load-balancing
[2] https://kb.vmware.com/s/article/1006580

Configure NLB

To begin, install the NLB role on the RRAS server by opening an elevated PowerShell window and running the following command:

```
Install-WindowsFeature NLB -IncludeManagementTools
```

Create NLB Cluster

Once complete, open the Network Load Balancing management console (nlbmgr.exe) and perform the following steps to create an NLB cluster:

1. Right-click Network Load Balancing Clusters and choose **New Cluster**.

2. Enter the hostname of the first VPN server to add to the cluster in the **Host** field.

3. Click **Connect**.

4. Select the network interface to be used for NLB. For multi-homed servers, configure NLB only on the external network interface.

5. Click **Next**.

6. Click **Next**.

7. Click **Add**.

8. Enter an IPv4 address for the new NLB cluster in the **IPv4 Address** field. This IPv4 address must be on the same subnet as the dedicated IPv4 address.

9. Click **Ok**.

10. Click **Next**.

11. Enter a descriptive name for the NLB cluster in the **Full Internet name** field.

12. When configuring NLB in a virtual environment, select **Multicast** in the **Cluster operation mode** section. Otherwise, select **Unicast**.

13. Click **Next**.

14. Click **Finish** (Figure 10-1).

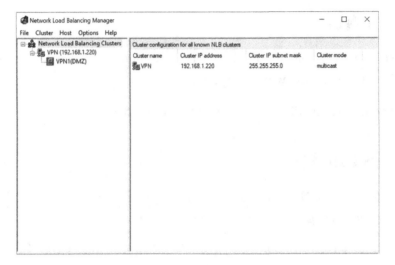

Figure 10-1. *Create an NLB cluster*

Add Cluster Nodes

Once the initial cluster configuration is complete, administrators can add additional cluster nodes by performing the following steps:

1. Right-click the cluster node and choose **Add Host To Cluster**.

2. Enter the hostname of the additional VPN server to be added to the cluster in the **Host** field.

3. Click **Connect**.

4. Select the network interface to be used for NLB. For multi-homed servers, configure NLB only on the external network interface.

5. Click **Next**.

6. Click **Next**.

7. Click **Finish** (Figure 10-2).

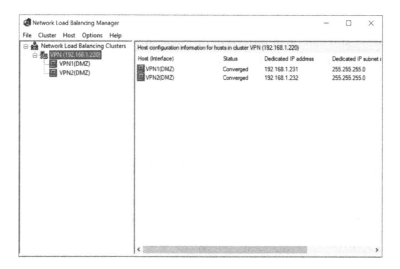

Figure 10-2. *Add cluster nodes*

Server Core

To configure NLB on Windows Server Core, install the NLB manager on an administrative server or workstation with a GUI to perform the previous tasks.

To install the NLB manager on Windows Server, open an elevated PowerShell window and run the following command:

```
Install-WindowsFeature RSAT-NLB
```

To install the NLB manager on Windows 10, open an elevated PowerShell or command window and run the following command:

```
dism.exe /online /add-capability /capabilityName:Rsat.NetworkLoadBalancing.
Tools~~~~0.0.1.0
```

External Load Balancer

Using an external load balancer is the preferred method of providing load balancing and high availability for VPN servers. External load balancers operate at layer three and above and do not use broadcast messages. They also offer more fine-grained traffic distribution control and better visibility and monitoring of load. When implementing an external load balancer, ensure the load balancer itself is redundant by using the appliance vendor's clustering feature. External load balancers are available from numerous vendors and can be deployed in physical or virtual form factors.

Using an external load balancer typically comes with additional costs associated, but some vendors offer "free" or "community versions" of their platforms that may be suitable for some deployments.

External Load Balancer Configuration

The configuration of external load balancers is outside the scope of this book, unfortunately. There are simply too many common platforms to fully document here. However, many popular load balancer configurations have been fully documented at directaccess.richardhicks.com.

- F5 BIG-IP Local Traffic Manager IKEv2 - `https://directaccess.richardhicks.com/2019/03/11/always-on-vpn-ikev2-load-balancing-with-f5-big-ip/`

- F5 BIG-IP Local Traffic Manager SSTP - `https://directaccess.richardhicks.com/2019/06/17/always-on-vpn-sstp-load-balancing-with-f5-big-ip/`

- Citrix ADC (NetScaler) IKEv2 - `https://directaccess.richardhicks.com/2020/01/20/always-on-vpn-ikev2-load-balancing-with-citrix-netscaler-adc/`

- Citrix ADC (NetScaler) SSTP - `https://directaccess.richardhicks.com/2020/01/13/always-on-vpn-sstp-load-balancing-with-citrix-netscaler-adc/`

- Kemp LoadMaster IKEv2 - `https://directaccess.richardhicks.com/2018/09/17/always-on-vpn-ikev2-load-balancing-with-kemp-loadmaster/`

- Kemp LoadMaster SSTP - `https://directaccess.richardhicks.com/2019/07/08/always-on-vpn-sstp-load-balancing-with-kemp-loadmaster/`

In addition, Kemp and LoadBalancer.org have published implementation guides for load balancing Always On VPN.

- Kemp LoadMaster - `https://support.kemptechnologies.com/hc/en-us/articles/360026123592/`

- LoadBalancer.org - `https://pdfs.loadbalancer.org/Microsoft_Always_On_VPN_Deployment_Guide.pdf`

NPS High Availability

High availability and redundancy for Windows Server NPS can be configured in one of two ways. The quickest and most straightforward way to enable high availability for NPS is to configure RRAS to use more than one NPS server. Optionally, administrators can place NPS servers behind a network load balancer for additional deployment flexibility and greater control of authentication traffic.

Prerequisites

To provide high availability for NPS, it will be necessary to deploy additional NPS servers using the same configuration. Once the additional NPS server is configured (role installed and server certificate deployed), open an elevated PowerShell window on an existing NPS server and run the following command to export the NPS configuration:

```
Export-NpsConfiguration -Path C:\NpsConfig.xml
```

Next, on the new NPS server, open an elevated PowerShell window and run the following command to import the NPS configuration:

```
Import-NpsConfiguration -Path .\npsconfig.xml
```

Once complete, review the network policy settings and validate the correct server certificate is selected for the EAP configuration.

Note   RADIUS shared secrets will be the same on each NPS server when exporting and importing the configuration. If unique shared secrets are required per NPS server, update the share secrets on the new NPS server after importing the configuration.

Update Client Configuration

Once a new NPS server is added to the VPN server configuration, Always On VPN client must be configured to authorize it. On a Windows 10 client configured for Always On VPN, open the Network Connections control panel applet (ncpa.cpl) and perform the following steps to add the new NPS server to the existing configuration:

1. Right-click the Always On VPN connection and choose **Properties**.

2. Select the **Security** tab.

3. Click the **Properties** button below the **Use Extensible Authentication Protocol (EAP)** drop-down list.

4. Add the new NPS server to the existing NPS server configuration by including the new NPS server hostname in the **Connect to these servers** field. Servers should be separated by a semicolon ";" with no additional spaces (e.g., nps1.corp.example.net;nps2. corp.example.net). See Figure 10-3.

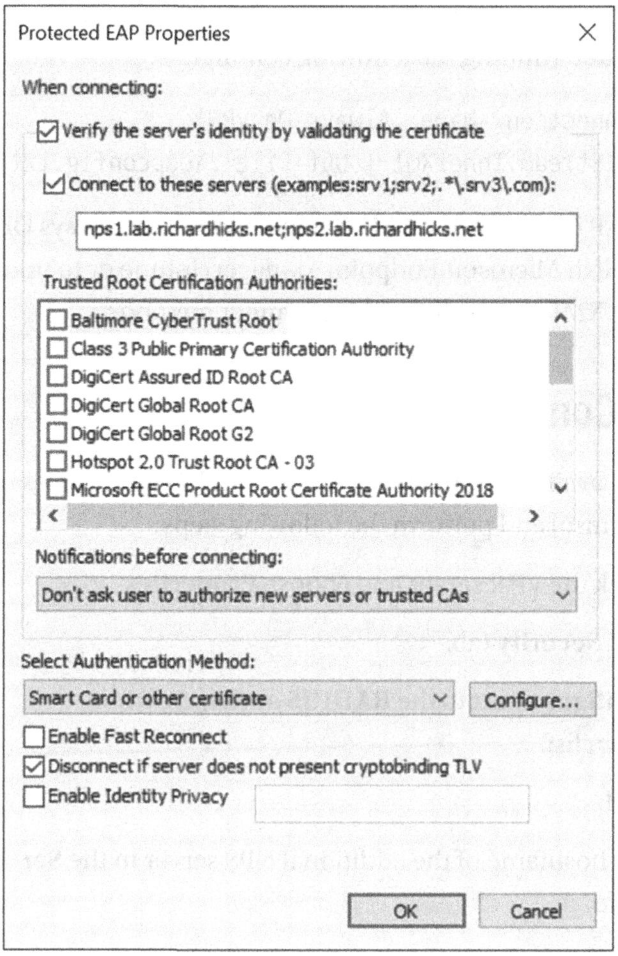

Figure 10-3. *Protected EAP properties*

5. Click the **Configure** button next to the **Select Authentication Method** drop-down list.

6. Add the new NPS server in the **Connect to these servers** field as outlined in Step 4 previously mentioned.

7. Click **Ok**.

8. Click **Ok**.

9. Click **Ok**.

Once complete, export the updated EAP configuration by opening a PowerShell command window and running the following commands:

```
$Vpn = Get-VpnConnection -Name 'Always On VPN'
$Vpn.EapConfigXmlStream.InnerXml | Out-File .\eapconfig.txt
```

Use this new EAP configuration XML data to update the Always On VPN device configuration profile in Microsoft Endpoint Manager/Intune or to update ProfileXML when using custom XML or PowerShell deployment methods.

Update VPN Configuration

To enable NPS high availability, open the Routing and Remote Access management console (rrasmgmt.msc) and perform the following steps:

1. Right-click the VPN server and choose **Properties**.

2. Select the **Security** tab.

3. Click **Configure** next to the **RADIUS authentication** drop-down list.

4. Click **Add**.

5. Enter the hostname of the additional NPS server in the **Server name** field.

6. Click **Change** next to the **Shared secret** field.

7. Enter the shared secret twice and click **Ok**.

8. If MFA is configured, enter **120** in the **Time-out (seconds)** field. Otherwise, accept the default value of **5**.

9. If one NPS server is preferred over another, adjust the **Initial score** value as required. NPS servers with a higher initial score are preferred over those with a lower initial score. Servers with the same initial score will be used in a round-robin fashion.

10. Click **Ok**.

11. Click **Ok**.

Note   It is essential to make these changes in the order outlined previously. If new NPS servers are configured on the VPN server before the client configuration is updated, some clients may not be able to connect. Always update the client configuration before configuring the VPN server.

NPS Load Balancing

One of the drawbacks to adding NPS servers to the VPN server configuration is that the client configuration must be updated each time this happens. This isn't difficult using Microsoft Endpoint Manager/Intune, but it can be more challenging when using other methods of deployment. To address this limitation and provide more deployment flexibility without requiring reconfiguration of Always On VPN clients, there are two alternative configuration methods that can be used.

DNS Alias

One option to avoid updating Always On VPN client configuration each time a new NPS server is introduced in the environment is to use a DNS alias for the NPS cluster. In this configuration, multiple NPS servers are configured, and each server's IP address is configured with a DNS "A" resource record resolving the cluster name (alias) to its IP address. For example, if two NPS servers have the IP addresses 172.16.0.215 and 172.16.0.216, two DNS records will be configured using the hostname, NPS, each resolving to the individual NPS server IP addresses, as shown in Figure 10-4.

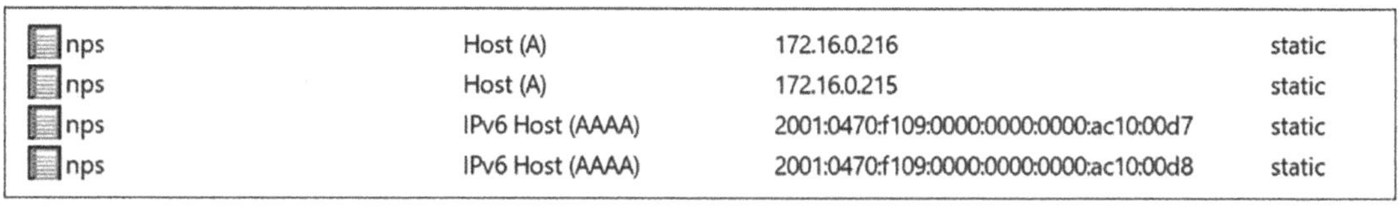

nps	Host (A)	172.16.0.216	static
nps	Host (A)	172.16.0.215	static
nps	IPv6 Host (AAAA)	2001:0470:f109:0000:0000:0000:ac10:00d7	static
nps	IPv6 Host (AAAA)	2001:0470:f109:0000:0000:0000:ac10:00d8	static

Figure 10-4.   DNS configuration for NPS load balancing

When Always On VPN clients are configured to use the DNS alias in their EAP configuration, NPS servers can be added and removed in the future without having to update the client configuration.

External Load Balancer

Another option is to use a single DNS "A" resource record resolving to a virtual IP address (VIP) running on a load balancer. The load balancer is then configured to distribute traffic to as many NPS servers as required. The load balancer is configured to load balancer UDP ports 1812 (authentication) and 1813 (accounting).

Certificate Configuration

Using either method described previously, each NPS server will require a custom server authentication certificate to be configured. Specifically, the subject name on the certificate must be the alias name, not the individual server's hostname.

The certificate template configuration is identical to the configuration outlined in Chapter 3, with the exception that the subject name must be configured to use **Supply in the request**. Additionally, certificate autoenrollment is recommended so the option **Use subject information from existing certificates for autoenrollment renewal requests** should also be checked (Figure 10-5).

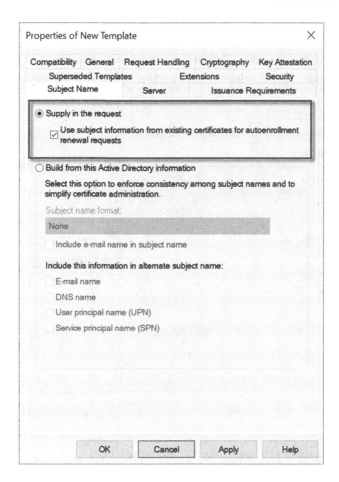

Figure 10-5. *Certificate template Subject Name configuration*

When making the certificate request on the NPS server, select the NPS certificate and click the **More information is required to enroll for this certificate** link. Provide the NPS server cluster FQDN in the **Subject name and Alternative name fields** as shown in Figure 10-6.

Figure 10-6. *Certificate request Subject Name settings*

Geographic Load Balancing

Deploying VPN servers in different physical locations may be required for disaster recovery or to ensure Always On VPN clients connect to a datacenter nearest their location for optimal performance. To support this, a Global Server Load Balancer (GSLB) solution must be used. GSLB can be implemented using cloud services like Azure Traffic Manager, AWS Route 53, Cloudflare, and many others.

GSLB is essentially "intelligent DNS". Instead of simply returning a static IP address based on a name resolution query, GSLB takes many factors into consideration, such as the health of the resource, source location of the DNS query, service response time, and more. Additionally, administrators can configure active/passive failover for disaster recovery or active/active load balancing with the option to distribute traffic evenly or unevenly.

Many load balancing appliances such as F5, Citrix, Kemp, and others also have GSLB features that can be optionally licensed on their platforms. Documenting the configuration of all these GLSB platforms and services is outside the scope of this book. However, the configuration of one of the more popular services, Azure Traffic Manager, will be covered here.

Azure Traffic Manager

Azure Traffic Manager is a cloud service that provides intelligent DNS for both Azure-hosted applications as well as external services. Azure Traffic Manager is a cost-effective alternative to dedicated GSLB appliances. However, most GSLB appliances have more advanced features and capabilities than cloud service offerings today.

Note   At the time of this writing, the cost for using Azure Traffic Manager is $0.54 per million DNS queries for the first 1 billion queries per month. Full Azure Traffic Manager pricing can be found here: `https://azure.microsoft.com/en-us/pricing/details/traffic-manager/`.

Azure Traffic Manager and IKEv2

Today, Azure Traffic Manager only supports HTTP, HTTPS, and TCP protocols for resource monitoring. The guidance that follows is designed to work with Always On VPN when SSTP is configured. If IKEv2 is used exclusively, Azure Traffic Manager can't be used. As a workaround, it is recommended to make at least one SSTP port available publicly for Azure Traffic Manager to monitor. Alternatively, a GSLB appliance can be used as they commonly include more advanced monitoring capabilities for non-HTTP and TCP workloads like IKEv2.

Azure Traffic Manager Profile

To create an Azure Traffic Manager profile, open the Azure management console (`https://portal.azure.com/`) and perform the following steps:

1. Navigate to the Resource Group where the Azure Traffic Manager profile will be deployed.

2. Click **Create**.

3. Enter "Azure traffic manager profile" in the search field and click **Enter**.

4. Click **Traffic Manager profile**.

5. Click **Create** (Figure 10-7).

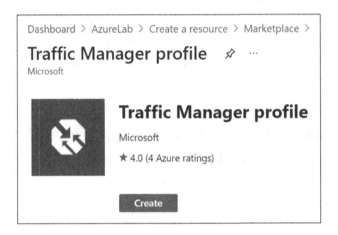

Figure 10-7. Create an Azure Traffic Manager profile

Next, perform the following steps to configure the Azure Traffic Manager profile:

1. Enter a unique hostname for the Azure Traffic Manager profile in the **Name** field.

2. Select an appropriate routing method from the **Routing method** drop-down list. For most deployments, selecting **Performance** is best. For disaster recovery (active/passive), choose **Priority**. Optionally, select **Geographic** to ensure Always On VPN clients are routed to the nearest VPN server to their physical location.

Note   A complete list of Azure Traffic Manager routing methods and their operation can be found here: `https://docs.microsoft.com/en-us/azure/traffic-manager/traffic-manager-routing-methods`.

---

3. Select an Azure subscription from the **Subscription**
   drop-down list.

4. Select an Azure Resource Group from the **Resource group**
   drop-down list.

5. Click **Create** (Figure 10-8).

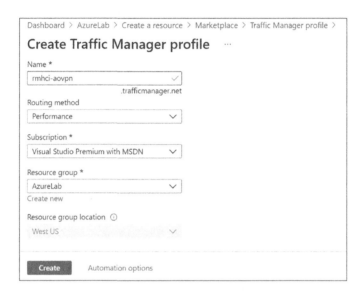

Figure 10-8. Azure Traffic Manager profile settings

Once complete, open the new Azure Traffic Manager profile and perform the
following steps to define the operating parameters for the profile:

1. Click **Configuration** in the navigation tree.

2. Select a routing method from the **Routing method**
   drop-down list.

3. Enter a value in the **DNS time to live (TTL)** field.

4. Select **HTTPS** from the **Protocol** drop-down list in the **Endpoint
   monitor settings** section.

5. Enter **443** in the Port field.

6. Enter /**sra_%7BBA195980-CD49-458b-9E23-
   C84EE0ADCD75%7D**/ in the **Path** field.

305

7. Leave the **Custom Header settings** field blank.

8. Enter **401-401** in the **Expected Status Code Ranges** field.

9. Accept the defaults in the **Fast endpoint failover settings** section.

10. Click **Save** (Figure 10-9).

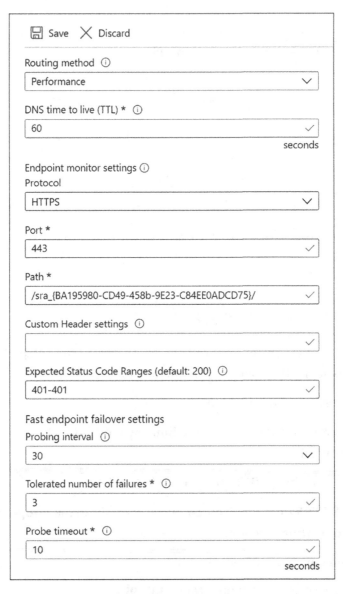

Figure 10-9. *Azure Traffic Manager profile settings*

Finally, perform the following steps to add VPN server endpoints to the Azure Traffic Manager profile:

1. Click **Endpoints** in the navigation tree.

2. Click **Add**.

3. Select **External endpoint** from the Type drop-down list.

4. Enter a descriptive name in the **Name** field.

5. Enter the FQDN or IPv4 address of the VPN server in the
    Fully-qualified domain name (FQDN) or IP field.

6. Select an appropriate location from the **Location** drop-down list.

7. Click **Add** (Figure 10-10).

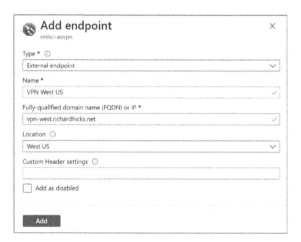

Figure 10-10. *Add an Azure Traffic Manager endpoint*

Repeat the steps earlier to add any additional VPN endpoints in the organization.

Validation Testing

Confirm operation of the Azure Traffic Manager profile by opening a PowerShell command window and running the following command:

```
Resolve-DnsName -Name <Azure Traffic Manager profile FQDN>
```

For example:

```
PS C:\> Resolve-DnsName -Name rmhci-aovpn.trafficmanager.net

Name                                Type  TTL  Section  NameHost
----                                ----  ---  -------  --------
rmhci-aovpn.trafficmanager.net      CNAME 60   Answer   vpn-west.richardhicks.net

Name       : vpn-west.richardhicks.net
QueryType  : A
TTL        : 270
Section    : Answer
IP4Address : 98.189.217.104
```

DNS Alias

Unfortunately, Always On VPN clients cannot connect to the VPN server using the Azure Traffic Manager domain because administrators won't be able to request a public TLS certificate for the traffcmanager.net domain.

To address this issue, a DNS CNAME record must be configured that maps a name in the organization's public DNS namespace to the Azure Traffic Manager FQDN. This name must match the subject name on the TLS certificate used for SSTP and on the IPsec certificate used for IKEv2 on the VPN server.

For example, a DNS CNAME for vpn.richardhicks.net mapping to the Azure Traffic Manager FQDN rmhci-aovpn.trafficmanager.net is configured here using Cloudflare DNS (Figure 10-11).

Type	Name	Content	TTL	Proxy status	
CNAME	vpn	rmhci-aovpn.trafficmanager.net	Auto	☁ DNS only	Edit ▶

Figure 10-11. *DNS alias configuration*

Once configured, clients are then configured to connect to vpn.richardhicks.net, which will resolve to the best available entry point determined by Azure Traffic Manager. The name resolution query results are as follows:

```
PS C:\> Resolve-DnsName -Name vpn.richardhicks.net
```

Name	Type	TTL	Section	NameHost
----	----	---	-------	--------
vpn.richardhicks.net	CNAME	60	Answer	rmhci-aovpn.trafficmanager.net
rmhci-aovpn.trafficmanager.net	CNAME	60	Answer	vpn-west.richardhicks.net

```
Name       : vpn-west.richardhicks.net
QueryType  : A
TTL        : 270
Section    : Answer
IP4Address : 98.189.217.104
```

Summary

The Always On VPN infrastructure (VPN and NPS servers) can be scaled out quickly and easily to accommodate additional capacity or to eliminate single points of failure. Administrators have a variety of options to choose from when it comes to local load balancing and failover. Native NLB can be used, but it is recommended that purpose-built load balancing appliances (physical or virtual) be deployed for optimal performance.

In addition, for large deployments with VPN infrastructure hosted in multiple geographies, the Always On VPN infrastructure can be made geographically redundant using a combination of native or external load balancing for local redundancy and cloud services or GSLB appliances for geographic redundancy. Administrators can configure active/passive failover for disaster recovery scenarios or active/active for best performance.

CHAPTER 11

Monitor and Report

Up to this point, all the VPN server configuration has been performed using the Routing and Remote Access Management console and various netsh.exe and PowerShell commands. Once the configuration is complete, and after transitioning to production, the RRAS VPN server can be monitored for system health and user activity using a variety of tools.

In addition, administrators may want to log and report on past VPN connections. Also, there may be times when current VPN connections need to be terminated. Here again, there are several options to accomplish these tasks.

RRAS Management Console

Administrators should now be familiar with the Routing and Remote Access Management console (rrasmgmt.msc), as it has been used frequently for configuring various options on the Routing and Remote Access Service (RRAS) server. In addition to making configuration changes, the RRAS management console can also be used to monitor system health and user activity. It can also be used to disconnect VPN sessions, if necessary.

Adding Servers

Opening the RRAS management console on the VPN server itself provides management control over the local VPN server. If managing a VPN server remotely, additional servers can be added to the console. This is also helpful for managing Windows Server Core remotely or if there is more than one server deployed for Always On VPN.

Perform the following steps to add a VPN server to the RRAS management console:

1. Right-click **Routing and Remote Access** in the navigation tree and choose **Add Server**.

© Richard M. Hicks 2022

R. M. Hicks, *Implementing Always On VPN*, https://doi.org/10.1007/978-1-4842-7741-6_11

2. Select **The following computer** and enter the IP address, hostname, or FQDN of the VPN server to be managed.

3. Click **Ok**.

4. Repeat these steps for each additional VPN server to be added to the management console (Figure 11-1).

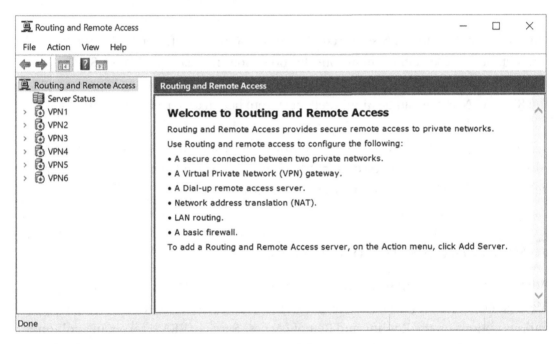

Figure 11-1. *Add VPN server to the RRAS management console*

Note   Opening the RRAS management console when a remote VPN server is not online or is otherwise unreachable takes an exceedingly long time. Be patient!

Firewall Requirements

If there is a firewall between the server or workstation where the RRAS management console is running and the VPN server itself, the following protocols and ports must be allowed for the management console to function:

- TCP 135 (RPC)

- TCP 445 (SMB)

- TCP 49172-65535 (ephemeral ports)

System Health

Viewing system health using the RRAS management console is limited to viewing the status of the RemoteAccess service only. Administrators can view the status of the RemoteAccess service by observing the icon next to the VPN server in the management console.

- Green – indicates the remote access service is running

- Red – indicates the RemoteAccess service has stopped

The RemoteAccess service can be stopped, started, paused, resumed, or restarted by right-clicking the VPN server and choosing **All Tasks** (Figure 11-2).

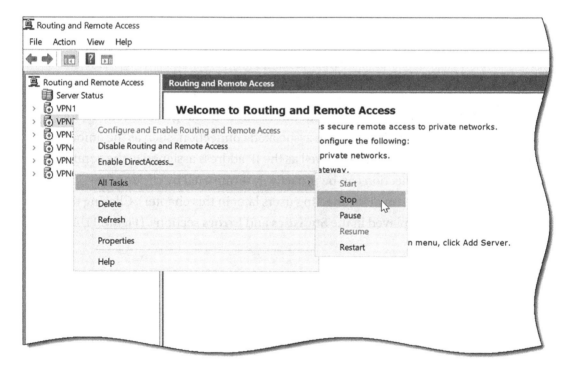

Figure 11-2. *Stopping the RemoteAccess service in the RRAS management console*

User Activity

Administrators can view which devices and users are currently connected by expanding a VPN server in the RRAS management console and selecting Remote Access Clients (Figure 11-3). Users are identified using their UPN (username@domain), whereas devices are identified with their FQDN.

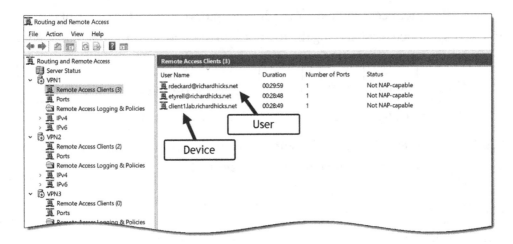

Figure 11-3. *User activity in the RRAS management console*

Double-clicking a connected user or device (or right-clicking a connection and choosing **Status**) reveals statistics for the associated connection, such as the amount of data transferred (sent and received) as well as the IP address assigned to the connection. In addition, the VPN connection can be proactively terminated by clicking the **Disconnect** button (more on disconnecting users later in this chapter). Clicking the **Reset** button resets the data displayed in the **Statistics** and **Errors** sections. (Figure 11-4).

Figure 11-4. *User activity details in the RRAS management console*

Remote Access Management Console

A better option for ongoing system health and user activity monitoring is the Remote Access Management console (ramgmtui.exe). This tool will be familiar to DirectAccess administrators, but it is also supported for use with the VPN workload on Windows Server RRAS servers. While the Remote Access Management console provides better visibility for system health and user activity, the main disadvantage to using this tool is that it can only be used to view a single server at a time. It does not support adding multiple servers as the RRAS management console does, unfortunately.

Overview

To monitor an RRAS VPN server using the Remote Access Management console, open the management console (ramgmtui.exe) on the VPN server. If managing the server remotely, click Manage a Remote Server in the Tasks pane and enter the hostname or IP address of the remote VPN server.

Click **Dashboard** in the navigation tree to view high-level operational status information and details about current connections (Figure 11-5). The **Operations Status** section will indicate service health status, and the **DirectAccess and VPN Client Status** section provides an overview of current VPN sessions on this server.

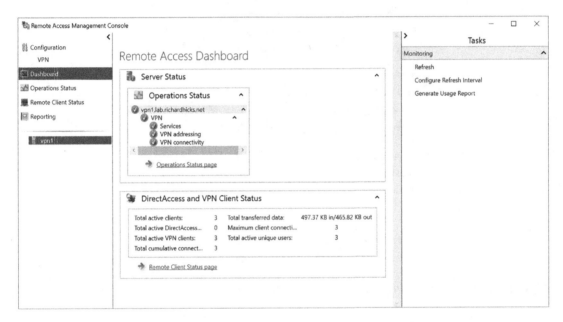

Figure 11-5. *Remote Access Management console dashboard*

System Health

For more detailed system health information, click **Operations Status** in the navigation tree (Figure 11-6). Highlighting entries provides more detailed information in the **Details** section. If a service or dependency has failed or is otherwise experiencing issues, the **Details** section will provide additional information as to what the problem is.

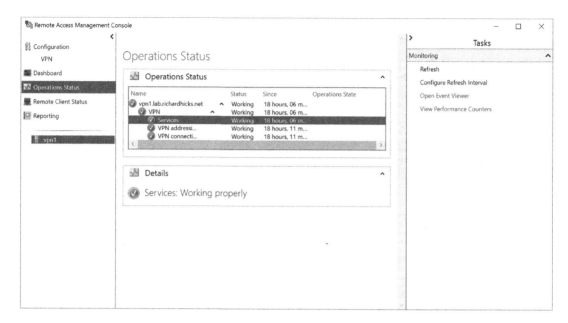

Figure 11-6. *Remote Access Management console operations status*

User Activity

Administrators can view current active sessions on the VPN server by clicking **Remote Client Status** in the navigation tree (Figure 11-7). Here, more detailed information is displayed when a user or device is highlighted in the **Connected Clients** section. Additional details about the connection and activity are displayed at the bottom of the window.

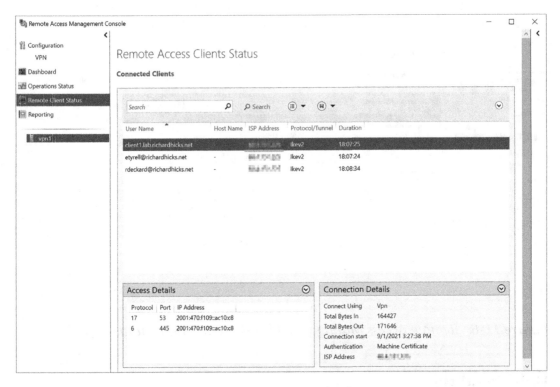

Figure 11-7. *Remote Access Management console client status*

Double-clicking a current session displays detailed information about the connection in a single window (Figure 11-8).

Figure 11-8. *Detailed client statistics*

Customize Headings

By default, only the username, hostname, ISP address, VPN protocol, and connection duration information are displayed in the **Connected Clients** section. Administrators can customize this view by right-clicking the header columns and selecting/deselecting fields to be displayed, as required (Figure 11-9).

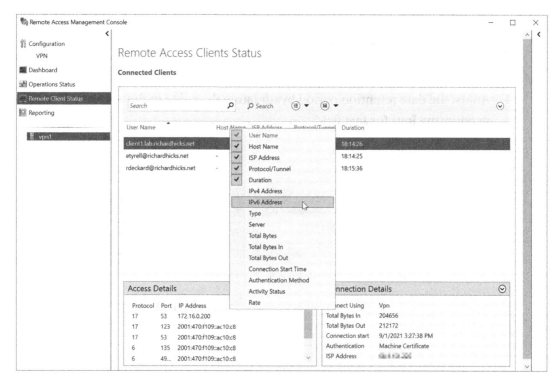

Figure 11-9. *Customize column headings*

Note   Information is never displayed in the Hostname field, so it is recommended to remove this column from the display. Adding the IPv4 Address and IPv6 Address fields will display the VPN client's assigned IP address, which is helpful. Connection Start Time and Authentication Method are also valuable to display.

Reporting

It is possible to configure the RRAS server to log user activity to a local database to enable historical reporting. Reporting is not enabled by default, however. Perform the following steps to configure Inbox Accounting and enable historical reporting on the VPN server:

1. Click **Reporting** in the Remote Access Management console navigation tree.

2. Click **Configure Accounting**.

3. Select **Use inbox accounting**.

4. Adjust the data retention period by updating the value in the **Store accounting logs for last** field.

5. Click **Apply** (Figure 11-10).

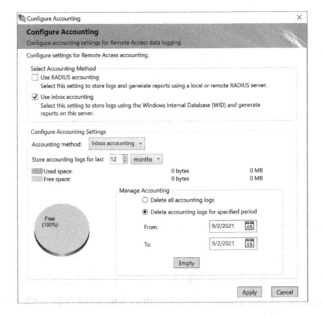

Figure 11-10. *Configure accounting*

Optionally, Inbox Accounting can be configured using PowerShell by opening an elevated PowerShell window and running the following command:

```
Set-RemoteAccessAccounting -EnableAccountingType Inbox -PassThru
```

After Inbox Accounting has been enabled, administrators can view past user activity information by clicking **Reporting** in the navigation tree, selecting a **Start date** and **End date**, and then clicking **Generate Report** (Figure 11-11).

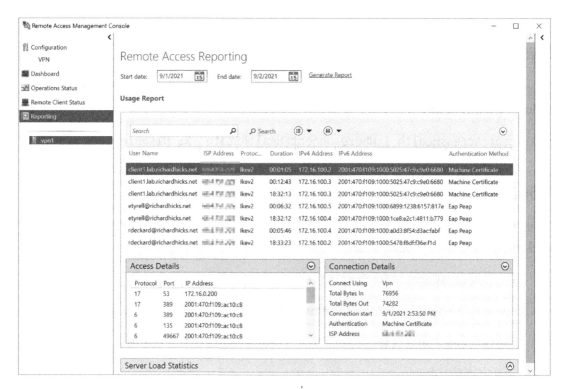

Figure 11-11. *Viewing historical reports*

Note   After configuring Inbox Accounting in the VPN server, a Windows Internal Database (WID) is installed on the server. This database is missing a crucial index on one of its tables which can result in high CPU usage under certain conditions. Also, this issue still affects Windows Server 2022. More details about the issue and a script to resolve the problem can be found here: `https://technet.microsoft.com/en-us/library/mt693376(v=ws.11).aspx`.

PowerShell

RRAS VPN system health and user activity information can also be viewed using PowerShell.

System Health

To view current VPN server health, open an elevated PowerShell window and run the following command:

```
Get-RemoteAccessHealth | Where-Object HealthState -NE Disabled
```

User Activity

To view current connections on the VPN server, open an elevated PowerShell window and run the following command:

```
Get-RemoteAccessConnectionStatistics
```

To view more detailed information using PowerShell, run the following command:

```
Get-RemoteAccessConnectionStatistics | Format-List * | Out-Host -Paging
```

Log Files

RRAS VPN server log files aren't necessarily important for daily administrative and troubleshooting, as they contain information that is already displayed in the event log or the UI management consoles. However, log files are commonly collected and fed to Security Information and Event Management (SIEM) platforms for log correlation and forensic analysis.

On the VPN and NPS servers, log files are stored in the C:\Windows\System32\LogFiles folder. They are in text format and begin with IN. Many vendors provide collector software that automatically monitors the log files and uploads data to the SIEM. Also, the files are stored in a standard format that many SIEM vendors can easily consume.

Disconnecting Sessions

Eventually, there will come a time when a user or device must be disconnected from the VPN. Sometimes it will be necessary to reset a VPN connection for troubleshooting purposes. In other scenarios, it may be required to permanently disconnect a session and prevent reconnection, as in the case of a compromised endpoint, lost or stolen device, or terminated employee.

Management Consoles

VPN users can be disconnected in the RRAS management console (rrasmgmt.msc) by expanding the VPN server in the navigation tree, highlighting **Remote Access Client**s and then right-clicking a user or device connection, and choosing **Disconnect** (Figure 11-12).

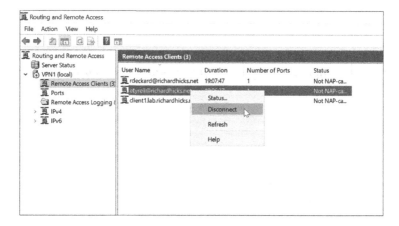

Figure 11-12. *Disconnect a session in the RRAS management console*

To disconnect a user or device in the Remote Access Management console (ramgmtui.exe), select **Remote Client Status** in the navigation tree, highlight the user or device in the **Connected Clients** section, and then click **Disconnect VPN Clients** in the **Tasks** pane (Figure 11-13).

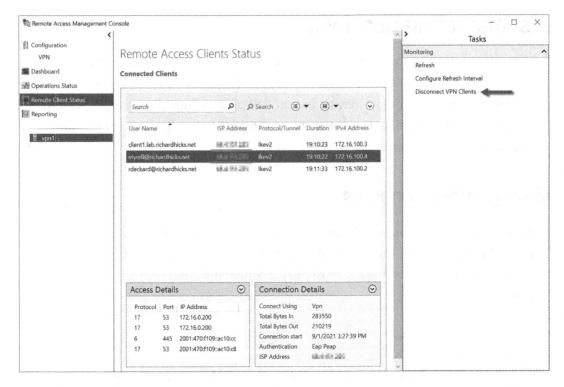

Figure 11-13. *Disconnect a session in the Remote Access Management console*

PowerShell

Users or devices can be disconnected from the VPN by opening an elevated PowerShell window and running one of the following commands.

To disconnect a VPN user:

```
Disconnect-VpnUser -UserName rdeckard@richardhicks.net
```

To disconnect a VPN device:

```
Device - Disconnect-VpnUser -UserName client1.lab.richardhicks.net
```

Permanent Disconnects

Always On VPN is just that – always on. Using the guidance earlier will terminate a user or device VPN connection, but the client will automatically try to reconnect by design. In some cases, though, it may be necessary to disconnect a user or device and further prevent them from reconnecting again. The process is relatively simple for user connections but more complex for device connections.

User Connections

Preventing a user from reconnecting to the VPN is as simple as removing their user account from the user group configured in the Network Policy on the NPS server for Always On VPN connections. Once the user is no longer in the group, NPS authentication will fail and access to the user will be denied.

While removing the user from the VPN Users group will prevent access, if client certificates are used for authentication, it is still recommended the issued certificate be revoked and a new Certificate Revocation List (CRL) be published immediately.

Device Connections

Preventing a device from reconnecting to the VPN is more involved. Always On VPN device tunnel connections are authenticated by their machine certificate. As such, revoking the certificate issued to the device would prevent access.

However, in practice, it is not that simple. First, certificate revocation checking is not enabled by default! To enable CRL checks for device connections on Windows Server RRAS VPN servers, open an elevated PowerShell window and run the following command:

```
New-ItemProperty -Path 'HKLM:\SYSTEM\CurrentControlSet\Services\
RemoteAccess\Parameters\Ikev2\' -Name CertAuthFlags -PropertyTYpe DWORD
-Value '4' -Force
```

Restart the RemoteAccess service for the change to take effect.

```
Restart-Service RemoteAccess -PassThru
```

Note   When enabling the registry setting to enforce CRL checks for device connections, Windows Server 2019 must have update KB4505658 installed, and Windows Server 2016 must have update KB4503294 installed. No updates are required to support this feature in Windows Server 2022.

Even with CRL checking enforced on the VPN server, revoking a certificate and publishing a new CRL will not immediately prevent a device from reconnecting. This is because CRLs are cached by endpoints locally until the CRL expires. Thus, revoking a certificate and issuing a new CRL may not be immediately effective.

To immediately prevent a device from connecting to the VPN server, export the device certificate only (no private key required) from the endpoint (if accessible) or from the issuing CA and perform the following steps to import it into the **Untrusted Certificates** store on the VPN server:

1. Open the Local Computer Certificates store (certlm.msc).

2. Right-click **Untrusted Certificates** and choose **All Tasks ➤ Import**.

3. Click **Next**.

4. Enter the path to the device certificate exported from the endpoint or the issuing CA.

5. Click **Next**.

6. Select **Place all certificates in the following store** and ensure that **Untrusted Certificates** is listed in the **Certificate store** field.

7. Click **Next**.

8. Click **Finish**.

9. Click **Ok** (Figure 11-14).

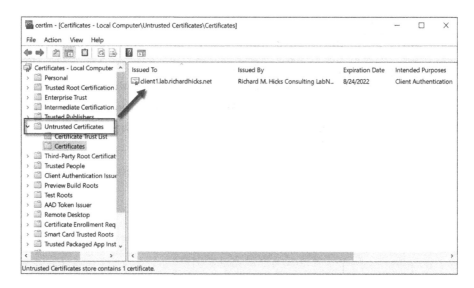

Figure 11-14. *Device certificate in the Untrusted Certificates store*

On Windows Server Core servers, a device certificate can be imported into the
Untrusted Certificates store by opening an elevated PowerShell window and running
the following command:

```
Import-Certificate -FilePath .\client1.cer -CertStoreLocation Cert:\
LocalMachine\Disallowed
```

Note   Be sure to repeat the previous steps on all VPN servers in the organization!

Once these steps have been completed, the device connection can be terminated
using a management console or PowerShell. When the device attempts to reconnect, the
connection will be denied.

Summary

Monitoring user activity on a production VPN server is essential in most organizations.
Understanding who is connected and what resources they are accessing is vital in
terms of security. Using the RRAS management console provides a bit of information to
support this, but clearly, the Remote Access Management console is the better choice as
it allows for much better visibility.

The VPN server can also be configured to log user activity information to a local database, allowing administrators to generate reports on past connections.

Of course, there may be times when users must be disconnected from the VPN server, either temporarily or permanently. Administrators have the choice of using GUI or the command line to perform these tasks. And don't forget, there are additional steps required to prevent device tunnel connections from accessing the VPN server.

CHAPTER 12

Troubleshooting

By diligently following the guidance provided in this book, administrators can save time and effort deploying Always On VPN and hopefully avoid many of the errors covered in this chapter. However, things don't always go according to plan, and invariably, problems will arise.

In addition, things often change even in working environments, resulting in connectivity failures and errors. Having a solid understanding of how Always On VPN works and how the individual infrastructure components operate is crucial. In addition, understanding the system interdependencies will speed troubleshooting efforts and allow administrators to identify issues and resolve them quickly.

A comprehensive review of every possible error code an administrator may encounter is outside the scope of this book. However, the troubleshooting and resolution of common error codes are provided here.

Common Error Codes

The error codes covered in this chapter can be found on the client in the Application event log from the RasClient event source. If a VPN connection fails, open the Application event log and locate the error. Double-click the event and note the error code returned on failure, as shown in Figure 12-1.

© Richard M. Hicks 2022
R. M. Hicks, *Implementing Always On VPN*, https://doi.org/10.1007/978-1-4842-7741-6_12

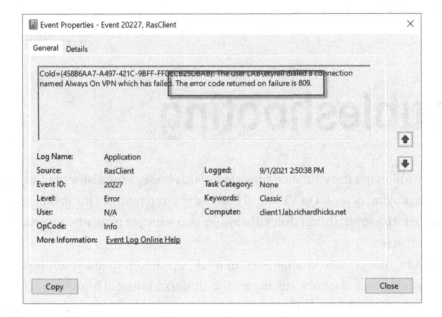

Figure 12-1. *Error 809*

Note   A comprehensive reference for all Routing and Remote Access Service error codes can be found here: `https://docs.microsoft.com/en-us/windows/win32/rras/routing-and-remote-access-error-codes`.

809

Error code 809 (ERROR_VPN_TIMEOUT) is commonly encountered by Always On VPN administrators when performing initial testing. The 809 error essentially means the VPN server failed to respond to the client's connection attempt.

Common Causes

There are numerous causes for this error, but here are the most common issues:

- DNS – Incorrect name to IP address mapping.

- Edge firewall – Incorrect or unassigned public IP address, firewall ACL missing, or not correctly configured.

- NAT – Missing or incorrect NAT configuration on the edge firewall.

- Routing – Internal VPN server not routing return traffic correctly (asymmetric routing).

- Load balancer – Missing or incorrect node configuration. For IKEv2, session persistence could be incorrectly configured.

- IP fragmentation – Most common when IKEv2 is configured; IP fragmentation may occur and, as a result, be blocked by the edge firewall or other intermediary devices as described in Chapter 2.

Testing

To validate connectivity from the Internet to the VPN server, open a PowerShell window on the client and run the following command:

```
Resolve-DnsName -Name <VPN server public FQDN>
```

Ensure the name resolves to the correct IP address.

Note   Using PowerShell and Resolve-DnsName is recommended over DNS test tools like nslookup.exe. When testing client name resolution issues in Windows 10, it provides more accurate and reliable name resolution query results.

If name resolution is working correctly, the next step is to attempt a TCP connection on port 443. To do this, open a PowerShell window and run the following command:

```
Test-NetConnection -ComputerName vpn.richardhicks.net -Port 443
ComputerName     : vpn.richardhicks.net
RemoteAddress    : 98.189.217.104
RemotePort       : 443
InterfaceAlias   : Internal
SourceAddress    : 10.0.0.1
TcpTestSucceeded : True
```

If the firewall is listening on TCP port 443, the output of **TcpTestSucceeded** will be **True**. If it responds **False**, it could indicate a firewall or routing issue.

Unfortunately, simply listening on TCP port 443 and responding is not an accurate indicator that networking is configured correctly. For instance, the firewall might be accepting connections on this port but not be able to establish a connection to the VPN server on the back end. Also, the NAT rule might be incorrectly configured and forwarding the request to the wrong internal resource.

Port Probe

To ensure the VPN server itself is responding on TCP port 443, a tool such as Nmap. exe can be used. Nmap is a free, open-source tool that can be installed on Windows machines for advanced network troubleshooting. Nmap includes a script that can accurately detect an SSTP VPN server response. Nmap can be downloaded here: https://nmap.org/download.html.

Once installed, run the Nmap.exe tool using the following parameters. If networking is configured correctly, the tool should respond with **SSTP is supported**.

```
nmap.exe -n -Pn -p 443 vpn.richardhicks.net --script sstp-discover
Starting Nmap 7.92 ( https://nmap.org ) at 2021-09-02 16:31 Pacific
Daylight Time
Nmap scan report for vpn.richardhicks.net (98.189.217.104)
Host is up (0.016s latency).

PORT     STATE SERVICE
443/tcp open   https
|_sstp-discover: SSTP is supported.

Nmap done: 1 IP address (1 host up) scanned in 0.50 seconds
```

Network Trace

Unfortunately, the earlier mentioned recommendations only work for TCP. As IKEv2 uses UDP, it is more difficult to troubleshoot. If the VPN server can be reached over TCP, network path issues can be safely ruled out. However, firewall ACL configuration could still be the issue. If IKEv2 connections are returning 809 errors, a network trace should be made on the VPN server to verify incoming requests. It is also recommended that a network trace be taken on the client at the same time to determine if traffic is being returned as expected.

A network trace can be performed on Windows servers and clients by opening an elevated command window and running the following command:

```
netsh.exe trace start capture=yes tracefile=c:\nettrace.etl
```

Once the administrator has reproduced the issue, stop the trace by running the following command:

```
netsh.exe trace stop
```

The output of the trace will be in .ETL format. Download the etl2pcap.exe tool to convert the trace file to a standard PCAP format for viewing in popular protocol analyzers such as Wireshark. The etl2pcap.exe tool can be downloaded here: `https:// github.com/microsoft/etl2pcapng`.

812

Error 812 (ERROR_SERVER_POLICY) is one of the more common errors that Always On VPN administrators will encounter. This error indicates an issue with authentication or authorization for the Always On VPN user tunnel connection.

Group Membership

The most common cause of 812 errors is incorrect security group membership. The Network Policy on the NPS server is typically restricted to a specific group in Active Directory. If the user connecting via Always On VPN is not a member of this group, access will be denied and an 812 error returned.

If the Active Directory group indicates the user is a member, confirm this on the client by opening a command window and running the following command:

```
whoami.exe /groups
```

Look at the output to ensure the correct group membership. The client may have to log off and log back on to update their group membership.

Authentication Type

An 812 error may also occur if the authentication configured on the Always On VPN client does not match the authentication type configured in the Network Policy on the NPS server. Review the authentication settings on the network policy and on the client to ensure they match.

NPS Communication

The error 812 can be quite misleading, unfortunately. For example, on the client, the user is presented with the following error message.

The connection was prevented because of a policy configured on your RAS/VPN server. Specifically, the authentication method used by the server to verify your username and password may not match the authentication method configured in your connection profile. Please contact the Administrator of the RAS server and notify them of this error.

The error states explicitly that the connection failed because "the authentication method used by the server to verify your username and password may not match." Implicitly this would indicate the NPS server denied the request. However, that is not always true!

This error message can occur when the VPN server is unable to communicate with the NPS server. Anything that prevents VPN server to NPS server communication should be investigated, including but not limited to the following:

- NPS server configuration – Is the NPS server configured correctly on the VPN server?

- Name resolution – Does the NPS server name resolve correctly on the VPN server?

- Firewalls and routing – Is the NPS server reachable from the VPN server? Is there a firewall blocking RADIUS traffic (UDP 1812) between the VPN and NPS servers?

Also, administrators should be aware of a bug in Windows Server 2019 that prevents RADIUS traffic from reaching the NPS server with the Windows Firewall enabled. As a workaround, open an elevated command window on the Windows Server 2019 NPS server and run the following command:

```
sc.exe sidtype IAS unrestricted
```

Reboot the server, and RADIUS traffic should flow correctly.

Note   This NPS bug affects only Windows Server 2019. It does not affect Windows Server 2022, and it does not affect Windows Server 2016 and older NPS servers.

Azure Conditional Access

Error 812 can occur when Always On VPN is configured to use Azure Conditional Access. Specifically, Azure Conditional Access issues short-lived certificates to authorized users that are used to authenticate to the NPS server. These short-lived certificates do not include a revocation URL. As such, the NPS server must be configured not to perform revocation checks in this scenario. If this step is missed, authentication will fail and return an 812 error.

To disable certificate revocation checking when using Azure Conditional Access, open an elevated PowerShell window on the NPS server and run the following command:

```
New-ItemProperty -Path 'HKLM:\SYSTEM\CurrentControlSet\Services\RasMan\PPP\
EAP\13\' -Name IgnoreNoRevocationCheck -PropertyType DWORD -Value 1 -Force
```

Restart the NPS server for the changes to take effect.

Event Logs

Another excellent source of information for failed authentication attempts (812 errors) is the event logs on the NPS server. Perform the following steps to view the NPS event logs:

1. On the NPS server, open the event viewer (eventvwr.msc).

2. Expand **Custom View ➤ Server Roles**.

3. Click **Network Policy and Access Services**.

In this log, look for events with **Event ID 6273** for failed authentication attempts. Important information is included in the **Authentication Details** section, specifically the **Reason Code** and **Reason**. These will give the administrator clues as to why the NPS server did not authorize the request.

If the event log does not record a disposition for the connection, allowed or denied, ensure NPS auditing is enabled by opening an elevated command window and running the following command:

```
auditpol.exe /set /subcategory:"Network Policy Server" /success:enable /
failure:enable
```

If there is more than one NPS server configured to support Always On VPN, ensure the command is run on all NPS servers.

Other Causes

There are several less common causes of 812 errors too. For example, an 812 error can occur if TLS 1.0 is disabled on old versions of Windows Server RRAS. 812 errors can also happen because of configuration conflicts between the NPS policy and the user's Active Directory account. Also, NPS configuration when multiple groups are configured can result in an 812 error. The following articles provide additional information on these errors:

```
https://directaccess.richardhicks.com/2018/02/26/troubleshooting-alwayson-
vpn-errors-691-and-812/
https://directaccess.richardhicks.com/2020/02/17/troubleshooting-alwayson-
vpn-error-691-and-812-part-2/
https://directaccess.richardhicks.com/2020/07/29/troubleshooting-alwayson-
vpn-error-691-and-812-part-3/
```

13801

Error 13801 (ERROR_IPSEC_IKE_AUTH_FAIL) indicates the authentication credentials used for IKEv2 are unacceptable. This can occur when the VPN server is configured to require certificates from a specific Certification Authority (CA).

Testing

To confirm the root certificate configuration for IKEv2, open an elevated PowerShell window on the VPN server and run the following command:

```
PS C:\> Get-VpnAuthProtocol
```

```
UserAuthProtocolAccepted       : {EAP, Certificate}
TunnelAuthProtocolsAdvertised  : Certificates
RootCertificateNameToAccept    : [Subject]
                                   CN=Microsoft Root Certificate Authority,
                                   DC=microsoft, DC=com

                                 [Issuer]
                                   CN=Microsoft Root Certificate Authority,
                                   DC=microsoft, DC=com

                                 [Serial Number]
                                   79AD16A14AA0A5AD4C7358F407132E65

                                 [Not Before]
                                   5/9/2001 4:19:22 PM

                                 [Not After]
                                   5/9/2021 4:28:13 PM

                                 [Thumbprint]
                                   CDD4EEAE6000AC7F40C3802C171E30148030C072

CertificateAdvertised          :
CertificateEKUsToAccept        :
```

Look carefully at the information listed in the **RootCertificateNameToAccept** field. Ensure the certificate thumbprint is correct and corresponds to the root CA of the PKI hierarchy used to issue device authentication certificates to endpoints.

13806

Error 13806 (ERROR_IPSEC_IKE_NO_CERT) indicates the client failed to find a valid machine certificate to use for authentication. This error can occur if a device authentication certificate has not been provisioned to the endpoint. It can also be caused by a missing certificate on the VPN server.

Missing Client Certificate

Open the Local Computer Certificates store on the client (certlm.msc) and expand Personal ➤ Certificates. Ensure a certificate issued by the internal issuing CA is present. Inspect the certificate to verify it is trusted, valid (not expired), has a private key, and includes the Client Authentication EKU. In addition, the subject name must match the hostname of the endpoint.

Missing Server Certificate

On the VPN server, open the Local Computer Certificates store (certlm.msc) and expand Personal ➤ Certificates. Ensure a certificate with the Server Authentication and IP Security IKE Intermediate EKU is present. Validate the certificate is trusted, not expired, and has a private key. Also, make sure the subject name on the certificate is the VPN server's public FQDN, not its hostname.

13868

Error 13868 (ERROR_IPSEC_IKE_POLICY_MATCH) indicates an IPsec policy mismatch between the client and the server. This occurs when using IKEv2, and a custom IPsec policy is defined on the server.

VPN Server

To confirm the IPsec policy settings configured on the server, open an elevated PowerShell window on the VPN server and run the following command:

```
PS C:\> Get-VpnServerConfiguration

AuthenticationTransformConstants : GCMAES128
CipherTransformConstants         : GCMAES128
CustomPolicy                     : True
DHGroup                          : Group14
EncryptionMethod                 : GCMAES128
Ikev2Ports                       : 128
SstpPorts                        : 1200
```

```
GrePorts                        : 0
IdleDisconnect(s)               : 300
IntegrityCheckMethod            : SHA256
L2tpPorts                       : 0
PFSgroup                        : ECP256
SADataSizeForRenegotiation(KB)  : 1024000
SALifeTime(s)                   : 28800
```

Compare these settings with those configured on the Always On VPN client.

Note   The SADataSizeForRenegotiation and SALifeTime values do not have to match on the client and server, and if different, they will not cause an IPsec policy mismatch error. The critical settings that must match are the AuthenticationTransformConstants, CipherTransformConstants, DHGroup, EncryptionMethod, and IntegrityCheckMethod values.

VPN Client

To confirm the IPsec policy settings configured on the client, open a PowerShell window and run the following commands:

```
PS C:\> $Vpn = Get-VpnConnection -Name 'Always On VPN'
PS C:\> $Vpn.IPSecCustomPolicy

AuthenticationTransformConstants : GCMAES128
CipherTransformConstants         : GCMAES128
DHGroup                          : Group14
IntegrityCheckMethod             : SHA256
PfsGroup                         : ECP256
EncryptionMethod                 : GCMAES128
```

Validate the settings on the client match exactly to those configured on the VPN server.

Registry Setting

If the client and server have been confirmed to have matching IPsec policy settings and the 13868 error persists, the problem could be a legacy registry setting on the VPN client or server.

There are guides published on the Internet that advocate for setting the following registry value on the VPN client or server:

`HKLM\SYSTEM\CurrentControlSet\Services\RasMan\Parameters\NegotiateDH2048_AES256`

13868 errors can occur if this registry entry is present with any value. It is recommended to delete this registry value if found.

NPS Configuration

13868 error can also occur if the NPS server policy is misconfigured. Specifically, in the **Encryption** section on the **Settings** tab for the network policy configured for Always On VPN, **Basic encryption (MPPE 40-bit)** or **Strong encryption (MPPE 56-bit)** must be enabled (Figure 12-2). If both are missing, a policy mismatch will occur.

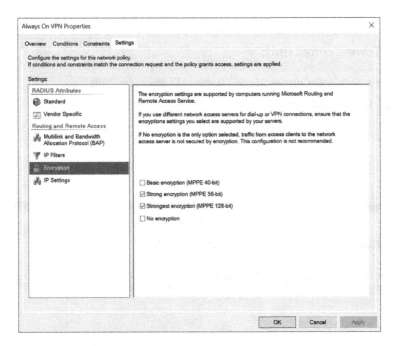

Figure 12-2. *NPS encryption settings*

853

Error 853 (ERROR_EAP_USER_CERT_INVALID) can occur when the Always On VPN client is configured to use Protected Extensible Authentication Protocol (PEAP) with Client Authentication certificates. Specifically, this error can occur because of a missing certificate on the NPS server.

Missing Certificate

For NPS authentication to function correctly when using certificate authentication for Always On VPN, the issuing CA certificate (not the root certificate!) must be present in the NTAuth certificate store on the NPS server. To confirm, open an elevated command window on the NPS server and run the following command. Review the list and ensure the issuing CA certificate is present (Figure 12-3).

```
certutil.exe -enterprise -viewstore NTAuth
```

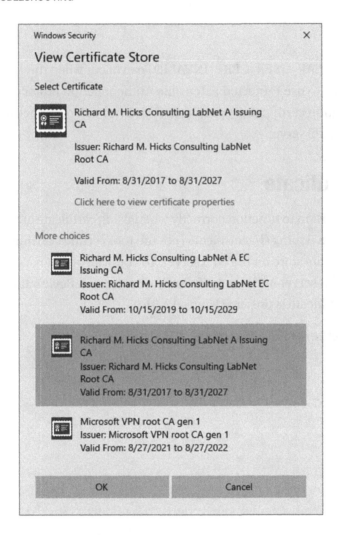

Figure 12-3. *View the NTauth certificate store*

If the issuing CA certificate is not present, it can be added by running the following command:

```
certutil.exe -enterprise -addstore NTAuth issuing_ca_certificate.cer
```

858

Error 858 (ERROR_EAP_SERVER_CERT_EXPIRED) occurs when the server authentication certificate on the NPS server has expired. Resolving this issue is as simple as renewing the certificate on the NPS server.

It is recommended to use certificate autoenrollment whenever possible. See Chapter 3 for more details.

864

Error 864 (ERROR_EAP_SERVER_ROOT_CERT_NOT_FOUND) occurs when NPS server certificate is not defined correctly on the NPS policy. This can happen if there is more than one certificate installed on the NPS server that includes the Server Authentication EKU.

Certificate Assignment

To confirm, open the NPS management console and perform the following steps:

1. Expand **NPS (Local)** ➤ **Policies**.

2. Select **Network Policies**.

3. Double-click the policy used for Always On VPN authentication.

4. Select the **Constraints** tab.

5. Highlight **Microsoft: Protected EAP (PEAP)** in the **EAP Types** section.

6. Click **Edit**.

7. Ensure the correct certificate is selected from the **Certificate issued to** drop-down list (Figure 12-4).

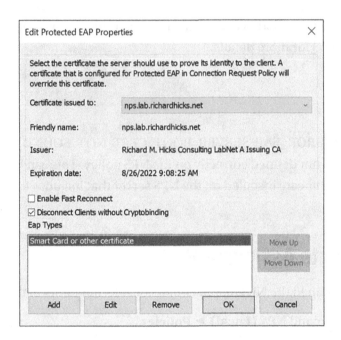

Figure 12-4. *Network policy certificate settings*

8.   Highlight **Smart Card or other certificate** in the **EAP Types** section.

9.   Click **Edit**.

10.   Ensure the correct certificate is selected from the **Certificate issued to** drop-down list (Figure 12-5).

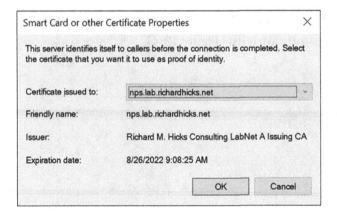

Figure 12-5. *Network policy certificate settings*

Root Certificate

In addition, ensure the NPS server has the root and any intermediate certificates installed in the local computer certificate store for the NPS server certificate issuing PKI.

798

Error 798 (ERROR_NO_EAPTLS_CERTIFICATE) can occur when the Always On VPN client is configured to use PEAP with client certificate authentication and the user does not have a user certificate in their personal certificate store. Open the users' local user certificate store (certmgr.msc) and expand Personal ➤ Certificates to confirm the certificate. The certificate must have the Client Authentication EKU and be valid, trusted, not expired, and not revoked.

Permissions

Certificate autoenrollment should be used to provision certificates to end users. If the user is unable to enroll for the certificate automatically, try enrolling for the certificate manually. If the template does not appear in the list, it could indicate a permissions issue.

TPM

If the end user has the correct permissions, certificate enrollment might be failing due to a missing or inoperable Trusted Platform Module (TPM).

Other Known Issues

There are myriad things that can go wrong when implementing Always On VPN. Here are some additional issues that commonly occur.

Clients Prompted for Authentication

After an Always On VPN client connects successfully, the user may be prompted to enter their credentials when accessing authenticated resources over the VPN connection. The most common cause for this issue is a missing Kerberos Authentication certificate on enterprise domain controllers. Ensure that all domain controllers in the organization have a valid Kerberos Authentication certificate that includes the Server Authentication, Client Authentication, Smart Card Logon, and KDC Authentication EKUs configured.

RRAS Service Won't Start

Another common issue after initial configuration occurs when the RemoteAccess service on the VPN server starts but then immediately stops. This can be caused by IPv6 being proactively disabled via the registry. IPv6 does not need to be configured on the RRAS server, but it cannot be disabled. Open the registry editor on the VPN server and look for the presence of the following value. If present, remove it.

`HKLM\SYSTEM\CurrentControlSet\Services\Tcpip6\Parameters\DisabledComponents`

Load Balancing and NAT

Load balancers are commonly deployed with Always On VPN to provide additional capacity and high availability for VPN and NPS servers. By default, most load balancers will proxy or NAT the traffic to the backend VPN servers. In this scenario, the VPN server sees the source IP address as the load balancer, not the client itself. This can cause problems for connection stability and reliability for Always On VPN clients.

It is strongly recommended to configure destination NAT (DNAT) only for Always On VPN. The VPN server performs more reliably when the client's original source IP address is passed. This also makes the log files more meaningful on the VPN server.

For more information on this topic and for remediation guidance for popular load balancers, visit `https://directaccess.richardhicks.com/2020/04/13/always-onvpn-ikev2-load-balancing-and-nat/`.

SSTP Connect/Disconnect

When using SSTP for Always On VPN user tunnel connections, users may encounter a scenario where the VPN connection establishes successfully and then immediately terminates. This can be caused when the VPN client is behind a network security device performing TLS inspection.

When the SSTP connection completes, the peers exchange information about the certificate used to establish the secure tunnel. If the certificates do not match, the session is assumed to be compromised, and the tunnel is terminated to protect against man-in-the-middle attacks. This is the case when a TLS inspection device provides a different certificate to the client than the one installed on the VPN server.

It can also occur if TLS offload is enabled for SSTP on the RRAS VPN server. If the TLS certificate is not installed on the VPN server, the configuration must be updated to include the correct TLS certificate installed on the upstream load balancer. Typically, it is not recommended to enable TLS offload, but there are some scenarios where it may be required.

A PowerShell script to properly configure the VPN server to support TLS offload with an external load balancer can be found here: `https://github.com/richardhicks/sstpoffload/blob/master/Enable-SstpOffload.ps1`.

Custom Cryptography Settings Ignored

Administrators may also encounter a situation where their defined custom cryptography settings for IKEv2 are ignored by the client. This can occur if custom cryptography settings are defined in custom XML and the **NativeProtocolType** value is set to **Automatic**. This issue is still present in Windows 11 at the time of this writing.

More detail about this specific issue can be found here: `https://directaccess.richardhicks.com/2019/01/07/always-on-vpn-ikev2-connection-failure-error-code800/`.

Summary

Ideally, administrators will configure the Always On VPN infrastructure and provision their clients without issue. That's not always possible, however. The VPN and authentication infrastructure is not trivial to configure, and it's easy to make mistakes. For larger deployments, the additional complexity can lead to configuration errors or overlooked steps.

Of course, it's always possible that something changed in the environment resulting in connectivity failures. Be sure to carefully document the environment when it is working correctly. This can be an invaluable reference in the future when and if things change.

Index

© Richard M. Hicks 2022
R. M. Hicks, *Implementing Always On VPN*, https://doi.org/10.1007/978-1-4842-7741-6

Printed in the United States
by Baker & Taylor Publisher Services